The ART of ADMINISTRATION

the Art of Administration

VIEWPOINTS ON PROFESSIONAL MANAGEMENT IN WALDORF SCHOOLS

edited by DAVID MITCHELL

THE ART OF ADMINISTRATION
© 1992 David Mitchell, Chairman, Economic Committee
The Association of Waldorf Schools of North America

Originally published by The Economic Committee of the
Association of Waldorf Schools of America
ISBN # 0-962-397-84-9

Reprinted © 2015 by Waldorf Publications
at the Research Institute for Waldorf Education
38 Main Street, Chatham, NY 12037
ISBN #978-1-936367-81-8

Editor: David Mitchell
Cover design: Elizabeth Auer
Design, Typesetting: Ann Erwin
Proofreading: Catherine Weld, Ann Erwin

All rights reserved. No part of this book may be reproduced in any form without written permission from the publisher, except for brief excerpts.

TABLE OF CONTENTS

INTRODUCTION – DAVID MITCHELL 7

CHAPTER 1 – TORIN FINSER
The Faculty Meeting 11

CHAPTER 2 – JAMES PEWTHERER
The College of Teachers... 29

CHAPTER 3 – CONNIE STARZYNSKI
Communication 45

CHAPTER 4 – SALLY VAN SANT
Committee Structure.. 55

CHAPTER 5 – DAVID ALSOP
The Roles of the Administrator, Business Manager, and Development Director ... 63

CHAPTER 6 – ANNIKEN MITCHELL
Admissions and Parent Education 75

CHAPTER 7 – CORNELIUS PIETZNER
Community Relations and Outreach 85

CHAPTER 8 – DAVID MITCHELL
Evaluation 99

CHAPTER 9 – CORNELIS PIETERSE
Working Together... 117

CHAPTER 10 – AGAF DANCY
The Board of Trustees 134

APPENDIX.. 145

INTRODUCTION
by David Mitchell

Contemporary educational reform has highlighted a need to establish "site-based management" in schools. Today's teachers see the results of their educational striving being condemned in the media as insufficient. They can be heard expressing a need to be empowered, self-directing and responsible for their own environment and curricula. American education is desperate for change.

Rudolf Steiner, in his address to the teachers at the beginning of the second school year in Stuttgart on September 22, 1920, said the following:

> The (Waldorf) school will have its own administration run on a republican basis and will not be administered from above. We must not lean back and rest securely on the orders of a headmaster; we must be a republic of teachers and kindle in ourselves the strength that will enable us to do what we have to do with full responsibility. ***Each one of you, as an individual, has to be fully responsible.****

Those of us in Waldorf education who have been working with this structure, and experiencing the resulting freedom, understand the longing of our colleagues in the public sector. We may also recognize that there is much that we could offer them through the successes and trials of the social management that we employ in our schools. On the other hand, there is much that we have to do within our own movement to refine our way of managing our schools.

In this book we explore this question of administration and management. It was written as a result of questions asked over the past several years that have been directed at AWSNA while I have served as chairman of the Eastern Region. These questions have come from schools both in their infancy and from schools over fifty years old. They take the following form: How are Waldorf schools administered? What is the role of the college of teachers in a Waldorf school? What is the purpose of consensus? How can we run a better faculty meeting? How do we evaluate our teachers, our students, our

---
*Rudolf Steiner, *Conferences, 1919-1920*, Steiner Schools Fellowship, 1986, p. 34.

schools? How do we determine mandates for committees? How should the phone be answered in the office? What is a Waldorf administrator, and what should he or she do and not do? What are the criteria necessary in the acceptance of children? How can we better present ourselves to the media and the greater community? How can we deal with the human complexities which arise when adults work together? What are the models for boards of trustees in Waldorf schools?

As one penetrates the questions, one soon realizes that there are no definitive answers, no recipes, no dogmatic responses which can serve our way of working. Living social organisms are constantly undergoing change. The forms we create are there only as a temporary, supportive framework. We must all learn to love the challenge of constantly improving upon what we have, and resist settling on any fixed final form which could lead to an individual power position and discord.

This book does not wish to dictate "how" to do things; rather it is hoped that the articles included in *The Art of Administration* will stimulate the reader's thinking so that an answer which fits their particular situation may become apparent. The answers to most of our questions reside within ourselves and we can find them if we develop the ability to observe carefully. To observe carefully means we have to try to study and understand Rudolf Steiner's intentions when he passed on the leadership of the Waldorf School in Stuttgart to the teachers.

We must go beyond a mere practical answer to our administrative questions and try to fathom that which is truly being asked of us. Administration in a Waldorf school calls forth the development of moral technique. It is through the active working with anthroposophy that we learn how to develop ourselves in this area. As we strive to understand moral technique, we begin to develop the capacity to meet those problems which come toward us with interest and love. At the same time we are strengthening ourselves so that we do not allow the arrows of critical opposition to penetrate our sensitivity. Rather we seek constantly for equilibrium, and in such a state of consciousness, we may then be able to intuit a solution to the problem. This way of working stands against that of the person who becomes immersed in the problem as a result of his own critical faculty. To develop this ability of intuition requires that individuals are willing to undertake their own inner development. Modern administrators can function in this way only if they have an understanding for their activity and recognize a deeper resource from which spring their responses.

The writing of this book was an interesting experiment. First, the questions were organized and then the chapter headings were developed. They were presented to the Delegates of the Association of Waldorf Schools of North America, who were asked to identify participants to concentrate on different aspects of the project. This list was developed further, and finally ten individuals from around North America, recognized by their professional relationship to a particular set of questions, as well as to their understanding of school administration as a whole, were asked to prepare a draft of a chapter. In September of 1991, all but one of that group, together with the Chairperson of the Pedagogical Section Council, gathered together around a round table at the Lexington Waldorf School and presented their thoughts to one another. Discussion, debate, and probing conversations followed, as the group struggled to broaden or contract the focus of each report. The intention was to look at each question from as many points of view as possible. It was hoped that when we left Lexington to go home to write the final revisions, something of all the other participants would live in each other's chapter.

We sincerely hope that this book can be of service, and we invite you, the reader, to give us feedback so that this work can develop into the future.

I would like to express my appreciation especially to David Alsop, but also to those other colleagues who have participated in this book and who have endured their editor's demands with warmth and humor!

David Mitchell
Wilton, NH
February 1992

It is aliveness that must be the guiding principle. Joy and happiness in living, a love of all existence, a power and energy for work ... The need for imagination, a sense of truth and a feeling for responsibility—these are the three forces which are the very nerve of education.

– Rudolf Steiner

Chapter 1
THE WALDORF SCHOOL FACULTY MEETING
by Torin Finser

Some years ago, the U.S. Department of Education reported a survey in which "as many as 45 percent of the teachers report no contact with each other during the workday; another 32 percent say they have infrequent contact. As a result, these teachers fail to share experience and ideas or to get support from colleagues. Isolation may undermine effective instruction."[1]

Many administrators and policy makers speak about fostering collegiality, setting aside time for faculty interaction, and involving teachers in setting school policies. However, few achieve this goal. The hierarchical structure in most schools, the absence of a shared, fully articulated philosophy of education, and the intrusion of school board politics all serve to undermine the implementation of meaningful faculty interaction.

From their inception in 1919, Waldorf schools were designed to place faculty collaboration at the heart of all policy formulation. Teachers in Waldorf schools the world over meet weekly, often on Thursday, to do the work needed in service of the children in their care. This work may include curriculum development, child observation, study, reporting, decisions on schedules, hiring, public events, etc. The meetings become real because the authority and responsibility of school direction rest with the striving teachers., Thus the faculty meeting represents simultaneously one of the greatest opportunities and one of the greatest challenges of teaching in a Waldorf school. The success or failure of the faculty meeting can be the determining factor in the health and growth of a school.

The challenge and opportunity become all the greater because there are no formulas. In their training, Waldorf teachers receive a comprehensive picture of the developing child, a philosophic basis out of which to work, and a curriculum full of countless marvels just waiting to be discovered and shared. However, working on a faculty of teachers remains, by its very nature, a new frontier. There are no guides for faculty meetings, nor should there be! Each group explores together, researches the possibilities and develops an organizational structure that fits the character and needs of the particular school. This ongoing, active searching is a crucial ingredient in all faculty work. The thoughts that follow are therefore intended as a stimulus for further exploration.

Why have faculty meetings?

A long, sedentary meeting in the traditional sense could rightly be viewed as anathema to the spirit of Waldorf education. Teachers work so hard already, planning lessons, holding parent/teacher conferences, serving on numerous committees, teaching long hours at low wages—is not a long afternoon of meeting just asking too much?

The answer might well be "yes" if the teacher feels she is merely fulfilling an obligation. If the content is not of interest, if the structure is not artistically organized, then time will weigh heavily on the minds of all participants. Everything depends on what colleagues bring to the meetings.

In an age characterized by Rudolf Steiner as the time of the Consciousness Soul, we can no longer let others do our tasks. Headmasters and principals cannot truly replace an active faculty of teachers. We need to emancipate ourselves, stand on our own "pedagogical feet," and abandon the old supports. To a large extent, public education has failed to do this and therefore remains fettered to an old system of governance that stifles initiative and actually impedes the real practice of pedagogy. A Waldorf school must first of all have a faculty that is free to set pedagogical policy. The responsibility is tremendous, but completely in harmony with the needs of our times.

Liberty, fraternity, equality: these three words served as a clarion call before and during the French Revolution, and they continue to resound in one form or another in the years since then. Yet, unfortunately, these three mighty ideals are often understood only in terms of physical realities, i.e., the redistribution of material wealth, freedom "from," and equality in the workplace. This materialistic interpretation, though valid in its own sphere, misses the main thrust of these ideals. We need to achieve *fraternity* on the physical plane, a real caring of one another's needs. However, *liberty* needs to be addressed in psychological terms, the ability to give space for the thoughts and feelings of others, the ability to be free in relationship. *Equality*, in the ultimate sense, is a spiritual matter. We are most equal in our striving as human beings, in our strenuous searching for insight. In a Waldorf context especially, it is our striving that brings us together.

A faculty meeting is a wonderful experiment, an attempt to implement the three ideals of the French Revolution in the sense described above. Certainly there is a "fraternal" aspect, known to all the colleagues who congregate around the snack table! During snack, everyday concerns are shared; genuine interest in the needs of others is furthered when the afternoon schedule allows for informal human interchange. In fact, much can be accomplished during what appears to be purely informal conversation. Concerns about family, housing, finances, and lesson materials are taken up. When faculty meetings are too tightly scheduled, often in the name of efficiency, one senses the lack of "fraternal" carrying in the school. Strangely enough, being too efficient is often inefficient.

Likewise, group work either enhances or impedes individual "liberty." A headstrong drive to reach consensus can stifle individuality (see "Making Decisions" section of this chapter), but when done well, a faculty gathering can be a time of inner freeing, a chance to truly share. Respectful of each colleague's insights and contributions, an atmosphere of psychological "liberty" deepens the pedagogical work of each teacher. In this atmosphere, Waldorf teachers can create a new language to meet one another out of enhanced anthroposophical insight. In striving toward this goal, colleagues can experience spiritual "equality."

Some years ago, Jørgen Smit asked a gathering of teachers in Garden City, "What are we doing so that the living spiritual substance can grow within the schools?" This question goes to the heart of our faculty and college work: the need to forge a new social form, a living vessel for spiritual/pedagogical inspiration.[2]

Continued Teacher Training

Faced with the constant press of business, the outer circumstances of school life can easily determine faculty priorities. A pressing issue of one sort or another always arises, such as, "What happened to the planning for tomorrow's assembly?" After some discussion of what went wrong, a group becomes immersed in the details of how many chairs to set up, where the display should go, etc. Yet all the "apparent" business, in the most amazing and varied way, obscures the central business of a Waldorf school faculty meeting: the self-development and continued training of the entire body of teachers.

In the Torquay lectures, among other instances, Rudolf Steiner spoke of the teacher's meetings as, "the heart and soul" of the work, a place and time when "each one learns from the other":

> "… We have our teacher's meetings in the Waldorf school which are the heart and soul of the whole teaching. In these meetings, each teacher speaks of what he himself has learned in his class and from all

the children in it, so that each one learns from the other. No school is really alive where this is not the most important thing, this regular meeting of the teachers."[3]

An active teacher is constantly learning from others. However, this general, indirect method is not enough. A faculty needs to consciously schedule a time for "sharing." The spontaneous outpouring about a successful lesson, a heart-rendering story of an especially difficult day, or the joyful sharing of lessons and newly discovered materials can reunite a faculty socially, all of which stimulates further growth. The class reports and child observations given at many faculty meetings also enhance teacher training, but the heart-inspired, spontaneous sharing is what I have found irreplaceable. Over and above setting aside a time in the meeting for spontaneous sharing, too much planning or structure forces the situation, and then everyone feels they have to say something profound, or worse yet, not speak at all.

The health of a school depends on the attitude of each teacher and the quality of group work in a faculty:

> Thus these constant staff meetings tend to make the school into an organism in the same way as the human body is an organism by virtue of its heart. Now what matters in these staff meetings is not so much the principles but the readiness of all the teachers to live together in goodwill, and the abstention from any form of rivalry. And it matters supremely that a suggestion made to another teacher only proves helpful when one has the right love for every single child. And by this I do not mean the kind of love which is often spoken about, but the love which belongs to an artistic teacher.[4]

It is interesting to observe how the content of the above quote is organized. The "organism" of the school depends upon the meeting of teachers in "goodwill," which in turn rests upon the love each teacher fosters for the children. When the children are carried in a living, loving manner, the whole organism is strengthened. We know that each child should come before the faculty in the course of a year, even if only for a few minutes. Teachers perfect their work, become true artists, by practicing child observation. This means sharing images of the child, characterizing behavior and school work, allowing differing perceptions to live in the circle, and carrying the child inwardly between meetings. Each child presents a sort of riddle, or a series of riddles, and from the human striving to understand these riddles come the soul forces a teacher needs to work effectively in the classroom.

Pedagogical work is an artistic activity that cannot be learned from a text. So often, the faculty study becomes a simple recapitulation of the lecture, and colleagues settle in for a brief inner nap. Of course a faculty study of lectures can be helpful, but it is the activity that results from the study that develops concrete teaching skills. Books are simply impulses for self-development.

A faculty cultivates the goal of becoming a new kind of university, a place where individual research is shared, ideas developed and insights fashioned out of conversation. Teacher meetings can become the life blood of a school when original work finds a respectful audience and an eager, appreciative circle of colleagues.

The soil for all the above-mentioned work is prepared through regular artistic activity. So many teachers observe their colleagues' talents and feel hopelessly inadequate. Yet most of those very talents were developed and refined through regular, not so glamorous practice. Everyone, in reality, still has areas that are in need of work. So when a faculty of teachers sings, draws, paints, moves and speaks together, the artistic configuration of the entire group blossoms, research is inspired, and issues are resolved.

Finally, when a faculty works to continue teacher training, the children sense it. Their teacher's striving, an intangible element, becomes food for the children. Lesson plans do not reach the class as effectively as the teacher activity that stands behind their preparation. Likewise, when the teachers stand up and sing together at an assembly, one observes a remarkable change in the children. One has just to look at their sparkling eyes and ruddy cheeks! In a few brief moments of singing together, a faculty strengthens the etheric sheath of a school.

Structure

All the aforesaid is possible only when the form of the meeting fits the content, when clarity and structure permit freedom and artistic expression. Thus the agenda becomes a crucial element in any faculty meeting.

Ideally, the weekly agenda reflects the life of the entire school. When a school is large, it may be advisable for two or three colleagues from different areas and with different responsibilities to contribute to the drafting of the agenda. For instance, when the faculty chair, administrator and college chair meet weekly to draft the agenda, they can also serve as an administrative committee to handle designated administrative tasks that need attention. Regardless of who forms the agenda, however, the key consideration is: What is occurring in the life of the school that needs to be brought to the full circle of teachers? Rather than have the agenda become a personal document, these guiding question helps raise the work to a more objective level, a service to the "whole."

Just as the human being works through the structure of its various "members," so too, the work of a faculty is enhanced through careful consideration of the several aspects of a meeting's structure. There are the physical needs and concerns, such as materials, room arrangement, time slots, report format and of course, snack. However, the etheric rhythm requires consideration of the life-engendering activities in a meeting: working with movement, speech and painting, perhaps for a month at a time. If the agenda takes into account the dynamics of the afternoon meeting, the astral element is engaged. Here the pacing of the agenda becomes crucial. For example, after a long, involved discussion, one might skip to announcements. The chairperson can conduct the agenda so that variety enlivens the session. Finally, one needs to carry constantly a consciousness of the process while it is occurring. Somewhat like "thinking about thinking," one is involved, yet aware of the nature of the process. This work with conscious perspective directly calls upon the human ego.[5]

Nothing, including the above, can be adhered to in a rigid fashion. A living form requires moments of contraction and expansion. Teachers often give this careful attention in their lessons, yet the structure of a faculty meeting deserves the benefit of the same insights. During the five years I served as a faculty chairman, I found that preparation made all the difference, especially in speaking ahead of time to those colleagues scheduled to give reports. Concise reporting upholds discipline and structure, while also allowing more time for classroom "sharing" and child observation. Needless to say, if one does not have to do much teaching, everything can be properly prepared and considered!

One of the major challenges facing Waldorf schools today is the health of our teachers. Not that we are all falling apart, but some issues have long been neglected. We need to lead healthy lives, even on Thursdays. Anthroposophical study and long faculty discussions are not a substitute for basic human needs, such as exercise, nutrition and artistic work. The physical well-being of teachers strongly influences relationships—with colleagues, parents and children. We often become so caught up in the periphery that we lose "the center." Teachers need a time to relate some personal elements, aspects of biography, during a faculty meeting. These need not be long, but even a conversation around the theme, "Where were you at age nine?" can help. Waldorf teachers deserve time to process childhood issues, while awakening to those of others. The exercise of looking back, whether on biography or at the end of a day, can strengthen the etheric.

Here are some possible agendas that attempt to incorporate some of the above considerations:

A. Eurythmy (30-40 min.)
    Pedagogical discussion and /or child observation (30-40 min.)
    Minutes of last meeting (5 min.)
    Reports, which might include: (30 min.)
        College of Teachers
        Lower School, High School, Kindergarten
        Parent/Teachers Association
        Board of Trustees
        School Committees
    Questions on the reports/discussion/free sharing (15-20 min.)
    Announcements (10 min.)

B. Opening Quote (5 min.)
    Minutes (5 min.)
    Reports—might be similar to the above (30-40 min.)
    Pedagogical discussion: class nights and parent/teacher work, all-school
        meetings (40 min.)
    Announcements (10 min.)
    Rehearsal of faculty play (60+ min.)

C. Opening Quote
    Faculty study—lecture from *Study of Man* (45 min.)
    Child observation (30 min.)
    Singing (15 min.)
    Minutes (5 min.)
    Reports —see above (30 min.)
    Announcements (10 min.)
    Review and Closing Verse

(In all the above examples, the faculty snack would precede the meeting, although many have scheduled it halfway through.)

Chairing a Faculty Meeting

Before examining the specifics of chairing, a few reflections on the role and concept of leadership, in general, may be helpful. For nowadays, all leaders are suspect. Partly because of the abuse of power in modern history, and partly due to the strong current of egalitarianism in the Western world, leaders are hardly given a chance anymore. If everyone is equal, so they say, then why have any leaders? This pervasive mindset influences everything we do, even in a Waldorf context. Part of our present-day challenge is to create a new definition of leadership.

A faculty of Waldorf teachers works as a group. Without the active participation of all teachers, pedagogical policy becomes an abstraction. However, group work does not preclude the need for leadership. In fact, to say, "We have no leaders here; we do everything ourselves" obscures the reality of the situation. In every discussion, in every decision, in every form of implementation, **there are leaders!** Not to recognize them means to deny them the conscious support they urgently need in carrying out the will of the school. However, a leader in one area of school life may not be suited for leadership in another. We need to learn to recognize our leaders.

We can do this by sharpening our perception of human capacities, learning to recognize talent and yet practicing inner discernment so those talents can be applied to the right tasks. Much can go awry when good people are given the wrong tasks. "But, so and so will learn to," is a refrain that does not succeed in administration. Of course, everyone can learn from experience, and for Waldorf **teaching** this is a central, pedagogical imperative. However, school administration should not, in my opinion, be the training ground for well-intentioned but otherwise ineffectual leaders. Teacher training, as described earlier, is a pedagogical affair. The damage done by misplaced administrative authority can be irreparable, not only for the circle of forgiving colleagues, but for the wider parent community.

The main task of a faculty chairperson is confidence-building. One can do this in so many ways, both large and small: encouraging colleagues with appropriate talents to take up new tasks, connecting people with each other, fostering an atmosphere of appreciation for the parents, board and colleagues, planning events and agendas that work, and developing a fine sense for "timing." A faculty chair facilitates, makes it possible for good things to happen in a school, keeps things moving. Confidence within and confidence without grows when issues are clearly perceived and the "warmth realm" is valued. (See "Social Challenge" section at end of chapter.)

A faculty chairperson should expect little glory and much detail work. The words of Robert Louis Stevenson help those who have been given the "Guardian Knot" of faculty chairing:

> We require higher tasks because we do not recognize the height of those we have. Trying to be kind and honest seems an affair too

simple and too inconsequential for men of our heroic mold: We had rather set ourselves to something bold, arduous, and conclusive... the task before us, which is to co-endure with our existence, is rather one of microscopic fineness, and the heroism required is that of patience. There is no cutting the Gordian Knots of life; each must be smilingly unravelled.[6]

Patience and humility are the rewards of faculty chairing.

Here are some practical suggestions for the faculty chair:

- Ask colleagues to submit agenda items at least a day in advance. The best agendas are destroyed by too many last-minute submissions.

- Post the agenda on the faculty bulletin board before the meeting. Expect that with advance notice, members will arrive prepared.

- Begin and end all meetings punctually. Teachers can be asked to follow the same high standards we ask of the children. Besides maintaining a regular rhythm, ending the meetings on time does wonders for family life. When punctuality is not observed and meetings frequently go past the allotted time, discuss it as a symptom. Is more time in fact needed? Is the faculty working as it should?

- Be an active chairperson. This does not mean dominating or doing a great deal of the talking (indeed, nothing is more annoying than a chairperson who holds forth by virtue of the position). Rather, the chairperson's activity should be in seeing and hearing. Know what's happening, anticipate events as much as possible, and draw things to a close with a firm hand. Advance preparation is crucial, as well as a healthy dose of intuition!

- When an issue or discussion starts to go in circles, call a break or do something else for a while. Even waiting a week can help everyone gain perspective. In the latter case, the key to subsequent discussion is for the chair to summarize the salient points of the previous conversation. If people feel that their views are acknowledged, there is a relaxing of "positions" and less chance of repetition.

- Compliments, when things go well and reports are clear, can be a marvelous tool for encouraging more of the same.

- One must be careful that reports and announcements don't turn into discussions. These "back-ended discussions" are often disorganized, too personal and generally inconclusive. When an issue "flares up," let the group know that it is recognized and will be placed on the agenda of the next meeting.

- Even when submerged in all the details of school administration, a faculty chair holds a vivid image of the big picture, and focuses the meeting on the things that in the final analysis matter most in a Waldorf school faculty meeting: child-centered activities, anthroposophy, and curriculum development. When the essentials are not given enough room, no mastery of the details can make up for it.

- If all the above is not enough, here is one last suggestion: Meetings are not just hard work, they can and will be fun, too! The goodwill and humor of the faculty chair can be wonderfully infectious.

Delegation

The faculty chairperson's task of confidence-building is furthered through delegation, which also develops the faculty as a working group. A faculty chairperson, indeed the entire faculty, can benefit from the conscious delegation of tasks. Delegation is actually the natural outcome of the heightened perception of human capacities mentioned earlier.

Once a task is assigned to a colleague or committee, trust becomes the vehicle through which they can function successfully. Trust does not mean blind faith—we cannot go back to the Middle Ages! However, when trust is exercised in this age of the Consciousness Soul, the questions and concerns one might have are properly directed to those individuals who have assumed responsibility. So much damage is done to the living being of a school when "parking lot" conversations prevail. Giving input to the designated individual(s) needs to happen early in the process, so that the final product reflects as much as possible the insights of the larger faculty. Thus, when a recommendation or report comes back to the full circle, acceptance occurs more readily. Equally important, if the recommendation is not agreed to, then the responsible individual or committee should be entrusted with making the necessary changes and reporting back again. Nothing destroys confidence more than working hard at a project only to hear afterwards that it is not wanted after all, or have a group of twenty-five people take apart and rewrite everything. At each stage, everyone must seek to build, not destroy, confidence.

The following is a "shorthand" delegation sequence that might be considered by a faculty of teachers:

- Imagine the need. Build a picture that is vivid enough and clear enough so that it lives in the whole faculty.

- Given the picture of what is needed, find the individual or group that can best help that picture incarnate. The selection should be based on talents in the subject or area under consideration, as well as the basic social skills of listening, working together and following through.

- Set a definite time frame so members can make timely contributions and the committee can report back to the faculty.

- Don't forget about them in the meanwhile. Extend trust and helpful suggestions. Visualize their success with the project, and it will happen.

- Hear their recommendations. Ask for their reasoning if the solutions appear problematic. Remember to extend gratitude for much-needed work done on behalf of the whole school.

Making Decisions

Groups do not make decisions. In our age of the Consciousness Soul, individuals make the decisions, and the group can recognize when a totality of individual decisions has occurred and consensus exists.

Arriving at a consensus is a magical moment. When true consensus lives in the room, one senses that something more than human willing and deciding is at work. A moment of consensus can be fleeting, yet when it arrives a special union arises between the divine spiritual and the struggling, earth-bound consciousness of those in the room. When true consensus is present, it can be felt, experienced. If it is not experienced in the feeling life of the colleagues, if there is any question about whether consensus was reached or not, then it is not a consensus decision.

Striving for consensus is part of the spiritual path of a Waldorf teacher. In aiming to realize consensus on an issue, one is really calling upon the hierarchies; colleagues experience something greater than their own ego. Consensus-building means fashioning the spiritual vessel whereby the hierarchies can become active in a school. They need our conscious efforts.

It is this spirit which matters above all. And if it is alive, it will engender enthusiasm, irrespective of the personnel or the leadership of the school. And then one can also have confidence that something of an objective spirit will live throughout the school, which is not the same as the accumulation of each teacher's individual spirit.[7]

There are many, many times during faculty work when consensus cannot be reached. This reality, when it occurs, needs to be recognized and not papered over. To represent a decision as the result of consensus when it is not is a serious injustice. Group manipulation by a few or the tyranny of the "majority" can wreak havoc in a cultural institution. Especially in our western world, the democratic rule of the majority creeps in wearing all sorts of disguises. One might say that the "rights life" as described by Rudolf Steiner is far too strong in the English-speaking world. In a cultural institution, the "truth" of the matter may find expression in the voice of a minority of one. Many times, I have heard all in the majority express the same opinion, only to have the tables turned when a previously silent colleague shares a few words of wisdom near the end of a discussion. Decision-making in a Waldorf school must thus be made on the basis of insight.

Again, there is no magic formula for making decisions on the basis of insight. Here are a few brief suggestions of a practical nature:

- Imagine. Do picture-building and share perceptions without the pressure of deciding. Separating the discussion/picture-building phase from the decision making opens up the sharing. Pressure kills true image-building. At this early stage, everyone should try to see all sides of the issue.

- Make sure everyone is heard from, even if it is only a "yes" after a colleagues' contribution. Decisions come unraveled when people save their words of wisdom for after the decision. Working with Rudolf Steiner's indications on the planetary influences can be helpful. (For instance, the "Mars" people are great initiators but need to appreciate more fully the "go slow" approach of the "Saturn" folks!)

- One way to "collect" the individual decisions, to see if consensus has occurred, is to go around the circle, asking each one to share, in a sentence or less, a summary thought on the subject.

- Use the element of time creatively. When issues are carried through the portal of sleep and back again, something is always gained. In the end, three weeks to process a decision is more efficient than making a series of quick but poor decisions.

- Let the "heart realm" speak. The web of thoughts can confuse and obscure. A decision may be intellectually correct, but if it does not feel right, if enthusiasm cannot be kindled, it can hinder the growth of a school. This is especially true with regard to hiring, where karma is so strongly at work.

- Review the school's decision-making process from time to time. Every group needs to renew its commitment to process, just as a violinist has to practice those scales again and again.

- Finally, no matter how important a decision may seem at the moment, one needs to keep perspective. A decision is really nothing more than a spiritual intention, a resolve to act in a certain way to achieve the desired goal. For every decision is really a challenge, a conscious moment when direction is given for implementation. All the "incarnating" work still lies ahead. Failure to plan the communication and implementation can render any decision useless.

As indicated earlier, a consensus decision is a kind of gift, one that calls upon the members present to move forward with common resolve.

Role of the Scribe

In many ancient cultures, the scribe held a sacred position. It was the scribe who preserved for humanity the spiritual wisdom of the gods. In ancient Egypt, the entire physical world was seen as the handwriting of the gods.

In a faculty meeting, preserving the "wisdom" of the discussions and recording the decisions require a special perspective and sense for the essence of each subject. Some colleagues are more able than others to distill the essence of the past.

A scribe can help the group review the meeting, as well as refresh teachers' recollections at the start of the next session. Reading the minutes before new reports are given is always helpful. Generally, minutes that are clear and simple with emphasis on major points and decisions work best. A pedagogical discussion is diminished by recording everything, especially when the children are discussed, since writing things down tends to fix and freeze the situation. The scribe can work closely with the faculty chair between meetings to ensure that items needing attention are carried forward to the next agenda and details receive the necessary follow-up.

The Waldorf School Faculty Meeting

Review of the Meeting

Rudolf Steiner hoped that the teacher's meetings would be a practical manifestation of anthroposophically-inspired pedagogy. A real meeting of Waldorf teachers is more than an exercise in communication. It is a workshop, a practical session in "applied" anthroposophy. How we approach each part of the meeting can strongly influence the development of spiritual insight in a school.

The review portion of a meeting can be considered in this way. Recollection calls for spiritual activity; it is not the preservation of old ideas or images, but a chance to perceive anew the events of the previous meeting. The goal is greater than a repetition of the old content. In reviewing, something new, less fettered by the "here and now" is created and then released. A good review can help colleagues "let go" of their personal attachment to previous events, while learning from the process.

A passage in *Theosophy* speaks to the development of new capacities through review:

> "When the human spirit encounters an experience similar to one to which it has already been linked, it sees therein something familiar, and is able to take up an attitude towards it quite different from what would be the case were the spirit facing it for the first time. This is the basis of all learning. The fruits of learning are acquired capacities."[8]

Thus, rigorous review is an archetypal schooling of new human faculties. This deep human insight and schooling of new faculties can affect modern relationships in a positive way.

The Social Challenge

Relationships today are increasingly difficult. Nothing can be taken for granted, all assumptions are off. Stripped to bare individuality, teachers and parents need to rebuild not only the educational structure for our children, but the very social fabric itself. The faculty meeting gives impetus for social healing in the community of parents and teachers.

> … Instead of taking interest merely in my own way of thinking, and in what I consider right, I must develop a selfless interest in every opinion I encounter, however strongly I may hold it to be mistaken. The more a man prides himself on his own dogmatic opinions and is interested only in them, the further he removes himself, at this

moment of world evolution, from the Christ. The more he develops a social interest in the opinions of other men, even though he considers them erroneous—the more light he receives into his own thinking from the opinions of others—the more he does fulfill in his inmost soul a saying of Christ which today must be interpreted in the sense of the new Christ language… In whatever the least of your brethren thinks, you must recognize that I am thinking in him; and that I enter into your feeling whenever you bring another's thought into relation with your own and whenever you feel fraternal interest for what is passing in another's soul. Whatever opinion, whatever outlook on life, you discover in the least of your brethren, therein you are seeking Myself.[9]

These words from *The Inner Aspect of the Social Question* by Rudolf Steiner provide the possibility for renewed colleagueship and renewed community work. Fraternal interest in others has the effect of drawing people forward, calling forth the highest in each individuality. Whenever a group is fortunate to have a body of knowledge unique in contemporary thinking, there is a danger of becoming ingrown, shutting oneself off from the "superficial" outside world. In the long run, a movement cannot be effective in the world unless it is capable of widening its circle. We need to draw people in, not push them away.

Teachers can do this by entering into the life of the community, joining local initiatives, fundraisers, town improvement projects, local libraries, etc. If every colleague in a school took up just one community endeavor outside of Waldorf education, what an effect that would have! The impulse for such involvement can come from the faculty meeting, when reports and contributions from outside the school are allowed to enter the circle, when colleagues actively practice the art of taking fraternal interest in each other and in the world at large.

When one practices inner tolerance and cultivates interest in the thoughts of others, something new unfolds. This can best be described as a heightened feeling of responsibility for every action one performs."[10] Not just the child/teacher relationship, but in fact, every relationship in the school community matters.

Once again, the child observation sessions can be a training, this time in a social sense. For when we "learn to listen to the revelation of spirit and soul in the growing child as they existed before birth," we see a journey that is greater and longer than we can fully comprehend with ordinary sense perception.[11] We can contemplate the path of destiny, strive to see the child's eternal core, and in so seeking, "our relationship to the eternal core of man's being will become less and less egotistical."[12] Child observation, when carried as an inner quest, lays the basis for an unegotistical mood of soul.

Thus the children help us become less egotistical. They promote renewal of the social life; they become our teachers. This attitude of soul, when present in a faculty meeting, works to the good of the entire community.

Much of the above may sound too idealistic, even impossible. Yet even when we do not succeed as we would wish, our struggles still help. For when the intention behind having faculty meetings lives strongly in a group, then the specifics and weekly details can better fall into place. The spiritual intentions of a faculty gathering, as well as the mood of soul, are the intangibles without which we cannot be Waldorf teachers.

The mystery dramas by Rudolf Steiner offer a lively example for a faculty's collective striving and group work. This concluding quotation could serve as a motto for faculty meetings:

> In future times it will behoove us
> As men to live each for the other
> — No longer through the other's being.
> So shall the cosmic goal be reached
> When man is rooted in himself
> And each gives to the other
> What neither wills as his.[13]

May men and women, working together in the context of the faculty meeting, find the insight, the fraternal interest and the good will to actively nourish one another and the community we serve.

Endnotes

1. U.S. Department of Education, *What Works?* 1986.
2. Jørgen Smit, June 1989, Garden City, notes of T. Finser.
3. Rudolf Steiner, Torquay Lectures, 19.8.24.
4. Rudolf Steiner, Manchester College Lectures, 16.8.22, 25.8.22.
5. Rudolf Steiner, *Philosophy of Spiritual Activity*.
6. Robert Louis Stevenson, *A Christmas Sermon*.
7. Rudolf Steiner, *A Child's Changing Consciousness*, 22.04.23.
8. Rudolf Steiner, *Theosophy*, Anthroposophic Press.

9. Rudolf Steiner, *The Inner Aspect of the Social Question*, R. Steiner Press.
10. Ibid.
11. Rudolf Steiner, *Education as a Social Problem*.
12. Ibid.

TORIN FINSER *is currently Director of Waldorf Teacher Training at Antioch New England Graduate School. He lives with his wife and two children in Keene, NH. Previously he was a class teacher for twelve years at the Great Barrington Rudolf Steiner School, where he also served as faculty chairman and Trustee for five years. He was, himself, a Waldorf school student, having attended the Steiner School in NYC, the Green Meadow Waldorf School, and Die Freie Waldorf Schule in Krefeld, Germany.*

The Waldorf school must be a true cultural deed through which the renewal of the entire structure of society must echo…

The teachers of the Waldorf school must follow their own initiatives but strive to always be in harmony with the entire group. This is something which needs to be learned…

It is everyone's task to be responsible and wakeful—this is the new challenge.

– Rudolf Steiner

Chapter 2
THE COLLEGE OF TEACHERS

by James Pewtherer

At the first Waldorf School in Stuttgart, Rudolf Steiner encouraged the original core of teachers to work into the future together by carrying the school forward in a new way.[1] He asked that they take on the rigor of establishing a new social form. He acknowledged that this task would be difficult, but he said that it was absolutely necessary for world evolution that preparation begin for mankind to experience a new way of working with one another. This form, often called the college of teachers, was to be based on a spiritual beholding of one another, a working out of consensus, and a conscious attempt by the teachers to align themselves with the "genius" or "being" of the school through disciplined meditative practice.

Perhaps no organ within the Waldorf school is more difficult to achieve than this college of teachers. On the one hand, the college of teachers can provide the most marvelous spiritual insights, bringing life to education. On the other hand, it can be inefficient, ponderous, even socially inept. Yet, we work in this way so that we may share the fruits of the spiritual world, and so that we may begin to understand what it means to work together out of freedom. What then is this college of teachers, a body which is unique to Waldorf schools?

We can only begin to answer this by trying to understand what the Waldorf school is all about. Rudolf Steiner characterized Waldorf education as an education which is designed to meet the needs of human beings in the fifth post-Atlantean epoch of earth evolution. This epoch is characterized as a time when our task as human beings is to develop the consciousness soul, that element in the human constitution which requires each one of us to stand alone and to experience oneself as an individual in day-clear consciousness. It is this experience that provides for the possibility for each man and woman to achieve the true freedom referred to in Steiner's book, *The Philosophy of Freedom*. However, the price for this possibility to experience oneself as an individual is that one must learn to live with the fact that there is a space, even an abyss, between oneself and the world, both the world of nature and the world of one's fellow man. So it is that at a certain point in life, each of us can feel himself to be completely alone. At the same time, this condition also leads each of us to strive to reconnect ourselves, and to overcome this gap that separates us from the world and the others around us. Before this can happen, though, and as this epoch progresses, the experience of subject/object will become ever stronger, while the experience of being alone will intensify. In light of this, we can see that our task for the present is to make use of this isolation and to develop capacities which will lead us from isolation into a new kind of community. This community will be timely, however, only if it is one based on true freedom.

This task of finding a new kind of community is one of the primary objectives of spiritual science. When we go further and look at our task as teachers working out of spiritual science, we see that our responsibilities include the guidance of children along their individual paths of incarnation. In normal development, they begin their lives in a state of natural unity with the world and then pass into the equally "natural" experience of separation from it around age nine.

However, from this point, and in light of the demands of this cultural epoch, we must begin to give them the tools so that they will have the possibility to establish anew a conscious connection with the world and the people around them. Yet, this connection can come about only when, over the course of their lives, they find the way as a result of individual, conscious effort. Each individual must make whole what is otherwise a polarity of self and world. This is an ideal for the future, however. We cannot expect to realize this reunification anytime soon. Yet as teachers, we need to point to its possibility for ourselves and for the children.

Here we come to see the unique challenge of the Waldorf school and the legacy which Rudolf Steiner left us in order to meet it. This legacy consists of the forms for our work together in the school, especially in the faculty meeting and the college of teachers. For our task is not only to create social forms so that these incarnating children find their way to each other and to the world. It is also to help them come to recognize, accept and learn to work with the destiny which they have brought with them. To be able to do this is through and through a matter of a spiritual development. It does not come out of nature, but can be acquired only through self-directed activity.

To cultivate this capacity in the children so that as adults they can develop their own spiritual perceptions in freedom, something is required of the teachers. They must first learn themselves to work with these factors in their interaction with the children, the colleagues, the parents and the entire school community. All this depends on achieving a degree of self-knowledge. Within a Waldorf school, an institution which is based upon an active working with the spiritual world, a very important condition must exist as a prerequisite to such work done on behalf of the children; we must create a vessel which can become a protected place in which these matters, matters which go far beyond the concept of "social" as we know it, can be rightly considered and worked upon. The college in particular should be such a vessel. It must be the place in which we can nurture, protect, and support the young people who have come to the Waldorf school in their quest to become true human beings. It must also provide something similar for the colleagues if they are to provide such support. Our central task, though, is the care of the children. How can this care lead them towards this new way of being together?

It is in the building of the class community that one of the first steps is taken by which the children learn to know each other. The teacher already begins on the first day of preschool to lay a basis for this class community. In their class over the years, the children learn to live together by learning to know and to love the others who live and work alongside them. In this process of learning to love the other, the teachers are indispensable. They must be the ones who create the possibilities for the children to learn this art of community building. Yet, we teachers are ourselves hardly able to know how this is to be done in our own lives.

So we face an apparent paradox. It is a situation in which the teachers need to help the child lay the basis for something which they are hardly able to achieve themselves, the building of community. It does not work to base this teacher-community on old forms; we must build a new kind of community out of our work together. This community-building demands quite clearly a particular effort on the part of the teachers themselves. True faculty work requires that we develop means of helping the children which go beyond our individual talents, abilities and efforts. Some of these methods of working are addressed in the first chapter on the faculty meeting.

In a college of teachers, however, we are asked to go even further in creating a new paradigm for work as colleagues. In this paradigm, it is the circle which must take ultimate responsibility for the school, yet, it must not be come a center of power in the usual sense of the word. It must be willing to make decisions which will have far-reaching consequences, but it must be impeccable in its processes, consulting and communicating wherever it is needed. It must be mindful of what the school has been, yet, it must actively seek to develop an imagination for what it needs to become.

This will be different for each school and therefore each college must find its way to spiritual insights out of true spiritual freedom. The college has to take responsibility for what happens in every part of the school, yet it must not let itself become merely an administrative organ which becomes so bogged down in details that it loses its sense for the whole.

The Spiritual Task of the College

Ultimately, the responsibility of the college of teachers is a spiritual one. That means we must recognize that the spiritual realities flow into all aspects of the school's life. Each action which affects the life of the school is, at bottom, the responsibility of the college. It is indeed like the heart organ of the school organism. As with the body, the heart does not take over all the functions of the various organs. Instead it senses and regulates the flow of life-bearing activity to each part as it is needed.

The college of teachers should strive to be a future-bearing social form. In such a form, the material and the spiritual world so interpenetrate each other that we are actively helping to shape this new paradigm for human interaction with both the content and the method. Again, though, all of this work is for the benefit of the children who come through the door to meet us each day. Its primary aim cannot be for our own personal development.

For this very important aspect in the life of each Waldorf teacher, one must turn to the work of the Anthroposophical Society which Rudolf Steiner formed as the instrument of the anthroposophical movement. Within the Society, each person must be willing to take his own schooling in hand. It is entirely a matter of personal freedom. Often this will mean work in a group and/or a branch of the Society in one's local area. Additionally, at some point in this self-education, the individual will find himself looking for indications as to his next steps. At this point, any person, but especially a teacher will wish to look into The School for Spiritual Science and especially its Pedagogical Section. Here, there are ample riches for self-development, opening up possibilities for tremendous personal growth.[2]

The Practical Tasks

Having looked at some of the broad ideals of the college of teachers, we now turn to some examples of the practical application of these ideals. The foundation of a college will ask different things of us depending upon the situation. In a new school, the faculty will most likely be rather few. All the teachers will share in the decisions as the school seeks to find its own, unique form. Here the founding impulses of the school will have a great deal to do with what the school becomes. In some cases, there will be a strong anthroposophical foundation. In other situations, it will be the parents' strong wish for a Waldorf school which will imbue the founding. Whether the school has come into being out of the work of parents or the hopes of anthroposophists in the area or out of the idealism of a few teachers will also have its effect on the early colleagial forms of the school. Whatever the basis though, the teachers will need to make the faculty meeting a vessel, however modest, where spiritual considerations are consciously cultivated. This may involve, for example, study of pedagogical texts, work on the festival life of the school, or learning how to study a child in a way which actively works with what the child has brought with him from the spiritual world before birth.

Forming a College in a New School

At a certain point in the school's growth, the size of the faculty, and the number of part-time teachers, new teachers and teachers new to the school may mean that the whole faculty no longer can carry the intimate inner work on behalf of the school. The press of business, faculty education, class discussions and so on will require that the centering and active carrying of the spiritual life of the school be done in a circle outside the general faculty meeting.

At this point, a college of teachers might well be considered. It would most likely be founded with the help of the Pedagogical Section of the Anthroposophical Society and by those members of the faculty who feel that they wish to take on the extra responsibilities which will be referred to below. It is critical, though, that this deed be carried and supported in spirit by the entire faculty. It needs to be clear that this is a work taken up on behalf of the whole school and that it is done out of a deep sense of service to the children and the faculty. It is a necessary step in the life of each school which often comes when its pioneer phase is complete.

Forming a College in an Established School

In founding a college in a more mature school, there is usually a history which must be addressed. Colleagues often know each other well, and it may be that matters within the school have become difficult, even so difficult that the work within the faculty goes badly. Or it may simply be that the faculty feels there is an aspect of the life of the school which needs renewal. Whatever the circumstances, the founding or refounding will need opportunities for deeper conversations in which the teachers can look at the current situation of the school. Such discussions might well include a look at the school's founding impulse, its current goals as a faculty, its present situation in regards to size, demographics, personnel, etc., and the particular challenges which the school is facing at the moment. Out of this kind of sharing and with the full participation of the faculty, the shared perception might well embrace the wish to strengthen and deepen the spiritual work of the school.

The process of founding a college can be invaluable. It is an opportunity for the teachers to renew their commitment as individuals to the spiritual foundations upon which the school and Waldorf education are built. Because new colleagues will have joined the faculty since its early days, the preparation for a founding allows each of the teachers to grow closer to the school without regard to "old" and "new" faculty members. This is not to say that all the teachers will join this new college but only that the opportunity to be apprised of the elements and process of the forming of a college will build a basis for confidence and trust throughout the faculty.

The founding and work of a college of teachers can be seen as a sign of the intent of the faculty to create an organ to insure that the life of the school, in body, soul and spirit, succors the young human beings for whom it exists. In some ways, the elements which make this possible are the "imponderables" to which Rudolf Steiner referred. Nonetheless, we can enumerate some of the conditions which make for a healthy, working college.

Description of a College

In such an enumeration, we can say that the basis upon which all college work is dependent is the individual commitment of its members to self-development, that is, to living anthroposophy. Still other factors are: the ongoing commitment of the members to work within a particular school; the commitment to work with the colleagues in this particular school; a determination to maintain the quality, depth and professionalism of the teaching; the resolve to create a protected space in which the karma of a child, a class, a colleague, or the school can be recognized and acted upon (it will be this recognition of the destiny of the school in particular which will allow the school to continuously reform itself as a living organism); and the resolve to make the "level" of the college meetings such that we create a forum in which spiritual beings will be interested and active in our work. All of these are crucial requirements for a healthy, effective college. These demands require more work of the teachers but if they are rightly tended, they are at the same time a source of endless creativity and strength.

What then, are the steps needed not only to establish but to maintain this college of teachers in a living way? Let us begin by stating that there is no one "right" college form. Even its name can vary, being called a *council* in one school, a *conference* in another, and a *collegium* in a third. At the foundation of any college, however, stands a circle of colleagues who bear the conviction that a living connection with spiritual beings is required if the school is to fulfill its responsibility to the children. Out of this conviction, some members of the faculty, who have committed themselves to inner work, will put this striving and its fruits at the service of the school. It is this which will form the basis for any college of teachers—a sacrifice of some individual freedom in favor of a higher freedom within a dedicated circle of teachers. This will be a circle of teachers who actively cultivate a consciousness which is greater than their own individual point of view.

And if a college is thus rightly constituted and formed, it will, like the heart, sense what is happening in every part of the organism. It will know how things are throughout the school. At the same time, this heart organ will intuit what the times are asking of the school today and what it will need to become in the future. The school will be a place in which children and young people will feel themselves to be part of an exciting endeavor, a place in which they can meet life. In addition, one will find that in such an organ, attention, true consideration, and productive activity will surely be devoted to those areas which are in need of it at that point in time. And miraculously, the effectiveness of the work will be more than the sum of the energy and capacities of the individual members of the college. Rather, it will be of a much higher potency because it will invite the interest and participation of both spiritual beings and those human beings who are on the other side of the threshold of the spiritual world.

The Individual's Commitment to the College

These experiences will come about, however, only when each individual has dedicated himself or herself to inner activity. Indeed, this inner commitment to become a meditant, to develop the organs of perception needed for the spiritual world, is a veritable foundation stone for a college of teachers. The important factor here is not how "spiritually developed" someone is. Rather, the important point is that I, as a college member, have recognized that I must transform my own being in such a way that I become an instrument for the spirit. Rudolf Steiner has given many indications for such an anthroposophical path.[3] More will be said on this later. Another valuable source for material on this topic is *The Meditative Life of the Teacher* by Johannes Tautz.[4]

Having made this commitment to oneself, the opportunity exists to join with colleagues in a new way. The circle is now made up of individuals who wish, out of something larger than what they are as personalities, to carry the needs of the children and the school. This means that one has the possibility of committing oneself to work with other colleagues to create a spiritual vessel for the school. This vessel is made up of the good intentions and of the actions born out of anthroposophical striving. To put it another way, it means giving up my personal wishes for myself, my class, and my school in order to discover what the spiritual tasks and needs of the school are as its own living organism. The only way in which these tasks and needs can be recognized is if each member works to create a protected space in which the college as heart-organ can perceive what the times are asking. For the individual members of the circle, this demands a fine balance between two gestures. On the one hand there is the needed inner and outer activity of each individual. On the other, there must be the willingness to hold back so as to hear what is living in the larger sphere of the cosmos. This reality may sound in one's heart, in the room, the school, the community or beyond. Indeed, it is not too much to strive to hear in this way what is being asked of all of us by the spirit of our time, Michael.

This kind of perception is possible when the social structures within the school allow for each colleague to contribute, communicate and consult with the others so as to maintain a living circulation within the school. This means that a soul-spiritual basis is engendered within the college such that the deliberations of the colleagues are based upon a mutual trust which has come from a real recognition of the others.

This is the meaning of decision-making by consensus. It does not mean that every member must agree to a given decision, but that the process has been one in which, for each individual, the best efforts to find the truth have been made. The process of working together must be timely but not hurried, thoughtful but not ponderous. Ideally, each member will come away satisfied with the decision. However, failing that kind of agreement, each will nonetheless stand behind the integrity of the process. It may mean allowing something to happen which is against my best judgment, but I then put my confidence in the wisdom of the individuals who make up this very special circle. I will stand behind the decision as the best which the college could do at that moment. If it should prove to be the wrong decision, I will take it as my own responsibility, too. This does not mean an "I told you so" attitude, but rather an attitude which sees the whole process as a path upon which I, as a member of the college, have learned something out of spiritual insight.

Such a way of working can also be engendered in meetings of faculty, board and parents if the college mood is also consciously carried into these meetings by college members. Within the college itself, building this trust will need time, self-knowledge and work. It will also need a confidentiality which allows for a full exploration of a subject without concern that parts of the conversation will be rumored about and taken out of context. It must also, however, avoid the risk of being seen as secretive. The answer lies in having the moral tact to know what to share, whom to involve and when to involve them in the deliberations.

In a meeting with such an atmosphere, the spiritual possibilities can be freely sounded, examined and decided upon without the danger of sympathy and antipathy becoming the determinants in a decision. Here, the results of individual anthroposophical activity in developing new capacities are experienced. Each member can feel that his counsel is not only the fruit of his own thoughts, but also the gift of those beings who stand behind the assembled colleagues and weave through their circle as the deliberations proceed.

Priorities

Since the school's reason for being is to serve the needs of the children, the quality and scope of the teaching is a matter to be carried by the college as well. While much of this work goes on in the faculty with all the teachers, it is the college which has the ultimate responsibility to ensure that the children's needs are being met. This charge encompasses many aspects: the continuing education of the teachers; preserving the role and direction of the festivals in the school; the work and study in the faculty meetings; the knowledge of what is going on in each classroom; overseeing effective teacher evaluation so that it is done with insight; the final responsibility in hiring or dismissing teachers. All these are realms in which the college must take a leading role. It is the sign of a healthy college that the work in most of these areas will involve the entire faculty in some aspects. Delegated committees will function with a good mix of college and non-college members, of kindergarten, elementary and high school teachers, of full and part-time teachers, and of experienced and newer colleagues. Not all elements need to be present on each committee, as Ernst Lehrs indicates in his article *Republican Not Democratic*.[5] A real leaven to the work will be experienced by the shoulder-to-shoulder striving of ever-changing constellations of people, each contributing his or her unique qualities.

It is also the college which must penetrate the programs and the curriculum of the entire school. It is first of all a matter of striving for a thorough understanding of why Rudolf Steiner formed the curriculum in the way that he did. It is also a matter of reading the times as well as the children and young people so that their expressed as well as their unexpressed needs are met by the school, as far as possible, in every aspect of its life. The curriculum was chosen by Rudolf Steiner with a deep wisdom, so that it takes long years of work and study to understand why something is taught at a particular time in the life of the child. As trends come and go in education, we must learn to see what sort of relevance each has in the light of spiritual science. Ideas such as new math, ungraded classrooms and multiculturalism must be researched and understood in the light of *The Study of Man* so that informed discussions can lead to decisions based on spiritual insight.

An intimate knowledge in regard to everything which is going on with each teacher and in each classroom throughout the school is also a college responsibility. Each colleague can then feel himself or herself recognized and supported by fellow teachers. Each teacher needs to feel, "I can count on my colleagues to help me grow beyond who I am." These same teachers will share observations, encourage and support study and development in identified areas, and then assess progress in such areas. While learning to critique our own performance and that of our colleagues is difficult, it is the only way that we can morally stand before the children, their parents and the community. It is a responsibility which we must strive to carry, for to do less is to say that this new paradigm for shared leadership is fatally flawed. We have no right to ask for the trust and confidence of the school community if we are not willing to carry the responsibility for knowing and striving to improve everything which is done with the children.

Let us now turn to the college as a place in which the destiny of the school can be considered. It is especially here that the individual meditative work bears fruit. Where anthroposophy becomes more than study and intellectual understanding, where it has become something which now comes from within us as a way of perception and action, from the "inside out" so to speak, we find that the true task of the school can be recognized. Just by working actively with anthroposophy as a way of life, our way of meeting the world becomes qualitatively different. It allows one to rise above the challenges of each day and see the historical context of the present moment as well as the possibilities for the future.[6]

In meetings on this level, we can maintain spaces in which the college of teachers can develop an overview which has both breadth and depth. From such a vantage point, it is able to articulate strong and clear intentions. Each member contributes, out of his own counsel, what he has held up to the clear light of spiritual reality. "Is what I bring something which is essential or non-essential? Does it speak to the eternal or only to the ephemeral? Is it in consonance with the true aims and purposes of the school and of Waldorf education?" Everything which we do can now be seen in a broader context. We cannot of course, remain on this level only. We must also make some practical decisions which need timely answers. If, however, our point of departure has begun by orienting ourselves spiritually, our journey will be much different indeed. Out of our practice of working together, we are able to intuit what are the right and necessary deeds.

We can avoid the pitfalls of endless details if the college sees that its task is to develop imaginations which can be shared with the school community. Then by rightly delegating tasks in light of these imaginations, the entire school community becomes actively involved, taking up each task in a broad context and thus in a healthy way. These imaginations can become like stars, beacons for the entire school community, providing everyone with the possibility to work in consonance towards the greater goals of the school.

The Relationship of the College to the Community

The interrelationship of the college of teachers to other circles in the school community are crucial to its success. In his book, *The Child, the Teachers, and the Community*,[7] Jørgen Smit recalls Rudolf Steiner's picture of the teacher's meeting as the heart organ of the school. Avoiding any conception that the heart is merely a pump, Mr. Smit builds upon the picture of the heart as an organ which senses and regulates the flow of the life-bearing blood to all parts of the organism. The heart ensures that the blood continues to move throughout the organism. If the teacher's meeting is to properly carry the above-noted responsibilities, we can well see that it must do just what we would want the heart to do.

We can expand upon this picture by thinking of the college of teachers as more of an etheric heart. As such, it is more of a formative or life bearing organ. It gives to the faculty, the physical heart in this analogy, its form, shape, and impulse. It cannot, however, be seen as a source of power in the normal sense of the word. It sculpts the faculty organ, infuses it with life, so that it can meet the needs of the school. It is therefore equally essential that the communication and consultation between the college, the faculty, and the other organs of the school flow regularly, freely, and effectively.

The Relationship between the College and the Faculty

The flow between the larger faculty and the college is perhaps the area in which the interaction must be especially good. It is important that the college processes be as transparent as possible. If all the teachers know how the college works—how it takes in members, how it considers important matters, and what its place in the school is—the relationship to it can be a healthy one. As many conversations as possible should be taken up in the faculty or in the committees mentioned above. When it becomes clear that some far-reaching decisions are needed, when an intimate conversation is necessary, then the college meeting will be recognized as the place where these sorts of things should happen. The weight of these matters and the resultant decisions should not be loaded onto those colleagues who feel that their main task in the school lies more narrowly elsewhere for the time being. If, however, the college looks to delegate as much as it responsibly can, always being mindful of its duty to the children and the parents, a good balance can be achieved between the smaller circle of teachers and the larger circle from which it draws its membership.

The college also needs to guide the colleagues in the ever-present need for continuing education, both for specific individuals and the faculty as a whole. Thus, part of the sensing task will be one of helping the school to anticipate the future by identifying and strengthening areas of activity and knowledge in the school. Furthermore, the recognition of particular needs or shortcomings in the work of a colleague might, at some point, need a more intimate circle of peers who can help the individual to address the problem in a positive way. Whether this colleague is a member of the college or not, the openness, trust and confidence in one's fellow teachers is enhanced when there is a strong, regular and transparent addressing of issues. Ensuring that the college makes teacher and class evaluations part of its normal process provides the entire faculty with the knowledge that the need for help will be noticed and acted upon as a matter of course. This can build tremendous confidence in the whole community.

The Relationship of the College to the Board of Trustees

The relationship to the board of trustees of the school is in need of much the same interaction. The board is usually given responsibility for the fiscal well-being of the school, so that it needs to let its deliberations be informed by the pedagogical aims, even by the imaginations mentioned above, of the college. While the interaction will not be as great as it is with the full faculty, the need to share hopes and concerns in terms of new programs, salaries and benefits, teaching spaces and so forth is important. Early and regular consultation is a vital element throughout the deliberations, especially those which have a major impact on the budget. The board can quite fruitfully be involved in conversations in which the vision of the future of the school is being developed by the college. Without this opportunity, the board will risk operating in a vacuum. Perhaps it will provide sound financial support, but it might well be at the cost of a detachment from the deeper aims and purposes of the school.

For a board to be effective, it needs to provide the college with effective fiscal guidance and leadership. The college needs to see it as a partner to which it can turn for honest opinions and ideas as well. In an ideal relationship, two extremes will be avoided. The board will not act alone without regular consultation with the full college. At the same time, it will exercise some independence so that the college has the benefit of knowing the full effects of its various pedagogical decisions. Ultimately, the college must be the final arbiter as to policy, even though this may not be the case legally. For without the spiritual leadership and support of the college, no financial support, no matter how generous, can truly help the school. Thus, at a certain point, the board needs to defer to the considered judgment of the college of teachers. However, if the deliberations in areas of common concern have been rightly carried by both circles, there will be very few moments when a consensus cannot be reached.

The Relationship of the College to the Parents

The interrelationships of the college must also include the circle of parents who, with the teachers, stand around the children. Without a doubt, the parents must also be recognized for the contributions which they have to bring to the school. In all circumstances, steps must be taken to be sure that the college of teachers does not appear as a mysterious group which makes decisions without the parents knowing how these things come about. As with the board and the larger faculty, the parents as a group also need to be consulted, kept informed, and can even be involved in deliberations where it is appropriate. The parents in particular need to feel that the college and the faculty are circles which have the characteristics of clarity, openness and warmth. The college can bring about positive attitudes and enthusiasm from the parents by enlisting their aid, asking their opinions, and providing opportunities for them to learn about the education and what stands behind it. This means creating regular meeting times, workshops, and other forms in the school which will ensure that there is ready access to this heart organ of the school. It also means that the college becomes a body which ensures that timely and decisive responses are made to any and all concerns. Once again, responsibility may well be delegated in some areas, but the parents need to know that, ultimately, they can count on the college to give them a fair hearing and decisive leadership which has insight as its hallmark.

Support for the College

Given all the above considerations, the tasks of a college of teachers can seem to be overwhelming. We must, though, always remember that all that we attempt to do in the Waldorf school should to be done out of a spiritual orientation. With this in mind, we must enlist the help and active participation of teachers, board, parents and community members in helping the school to fulfill its goals. These goals are of real importance, for they are taken up on behalf of society, indeed, on behalf of all mankind. They require social skills which we are only beginning to develop. They also involve the development of spiritual insight out of the strivings of a circle where one standing alone is no longer up to the demands of the times. However, these efforts will succeed only if we also invite spiritual beings to share this work. If these invitations are real, if they are evident in our deeds as well as in our words, then we will give children the possibility to become full human beings.[8]

This, in the final analysis, is why the college is there. Each of us must decide whether this living imagination is something into which we will put our individual initiative and effort. Only with this kind of commitment can the school become a free community of teachers working together for the future of humanity. Only by working and striving together can we hope to carry the weighty responsibility which we assume when we take up the profession of a teacher.

ENDNOTES

1. See Rudolf Steiner's *Conferences with the Teachers of the Waldorf School in Stuttgart*, Volume 3, 1922-23 and Volume 4, 1923-24, Steiner Schools Fellowship, England, 1988.
2. For more information on The Anthroposophical Society see *The Life, Nature and Cultivation of Anthroposophy* and *The Constitution of the School of Spiritual Science*, both by Rudolf Steiner. These are available from the Anthroposophic Press. Additional information can be found by writing to The Anthroposophical Society in America, 529 West Grant Place, Chicago, IL.
3. Indications can be found in *Knowledge of the Higher Worlds and Its Attainment*; *Occult Science, An Outline*; *Theosophy*; *Guidance in Esoteric Training*; *Esoteric Development*; all by Rudolf Steiner. Most are available for purchase from the Anthroposophic Press, Star Route, Hudson, NY 12534. They can also be borrowed from The Rudolf Steiner Library, RD 2, Box 215 Harlemville, Ghent, NY 12075.
4. Available to active Waldorf teachers from the Pedagogical Section Council, c/o Hawthorne Valley School, R.D.2, Box 225, Harlemville, Ghent, NY 12075, $8.00 postpaid.
5 Available from the Publications Committee of The Association of Waldorf Schools in North America, c/o The Hartsbrook School, 94 Bay Road, Hadley, MA 01035.
6. For a fine exposition of the world historic context of Waldorf education, see *The Founding of the First Waldorf School in Stuttgart* by Johannes Tautz. Pedagogical Section Council, 1984.

7. Available from the Pedagogical Section Council, c/o Hawthorne Valley School, RD 2, Box 225, Harlemville, Ghent, NY 12075, $8.00 postpaid.
8. See *Towards the Deepening of Waldorf Education*, second edition. It provides a comprehensive picture which will be invaluable to all teachers. It will be available from the Pedagogical Section Council to serious, active Waldorf teachers. Inquiries can be directed to the aforementioned address.

JAMES PEWTHERER *was a founding teacher of the Hawthorne Valley School in 1973. He has taken two classes through from first to eighth grade as well as serving on the school's college of teachers since its inception and representing Hawthorne Valley to the Association of Waldorf Schools of North America. He serves on the Association Coordinating Committee and is also a member of the Pedagogical Section Council of the Anthroposophical Society and of the Hague Circle, which serves the international Waldorf School movement. As such he has helped with the founding of colleges of teachers at other schools.*

When we bring the child, just at the right moment, matter appropriate to his faculties, to his disposition, then what has thus been introduced will become a re-creating source of refreshment for the child throughout the whole course of his life.

If the parents of our children perceive that we have the will to work in such a way that we place into the decades lying before us people capable of dealing with ever-increasing difficulties of life—but still having questions to ask of life—then the parents will stand in the right relationship to the school. For it is upon the parents' understanding that we must build. We cannot work, as do other schools, protected by the state or by any other authority. We can only work supported by a community of parents who have this understanding.

We love our children; our teaching is inspired by knowledge of man and love of children. And, another love is being built around us, the love of the parents for the true essence of the school. Only within such a community can we work towards a future of mankind able to prosper and withstand.

– Rudolf Steiner

Chapter 3
COMMUNICATION

by Connie Starzynski

Communication is the key element in any relationship—personal or professional. How we speak to each other, listen to each other, understand each other determines how well we live and work together, whether it is a friendship, marriage, working relationship, parent to child relationship or teacher to child relationship.

My friend and I are going out to dinner; she hasn't been out of the house for six weeks since she had her new baby. She has her heart set on a restaurant where I don't particularly like the food. Serious dilemma? Not really. I can always find something to eat, and my friend is a happy person.

I am irritable and nervous. The book chapter I promised to write is due in a week. The children have music lessons, Halloween is almost upon us, and everybody has to eat. My husband is a busy person as well, but he "hears" my unvoiced cry for help. He takes the children out for the weekend and leaves me free to meet my deadline.

A colleague comes into my office to discuss a complicated issue. I can see that he is not having a good day. Is this the time to discuss it? No! It is not fair to him, myself or the issue. I suggest that we talk tomorrow over coffee and cake. Sharing a meal or dessert adds warmth to the process of communication. Does this mean that we will agree on the issue? Maybe not, but we may more easily come to a compromise.

My children are nine and twelve years old. During their early years we were very conscious and conscientious about diet, medical advice, clothing, toys and the media, but as they grow, can we keep reflexively saying no to all their requests? Probably not. So we begin regular family meeting sessions to discuss allowance, limited TV viewing, their responsibility around our home. Discussing the issues together, we come to a compromise. Everyone is happy until the next meeting when a new issue comes up!

It is important that we are sensitive to the other person or people in a working group. It is so convenient for us when all we can see is our own agenda. It requires

Communication

consciousness and skill to actively listen. In reading a newsletter from the Green Mountain Waldorf School, I came across a statement by Carl Rogers:

> The major barrier to interpersonal communication lies in our very natural tendency to judge; to approve or disapprove of the statements of the other person, or to evaluate them from our point of view.

Every chapter in this book addresses communication in some way. The successes and difficulties of any of these groups or processes all depend on how we relate to one another, how we truly hear what our colleague is relating to us as individuals and in a group, and how we speak to each other. For the purposes of this chapter, however, we will focus on the office staff and their relationships to the other working groups in the Waldorf school

The Role of the Staff

As a school grows from a small kindergarten to a full grade school, later adding on a high school, the administrative needs grow as well. The work may begin on and around a kitchen table, but soon the need arises for a real office with a desk, file cabinet, telephone, copy machine, etc., and all the human beings that go along with it.

The members of the office staff hold a unique position in the Waldorf school. It is important that they communicate effectively to other members of the community and that they support the communications of others. They have both a special ability and a special responsibility to keep lines of communication open among teachers, among families, between teachers and families, and between the school as a whole and the outside community.

In a young school, the office staff may be one person. This person may be receptionist, secretary and bookkeeper all in one. As the school grows, the need for office staff grows so that in a school of 260 children there may be four full-time office persons. The Chicago Waldorf School currently has a full-time receptionist/secretary, a bookkeeper, a development officer and an administrative chairman. (See Appendix for sample job descriptions.) Each of us has specific responsibilities, but there are times when those are shared.

The fact that we employ four full-time people in non-teaching roles might seem to depart from Rudolf Steiner's intention for school management. He said,

> The nature of the art of education demands that the staff divide their time between teaching and school administration. This ensures that

> the running of the school will be thoroughly saturated by the whole
> spirit arising from the attitude that exists when every individual
> teacher unites to form a teaching community.

Do we, perhaps, undermine this school spirit that Steiner envisioned when we exempt teachers from administrative responsibility and employ administrators who have no teaching responsibility? I believe that we do. I think therefore that not only should every faculty member participate at some level in major administrative decisions, but every staff member should have regular connections with the children. In our school, the office staff often serve as substitute teachers. It is also the case in other Waldorf schools that office staff have a part-time class responsibility such as handwork teacher, handwork assistant, maybe some skill classes with upper grades.

Telephone Communication

"Good morning, Waldorf School. This is Mary. May I help you?"

These words, repeated dozens of times daily, form an essential strand in the web of communications that supports the life of a school. Spoken in a friendly tone, they invite callers to frame their questions, state their business, express their concerns. At the same time the greeting is professional, clear and informs the caller who is taking the call. It is so very important that people answering the phone follow this protocol.

The caller might be a prospective parent making a first contact with the school, or it might be a regulatory agency calling to check fire safety or immunization records. A parent might be calling to suggest a fundraising idea. Perhaps it is a parent calling to relate a tangled tale of misplaced lunches or carpools gone awry. It could be someone from another school seeking information, or inspiration, or support. Or it could be a local newspaper reporter responding to a press release. Personal calls come in for teachers, and messages must be relayed. The number and variety of calls reflect the complexity of the communications network that the school office must maintain.

Of course the receptionist has primary responsibility for answering the phone, but there will be times when each one of us needs to respond to a persistent ring. It is important that the person answering the phone is friendly and has some relationship to the Waldorf school. If the receptionist cannot fully respond to the caller, he or she needs to direct the call to the proper person.

Many schools expedite this process with an information request form listing common questions and requests and with a space for comments. These can be easily routed to the proper person for a response. (See Appendix for an example.)

Communication

A school receptionist also keeps a log book where all messages for teachers and staff are recorded. Teachers and staff are then encouraged to form the habit of checking "the log book" several times a day. Some schools feel that a log book is too public for teachers' messages and prefer the privacy of placing messages in teachers' mail boxes. A more complete phone log that records all calls received can also be a useful tool for keeping track of the many types of calls and insuring that each has been responded to properly.

Another minor but essential aspect of telephone communications is the phone tree. We have a schoolwide phone tree for quickly disseminating emergency information such as school closings. We also have a room parents' phone tree to quickly relay requests for services (bakers, drivers, sewers, etc.). Individual classes usually have their own phone trees for conveying information about class business.

Printed Communication

The most tangible forms of communication involve the printed page. Many schools publish some or all of the following: weekly bulletins, monthly calendars, quarterly newsletters, annual reports, a parent handbook, and a faculty handbook.

A **weekly bulletin** is typically typed and xeroxed in the office and sent home with the children. Often it is, as its name implies, a "bulletin board," notifying parents of upcoming events, calling for volunteers, reminding of school regulations, perhaps carrying classified ads. In some schools, the weekly bulletin might also be a vehicle for letters, reaction and discussion. The weekly bulletin is usually staff-written, but volunteer help is welcomed for collating, stapling and distributing.

A **calendar** most often comes home with the bulletin at weekly or monthly intervals. It is a convenient visual reminder of upcoming events and also insures that events don't overlap or conflict. Keeping the calendar up to date and making sure events are scheduled appropriately are important office tasks.

Quarterly newsletters often carry longer articles by parents or teachers. They may report school events in more detail, describe an aspect of the curriculum, address issues of interest to the whole community, or show examples of student work. They usually contain photographs or artwork. Newsletters occasionally reprint articles from other schools, forming a valuable communication link with the wider Waldorf community.

Volunteer parents typically take a large part of the responsibility for producing a quarterly, and sometimes for that reason it may flourish one year and wither the next. Newsletters are not usually produced "in house." Schools may pay for outside layout and printing, or these services may be donated. A staff or faculty member may have a large or minimal responsibility for overseeing the newsletter, suggesting content and approving articles.

An **annual report** is often an integral part of a fundraising drive. Some are brief pamphlets, giving only a financial picture of the school and listing donors. Others are longer, giving a broad picture of school life as well as presenting economic information. Virtually all are professionally produced and printed under the supervision of a member of the administrative staff.

The **parent handbook** appears each fall in most schools, slightly updated from the year before. It is an important communication tool, as it lays the groundwork for community life. (It would be a more effective tool if it were more widely and carefully read.) It addresses the school's expectations of its families in areas ranging from media viewing and dress code to tuition payment; it explains the organization of the school community and suggests opportunities for involvement. Some schools incorporate community addresses and phone listings into the parent handbook; others publish these separately.

Most parent handbooks are faculty- or staff-written. Often there is substantial parental input. At least one school issues the handbook to new parents in a looseleaf binder, then issues only those pages containing revisions or additions to returning parents each year. Some handbooks are typewritten and xeroxed in house; others are printed professionally.

The Chicago Waldorf School may be unique in that we also have a Room Parents' Handbook. This booklet, written by and for room parents, stresses their important job of listening and occasionally mediating in the school communications network. It also gives a chronological review of the year, listing all the occasions when a class teacher might need the room parent's services. The office staff needs to work closely with the room parents to be constantly aware of issues that arise among the parent body.

The **faculty handbook**, like the parent handbook, lays down guidelines for teachers and staff. It addresses salary and contract issues and delineates what is expected from all staff in the area of meeting attendance, school involvement, continuing education, etc. Ideally, the faculty handbook should be teacher-written, but often this responsibility devolves upon a member of the office staff. Or, at least, the office staff often must take on the yearly job of revising and updating a faculty-written original.

Then there are the written communications to the community outside the school: the prospectus or information packet, the press release and the advertisement.

Communication

The **information packet** is sent to inquiring parents and creates an important first impression. Some schools describe themselves in detail with a professionally produced prospectus. Others have only a brief pamphlet describing their school and then add to it material describing Waldorf education in general.

A typical information packet might include a general letter welcoming the inquirer's interest, a pamphlet or booklet describing the school, a tuition schedule with scholarship information, a calendar or flyer listing upcoming events, and a reprinted article describing Waldorf education.

Depending on the receptiveness of local media, **press releases** can alert the public to the school's existence, to upcoming festivals, workshops or lectures, to newsworthy developments such as a change of location or a new building. A feature article in a newspaper or a short spot on the evening news can stimulate local interest in a school. Press releases are most often written and sent by a development director. In the case of a special event such as the Holiday Fair, a volunteer parent may take on this responsibility.

Advertisements can be similarly useful. They have the advantage that the message can be closely controlled, and the disadvantages of higher cost and lower credibility than news coverage

Meetings

As important as written communication is, human contact most surely integrates our feeling and will life. Face-to-face discussions, whether it is one-on-one or group, may be regularly scheduled or impromptu, community-wide or for select groups, but meetings, with their attendant discussion, dissension, compromise and consensus, are essential for the community to thrive.

Most of the following meetings are familiar to all Waldorf schools: faculty meetings; staff meetings; college, board and committee meetings; all-school meetings; parent/teacher association meetings; class nights and orientation mornings. Administrative support is essential for the schedule of meetings to run smoothly.

As a cornerstone of Waldorf school administration, the **weekly faculty meeting** has its own chapter in this book. For the purpose of this chapter, however, we should add that it is most helpful to the communication network for the administrative staff to attend and contribute in faculty meetings. In this way they can better promote understanding between parents and faculty.

Furthermore, while it is well accepted that Waldorf teachers need to work out of an ever-deepening understanding of anthroposophy, when it comes to the office staff, a grounding in these principles may be viewed as less important. I believe that at least a basic sympathy with the anthroposophical outlook is essential for the office staff to communicate effectively within the school and to represent the school to the public. One way of deepening staff understanding of anthroposophy is for them to attend faculty meetings and participate in faculty group study. In some schools the office staff presents the **preview of events** for the week ahead. Administrative reports to the full faculty describing the nature of the ongoing work are also important.

There should also be separate **staff meetings** on a regular—perhaps weekly—basis. Many daily nuts and bolts decisions about school operation need to be coordinated. And, more important, regular discussion helps over time to build a constellation of people who work together smoothly and share responsibility easily.

Each school will have its own distinctive roster of **board meetings**, **college meetings**, and many and varied **committee meetings**. At many of these meetings it will be helpful to have a representative of the administrative staff. The administrative staff can also enhance the functioning of committees by typing and distributing minutes, reporting decisions and developments in the weekly bulletin and by other appropriate channels, and by monitoring the calendar to ensure that meetings are scheduled appropriately.

Many schools hold **all-school meetings** one, two or three times a year. Some of these meetings are almost purely social; others are more informational, reporting on financial issues, for example, or discussing concerns of the moment. Whether or not a great deal of information is formally transmitted at all-school meetings, they are an important element of a posture of openness and sharing. They also provide valuable opportunities for informal sharing and communication. Staff members may or may not have an important role to play in running the all-school meetings; however, it is essential that office staff attend these meetings.

Another forum for a general meeting might be offered by a school **parent-teacher organization**. Parent-teacher organizations, associations, or forums often host quarterly, bi-monthly or monthly meetings. In some schools these are well attended, in others not. It is important to make them vibrant and alive. They may be the setting for wide-ranging discussions; they may stick to a featured topic; they may host a guest lecturer. Many variations on these themes are possible. For many parents, meetings of a parent/teacher organization offer a way in to deeper involvement with the life of a school.

Communication

The **class night**, where teachers meet the parents of their students in the classroom, is a highly effective setting for communication. It is usually held two or three times a year in each grade. Here parents and teachers learn from each other, and the class as a whole gains a sense of itself and is strengthened socially. In contrast to other parent evenings, class nights are nearly always well attended.

Many schools also regularly hold a sort of "open meeting" for the outside community. These are **orientation mornings** or **open houses**, often held monthly, for prospective parents, teachers from other schools and interested members of the community. They hear a short presentation on Waldorf education, tour the classrooms, and have an opportunity to ask questions. In some schools a member of the administrative staff may conduct the orientation; in others it may be taken by a faculty member. In either case, the administrative staff generally carries responsibility for publicizing and facilitating these mornings.

Informal Communication

Both the printed word and the formal meeting are, in a sense, "controlled" communication. Every school is also familiar with the power of the "uncontrolled" communication of informal social interaction, the chat outside the school doors in the morning, the spur-of-the-moment phone call, the "meeting after the meeting."

Such communication can be a wonderful strengthening force in a community. As ideas are shared, friendships form and deepen, and the social fabric of the community is more closely knit. For this reason, it is important to provide many arenas for social interaction—from the doll-making workshop or the spring picnic to the kindergarten tea. The opportunities are endless, and the administrative staff can play a crucial role in supporting them.

However, "uncontrolled" communication can also be a weakening force. We are all familiar with the potentially devastating effects of the "rumor mill." Here the administrative staff is in a unique position, by a posture of openness and accessibility, to defuse harmful communication.

Listening is an important part of the administrators' job. The office is an easy and accessible place to drop in to share an idea or voice a concern. Sometimes a sympathetic ear is all that is needed or wanted. Other times some simple clarifications may be in order. When the issue is more complex, it is important for the office staff not to usurp the role of the faculty, the college or the class teacher. Sometimes our role is simply to put the concerned party in touch with the person they really need to talk to.

It may be difficult for the office staff to balance work pressures and deadlines with the needs of the unexpected visitor or caller. It is important for us to remember that communication, both planned and unplanned, is our job. As one administrator puts it, "People tell me I should close my door. I don't think I'm here to close my door. I'm here to listen." Another administrator told me, "You should never be too busy to listen." If we are able to truly listen and to faithfully and responsibly act on what we hear, we members of the office staff will most effectively help our schools to grow and flourish.

Although we are all guided by Rudolf Steiner's indications, a Waldorf school each has its own unique way of working. As a teacher, parent and administrator, I have found it most valuable to visit other Waldorf schools, to observe classes and faculty meetings, and to just informally chat with office staff. Consider the following example: In a recent visit to the Waldorf School of Lexington (MA), the primary purpose being a meeting with other colleagues to discuss the content of this book, I took the time before the meeting to visit a kindergarten class, speak with their office manager, and attend a faculty meeting. In that short period of time, I brought home new ideas from each experience:

1. The kindergarten teacher had so wonderfully arranged her playstands in such a way that the children were surrounded by the rainbow colors. I most certainly felt as a visitor held by the warmth and color in this environment.

2. As I sat in the office observing the comings and goings, I noticed several three-ring binders artfully covered with children's paintings. Each binder displayed various articles of a particular theme: newsletters, curriculum guides, samples of children's reports, articles on Waldorf schools, Waldorf education, family life and parenting. Such a simple task! I spent years trying to figure out what to do with articles and newsletters from other Waldorf schools aside from leaving them on faculty room tables or loosely displayed on a rack in the school entrance. I immediately implemented this idea at our school, happy to know these valuable pieces of information are protected and available to visitors.

3. It was a relief to sit in another school's faculty meeting and objectively observe the dynamics. I felt quite at home and chuckled inwardly at times during the discussions. It was all so familiar. The experience gave me the opportunity to reflect on our own faculty meetings and experience a new perspective.

Every school needs to constantly analyze and review its communication patterns in the professional meetings at the end of each year. We must ask the question: How can we do it better? We must realize that we create the role model for our children who are being guided and formed by the manner in which adults around them communicate.

Communication

CONNIE STARZYNSKI *is the Administrative Chairperson at the Chicago Waldorf School, where, with her husband, Jim, she was a co-founder of the elementary school. She was first a kindergarten teacher, then a member of the board of trustees, and has been very active in committee work such as special events and finance. She has represented AWSNA as a member of the committee which has guided the Urban Waldorf Program in Milwaukee.*

Chapter 4
COMMITTEE STRUCTURE
by Sally van Sant

In my research of the committee structure of many Waldorf schools around the country, I have found that most schools have organizational charts and outlines of the functions carried out by their committees. I was left with the question: Once the skeletal structures of our organizations are in place, what are the next steps in forming healthy, working communities within our schools?

The framework of this chapter is best stated in the following:

> The spiritual life forces of a Waldorf school are twofold, or we could say, there are two motives for its existence. On the one hand, it is the starting point for a renewal of education based on a spiritual knowledge of the whole human being (the teacher's vocation as such). On the other hand, and at the same time, it is the working model for a social community, it is an institution of the free life of spirit.[1]

It is this working model for social community which is the basis on which committees should be structured. In this model we find an opportunity to develop an understanding of and a forum for active participation into the ideas and realities of social interaction. In this age of the consciousness soul, our challenge is to transform our relational life from the individual to the group. I will be sharing from my own experience as an administrator, and I hope to spark some ideas for others to experiment within their own unique schools.

Purpose of Committees

In order to create a network of support for the educational philosophy, it becomes important to understand the concepts of spirit (identity), soul (relationship), and body (structure) in relation to the committees. In the *dialogue with the spirit,* we encounter the thinking life of the school and this involves clarity of mission and goals. Does the

Committee Structure

activity of the committee reflect the educational philosophy and shared goals of the organization? When a person serves on a committee, he or she should find personal fulfillment. At the level of committee work, one can find expression for his or her own individual inner growth and an opportunity to create a living reality as a group. In the *dialogue with the soul life* of the school, we experience how we relate to each other within committees, how our committees relate to other committees, and how the committees relate to the community at large. Is space provided to get to know each other, perhaps through sharing of biographies? Is there an awareness and mutual recognition of our relationship to other committees and is our work being communicated? In *dialogue with the body*, we find the actual structure and organizational charts where the material we work with is visible. Does the budget accurately reflect the needs of the committee? Are reporting procedures clearly outlined?

The scope of work being carried out by Waldorf schools today is greater than can be accomplished by the faculties alone and requires the assistance and cooperation of the whole community in order to address the many areas of concern needing attention in the school environment. A committee serves to fulfill the needs of the community to participate in the life of the school. Parents want interaction with the faculty, and a healthy working relationship can increase understanding for both in serving the needs of the children.

Committees serve to identify and expand the cultural life around the school. When we bring people together behind a common purpose, the creative potential is increased from the individual to the group. We begin to experience the building of a living reality as a group. Karmic connections force us to confront each other and awaken to our mutual destinies. We must bring to consciousness the questions: Why are we together? What do we bring each other?

Committees function to share in the burden of responsibility. Rudolf Steiner's motto (as expressed in *Republican, Not Democratic*) for spiritually responsible human collaboration is: "To sacrifice freedom for the sake of higher freedom." Once a committee has been charged with an assignment, it must be allowed to give its best to the task and the freedom to work out of a group consciousness.

Committee Organization

When bringing together a group of individuals to carry out specific tasks as mandated by faculty and/or board of trustees, questions of size and talent must be addressed. Determination of the scope of work will suggest an efficient working number. A group larger than eight people begins to necessitate the formation of sub-committees.

Sub-committees serve to focus attention on specific areas of the tasks carried by the committee. An example is a Safety subcommittee as an active part of a larger Buildings and Grounds Committee. Subcommittee work encourages active participation, a closer working relationship and the possibility of greater personal fulfillment. Finding activities in which all can find fulfillment requires periodic evaluation of efficient working size.

I imagine a healthy organization resembling a tree in nature. In the root system, we find many off-shoots searching for nourishment in the earth. Subcommittees are like the roots. The roots then support the trunk and branches above. The trunk is the funneling of activity through the committees, working to link the growth of the branches with the life-giving work of the roots. The upper part of the tree has two main branches which reach out to the world beyond. The health of the whole is accomplished when all systems feed each other and their activities are in harmony.

Individuals entrusted with carrying out specific tasks must be assigned those activities which best suit their talents. Having tried to bring a person onto a committee to enable them to change their perspective or to feel included has resulted in energy being spent on the person, often at the expense of the work at hand. Conscious thought must be given to selection by talent, rather than the personal growth of individuals. A well-balanced committee includes individual with varied life experience. One might seek a professional viewpoint or an understanding of the pedagogy. A parent of a graduated student might have a different perspective from a parent new to the community. It becomes the responsibility of the faculty and board to guide the process of selection to committee, bringing an awareness of temperament, male/female, and a balance of community, faculty, parents, and friends.

Forming Committees and Establishing a Mandate System

The faculty and board of trustees are entrusted with the task of determining the needs of the organization. Through the classroom experience, faculty meetings and pedagogical committees, the faculty deepens its understanding of the core needs. The board of trustees works to financially and legally build an organ which reflects these ideals. A mandate is the clear articulation of a task and its purpose.

Once the needs of the organization are determined, questions to address are:

1. Does a committee already exist which can expand to include this task?
2. Is a standing committee of committed individuals functioning for ongoing work needed?
3. Would a time-limited, ad hoc, committee serve the need?

Committee Structure

Each committee should have a charter or mission statement which is endorsed by both faculty and board, to be reviewed and revised yearly. A three-year term of office enables new talent and initiative to develop. Staggering the rotation of committee membership allows for better continuity. Clearly defined areas of responsibility, with delegation of duties, will promote the individual's freedom to act in his or her area of interest. The committees are encouraged to make decisions on behalf of the whole when the leadership of the organization clearly shares the vision and purpose of the work.

An understanding and mutual listening between committees and board or faculty is of primary importance in maintaining trust in the organization. Committees should take specific decisions to the board or faculty in cases of uncertainty.

Many schools have well-developed committee structures which can be transformed into a mandate system with more conscious articulation. The governing bodies of the organization work toward clearly defining policies and procedures for the committees. When understanding and a common definition are reached, the mandate will be apparent. Work in areas of policies and procedures can be followed by the building of common definitions of mandated tasks.

Guidelines for Proposed Mandate

1. Each committee needs to write up a proposed mandate, including definitions of duties, limitations and accountability such as

    a. The _____ Committee is empowered to make decisions and follow through to implementation and review in the following areas of responsibility:
    b. The _____ Committee would act in an advisory capacity and make recommendations to _____.
    c. From whom would committee members expect to seek advice before making a decision and implementing it?
    d. To whom is the committee accountable?
    e. What tasks are presently within the committee's domain that you recommend be shifted to another group or individual?
    f. What tasks currently carried by another group ought to be within the committee's domain?

2. Faculty and/or board will review and refine these proposed mandates. Conversations between committees regarding the proposal may be needed.

3. Approval from governing bodies to the mandate will be the result of this work.

The Meeting

The social/relational work takes place at the point of meeting in committee. Three elements important to group work are:

        Study   Thought Life
        Social   Feeling Life
        Work   Will Life

When all three areas of interaction are exercised, individuals find fulfillment and energy for their work. Each meeting can provide an opportunity for inner development as well as outer activity when a living consciousness of content, relationship and procedure are carried. A well-planned meeting with agenda preparation and distribution in advance is essential. Are the aims clearly defined for discussion? Is there time allocated for discussion and analysis? Was a decision reached? Who needs to be communicated to? At the conclusion of each meeting, a period of review and reflection on the experience helps to foster group loyalty. In the review process we develop a sense of balance between procedural consciousness and lively engagement.

Policy

Each committee should set a definite day and time to meet regularly. The frequency of meetings is determined by the scope of work. Meetings should not be canceled. Even when there appears to be no pending business, just getting like minds together can sometimes produce a spark of creative energy. Each meeting needs set times to begin and finish; too long a meeting can be wearing. Clarity, precision and punctuality honor the commitment to the freely-given time of volunteers.

Membership on a committee means responsibility and commitment. If a person cannot attend meetings regularly, the whole group is affected. After three missed meetings, the person will be asked to step off the committee to be replaced by someone who is willing to participate on a fuller level.

Procedures

Minutes taken at each meeting provide a means of communication among the committee members and with others in the school. Distributing the minutes prior to the next meeting acts as a reminder for the date and time of the next meeting as well as a written review of the work completed and in process. Minutes of all committee work filed in the school office serve as a means of consistent record keeping. An agenda distributed before the meeting allows members to come prepared for the work at hand.

Committee Structure

Format

Setting goals for the group, with periodic review, encourages continuity and ownership of the work. Time allowed for open discussion and analysis helps the group reach a more unified decision. Consciously observe rules of decorum. Interrupting, talking while another is speaking, arriving late—these and other behaviors are disruptive to the group process. Committee work can be fun. Involve everyone, encourage all to participate and interact. Remember to give members rewards and show the committee they are recognized. Publishing the committee's accomplishments in the school bulletin and occasional social get-togethers helps to raise awareness of the committee's function.

Communication

Defining clear avenues of communication throughout the organization promotes healthy growth. Being aware of which decisions need input from faculty, board, parents and/or other committees can prevent misunderstanding as well as overlapping of responsibilities. Timing of the communication is also essential. Before a final decision affecting another group in the organization is reached, space for information gathering is needed. Finding avenues to communicate the process undertaken by a committee before reaching a decision will strengthen the final outcome. At all levels of activity, the following qualities are important: accountability, authority and responsibility.

Accountability

Accountability is the key area which requires strengthening throughout our Waldorf schools. Built into the fabric of an organization, without a single person "in charge," is the potential for lack of ownership. Delegation of tasks followed by clear and accurate reporting provides increased awareness and understanding of committee activity.

Within the whole of the organization there are those with the authority to lead and guide the process. The role of leadership in a Waldorf school is one of facilitator rather than "Boss." We work towards consensus in the decision-making process in order to reach a stronger and better supported outcome. In an interview with M. Scott Peck, the author of *The Road Less Traveled*, a group of physicians came up with this definition of consensus:

> Consensus is a group decision—which some members may not feel is the best decision but which they can all live with, support, and commit themselves to not undermine—arrived at without voting,

through a process whereby the issues are fully aired, all members feel that they have been adequately heard, in which everyone has equal power and responsibility, and different degrees of influence by virtue of individual stubbornness or charisma are avoided, so that all are satisfied with the process…[2]

Being a committee chairperson requires the ability to be conscious of each individual's contributions and needs, focusing on enhancing the abilities of the group and sharing observations. A person acting as facilitator keeps the committee members active and engaged. A good facilitator has an open awareness of the individuals interacting within the group. When a person sits quietly through a discussion, ask him to share his thoughts before moving on to the next topic. Being aware of everyone's need to participate in, and own, the process is a primary focus for the person leading the discussion.

In order for the organization to fully promote responsible action in committee work, levels of trust and clarity need articulation. The ability of the governing bodies to guide through delegation is essential, along with the commitment to review and revise the direction when necessary. When trust and confidence are in question, we must have the courage to confront issues. Allowing time for the differences in perspective to find expression can help prevent misunderstanding and hard feelings. Support the action of a committee. During the review process, find the insight for improvement for the future if needed. Finding ways to express the ideals of a Waldorf school will enhance the work in the committees. Fundamental questions need to be addressed: How do we foster inner work? How do we balance the individual's needs with the needs of the group?

Conclusion

I am aware of the need to develop courage and enthusiasm for relationship building. When the awareness is clear and focused on the group, one can best facilitate and guide the work in committees. People volunteer in search of fulfillment and an inner desire to connect their wills with others. The schools have work to be accomplished, and when volunteers are allowed to serve the organization, the work in the classroom is strengthened. The teachers can focus their attention on lesson plans and the deepening of the pedagogy when a shared confidence in the environment is living. In order to provide a working model for a social community, we strive to be a reflection of the principles carried by the teachers.

Committee Structure

ENDNOTES

1. Manfred Leist, *Parent Participation in a Waldorf School*, AWSNA, Great Barrington, MA, 1987, page 13.
2. M. Scott Peck, Context/No. 29, Valley Diagnostic Medical and Surgical Clinic, Inc., of Harlington, TX, and the Foundation of Community Encouragement, Knoxville, TN, 1989.

SALLY VAN SANT *is the Administrator at the Great Barrington Rudolf Steiner School. She is on their board of trustees and serves as a Council member and advisor to five board committees. She is the mother of five children, three of whom have graduated from the Steiner School. Her husband is a class teacher.*

Chapter 5
THE ROLES OF THE ADMINISTRATOR, BUSINESS MANAGER, AND DEVELOPMENT DIRECTOR

by David Alsop

It must be stated at the outset that this survey is based almost entirely upon my own experience and observations.

In every organization that works to find its correct relationship with the surrounding community, certain functions quite naturally arise. In schools, the primary function is the pedagogical work that takes place between the students and their teachers. This work cannot take place in a vacuum, however. It must be supported by a clear vision of the pedagogy and how that pedagogy can best meet the needs of that particular community. It must be enabled to grow and prosper with the benefit of sound fiscal policies and responsible fiscal management. It must be enhanced by appropriate physical facilities, capable of providing a living environment for the activities of the students and the community. Communication, coordination, resource management, fiscal management, fundraising and friend-raising are some of the key elements which require attention in the working of a school. As the school grows more complex with each passing year, it soon becomes necessary to consider the question of administrative structure and positions.

In many Waldorf schools, the process of addressing these tasks and responsibilities has led to, among others, the positions of administrator, business manager and development officer. This chapter will attempt to explore some aspects of each of these functions. Sample job descriptions can be found in the Appendix.

Administrator

In the preface to his book, *Towards Social Renewal*, Rudolf Steiner wrote:

> The nature which spiritual life has assumed requires that it
> constitute a fully autonomous member of the social organism.
> The administration of education, from which all culture develops,

must be turned over to the educators. Economic and political considerations should be entirely excluded from this administration. Each teacher should arrange his or her time so that he can also be an administrator in his field. He should be just as much at home attending to administrative matters as he is in the classroom. No one should make decisions who is not directly engaged in the educational process. No parliament or congress, nor any individual who was perhaps, once, an educator, is to have anything to say. What is experienced in the teaching process would then flow naturally into the administration. By its very nature such a system would engender competence and objectivity.[1]

In recent years, more and more Waldorf schools have created the positions of Administrator, Administrative Chairman, Administrative Coordinator, Administrative Director, and so on. How can this be reconciled with the closely held conviction that Waldorf schools must be "faculty run" which has arisen from study and appreciation of the above excerpt and much more? What happens if this reconciliation is not forthcoming?

There is much in a name, and the school should take great pains to ensure that the community understand what the role of the administrative person is in the school. Is it an actual administrator, according to the dictionary: "one who manages or directs," and if so, what is the extent of this direction? Is this position in any way related to a headmaster or a principalship? Care must be taken to inform the school community that the Waldorf school is not managed "top down," and there is no one person responsible for all decision making. Rather, individuals are appointed to care for aspects of the school's life, and one of those aspects is the administrative work. For this reason, I have always felt the most appropriate title for the administrative position to be administrative chairman, for then it is clear that just as the faculty has appointed an individual to watch over and assist the pedagogy and the faculty (faculty chairman), so too has it been acknowledged that an individual has assumed responsibility for the administrative function (administrative chairman), and that these two, along with others (board chairman, college chairman, high school chairman, etc.) are working side by side.

Clearly, the administrator must have or establish a living relationship to the spiritual impulses working within the school, and the best way to attain that is by being a practicing Waldorf teacher, in the classroom. The number of class hours is not the important thing—what matters is a strong practical connection to the pedagogical needs of the school's students and faculty. This is only one aspect of what the administrator will have to carry in consciousness, but it is critical to understanding the fabric into which all decisions affecting the school must be woven.

There may be several ways in which the administrator maintains his living connection with the heart of the school. In his essay "The Riddle of Leadership," John Gardner writes:

> In a school community, there are other needs for teaching besides those in the classroom. The parents need education in the purpose and methods of their school; there are always beginning teachers who must be helped along; and the need of even more mature teachers for friendly counsel, both as seekers after knowledge and as human beings, never ceases.[2]

Engaging in these teaching activities is certainly valid as a way to remain in touch with the pedagogical impulse.

Isn't it obvious that for the school to be truly faculty run, those engaged in the running of it must be truly faculty? Perhaps, but is teaching the only avenue to understanding and furthering the spiritual impulses of the school, and assuming a responsible position side-by-side with ones' colleagues? I think not. There are individuals who through prior connections with the schools as parents or trustees have been able to assume administrative positions in their communities and who have been very successful. They enter the position with an awareness of the unique nature of the Waldorf school, and have an appreciation of the role of the administrator in the school. They are known, and readily accepted.

It seems that the most difficulties arise when a Waldorf school tries to hire a "professional administrator" from outside the circle of the school. Usually, this comes as the result of some segment of the community feeling that it is time to "get professional," and even if this is not directly said, it is felt by the faculty to imply weakness or failure. There is often the feeling that the school is a business, and as such needs professional management as such. It is important to acknowledge that the school has many business-like aspects, but fundamentally it is not a business. It is a cultural/spiritual institution, working, with the energy of teachers, parents, and other community members, to provide an unencumbered environment for the education of children. For those who worry that this is inefficient, Rudolf Steiner offered the following, again in the preface to *Towards Social Renewal*:

> Of course, one could object that such a self-governing spiritual life would also not attain to perfection. But we cannot expect perfection;

we can only strive toward the best possible situation. The capabilities which the child develops can best be transmitted to the community if his education is the exclusive responsibility of those whose judgment rests on a spiritual foundation. To what extent a child should be taught one thing or another can be determined correctly only within a free cultural community. How such determinations are to be made binding is also a matter for this community. The state and the economy would be able to absorb vigor from such a community, which is not attainable when the organization of cultural institutions is based on political or economic standards.

This book will necessarily arouse many prejudices, especially if the consequences of its thesis are considered. What is the source of these prejudices? We recognize their antisocial nature when we perceive that they originate in the unconscious belief that teachers are impractical people who cannot be trusted to assume practical responsibilities on their own. It is assumed that all organization must be carried out by those who are engaged in practical matters, and educators should act according to the terms of reference determined for them.

This assumption ignores the fact that it is just when teachers are not permitted to determine their own functions that they tend to become impractical and remote from reality. As long as the so-called experts determine the terms of reference according to which they must function, they will never be able to turn out practical individuals who are equipped for life by their education. The current anti-social state of affairs is the result of individuals entering society who lack social sensitivity because of their education. Socially sensitive individuals can only develop within an educational system which is conducted and administered by other socially sensitive individuals.[3]

This implies that the ideal source to find individuals who could serve the school well in the administrative functions would be from within the school's faculty. Rudolf Steiner wanted the teachers involved in the administration of the school for precisely the reason that it would help them to be better teachers! We are experiencing a growing tendency in the Waldorf movement to try to protect the teachers from everything except their teaching. Perhaps instead of adding more administrative staff, we should be concentrating on adding more teachers, so the loads could be managed and each teacher could make their reasonable contribution to the administrative needs. However, we must use caution and remember that an appointment to an administrative position should also be based upon a recognition of capacities. Just as the school would not ask a teacher lacking musical ability to teach choir, it should not ask the impossible of colleagues in the administrative realm, either.

The administrator, therefore, should be first and foremost an educator, steeped in Waldorf pedagogy and committed to the spiritual development of himself and those around him. He also needs a good heavy dose of common sense and the ability to work well with people!

What is he actually to do? What is the task at hand? This can be divided into two quite different functions, and this an area where much difficulty and misunderstanding can arise. These two functions are administration and management. The administrator must handle each, and often with different temperaments!

First, the administrator is called upon to "minister to" the school. This implies a school-centered consciousness, where the task is to listen, filter, sort out information, make suggestions to be responded to by others, and act as a conduit for information and the impulses of others—in short, to bear witness to the life of the school and help to make it visible to others. The administrator becomes a sense organ for the school, and informs the school about its inner and outer environment. This is made possible by the fact that the administrator is involved with so many diverse groups within the school community and attends many meetings. This is the "selfless" function, and the task is one of vision, imagination, exploring next steps in the growth and development of the school, enabling the school to move forward. A key task here is that of communications. The administrator must be able to share that which he sees with all constituents of the school community: faculty, board and parents. He should be able to function as an information bridge between board and faculty—an important reason why he must be fully involved in the work of each! He cannot be perceived as the agent of any one constituency, but instead as there working to further the school as a whole.

One of the greatest challenges to the Waldorf school administrator is the fact that he/she does in fact have responsibilities to both the board and the faculty. The ability to look beyond this, and not to get stuck on the concept of "having two bosses" is crucial for success in this position. It is simply a fact of life that a new form is being worked with and old models will not be of support.

The second major function of the administrator is management. This is where responsibility is assumed for those tasks mandated by the faculty and the board.

Decisions must be made, deadlines must be met, and action must be taken. This is the arena of executing policies and seeing that the work is done. Typically, the areas of primary responsibility are the non-teaching staff and their tasks, the maintenance of the physical plant, and the school finances, including the development and fundraising programs. It could be said that the essential nature of the work is "resource management." Please refer to the sample job descriptions in the Appendix for more detail.

The art of being a Waldorf school administrator lies in finding the proper balance between listening and acting, responding and initiating, holding back and taking charge. He must find the proper relationship to every new challenge that comes his way, and he must find it out of his own imagination, precisely as the teacher must meet every new situation with a child, without prejudice or preconceived answers. By working in such a way, the administrator will be providing leadership of the best possible kind for the school community. He will not be perceived as heavy-handed or insensitive, nor will he be labeled ineffective or titular, but rather he will inspire confidence within the school community.

Business Manager

As stated earlier, the Waldorf school, while not essentially a business, does have numerous business aspects, all of which need careful attention if the school is to succeed. In the beginning stage of the school's development, these things are often managed by the Trustees, with the assistance of a bookkeeper and the involved interest of an experienced faculty member. The healthy development and increasing complexity of the school's operations will challenge the community to find the appropriate form of operation, and, for better financial management, many schools have implemented the specific position of business manager.

It needs to be emphasized again that each school must find the constellation of administrative and staff positions which are appropriate to that particular school. It would not be healthy to create positions simply because some other school has them. The vision that lives in a particular school—which must be articulated by that school—the biography of a particular school, and the abilities of involved community members will lead to particular and distinct administrative organization. The functions, however, exist in all schools and must be attended to, whether it is by a finance committee, a board treasurer, an administrator in concert with a bookkeeper, a faculty finance liaison, or a business manager.

What are those functions? Essentially, insuring that the school's finances are being managed responsibly, that the financial policies are being faithfully executed, and that the school is fiscally responsible to the wider community—including federal, state and local agencies.

The business manager plays an essential role in the formation and implementation of the school's annual budgets. He is the one with the most intimate and immediate knowledge of the successes and failures in the fiscal plan, and can suggest corrections and refinements as the year proceeds and in the preparation of the upcoming budget. He bears the responsibility for providing the board and faculty with accurate and timely information about how the finances are unfolding, through monthly and/or quarterly reports. He must ensure that all continuous obligations incurred by the school are being met, such as payrolls, payroll tax deposits, insurance premiums, payable bills of all sorts; and, he must ensure that those obligated to the school are meeting their commitments, such as tuition payments, fees for day care, fundraising pledges, and so on. In short, he must be watchful of the income and outflow of funds.

In addition to current financial activity, the business manager needs to plan and act for the long-term financial health of the school. This entails such activities as building an investment portfolio, with which to manage the schools more liquid assets, and the management of the retirement fund for faculty and staff. It also means ensuring that the school is carrying adequate coverage on a number of insurance policies—on everything from general liability to school buses.

The business manager bears responsibility for making sure that the fiscal policies of the school are visible and understood by all concerned, by making sure that the faculty handbook is up to date, and that the information given to parents is accurate and clear. For faculty and staff, what are the policies regarding sick leave, severance pay, reimbursements, and so on. For the parents, what are policies regarding tuition cycles, late payments, failure to pay, discounts for prepayments, and so on. The business manager is often the first to know when a new policy is needed, or an old one needs revision, and will suggest possible revisions to the faculty and/or board.

While all Waldorf schools are non-profit and tax-exempt, this by no means absolves them of the responsibility to file tax returns on state and federal levels. The business manager, in cooperation with the school's accountant, will be very involved in the process of filing these documents. It is advisable for all schools to undergo a financial audit at least every three years, and many schools do this every year. This can be a long, difficult, expensive process if the record keeping is not immaculate (even if it is correct!), and the business manager will assume responsibility for the preparation of the audit materials for the accounting firm.

The business manager will also be the school representative to the school's bank, and this relationship must not be taken too lightly. Much can depend upon the confidence of and in individuals in this relationship.

The accuracy and availability of financial information is extremely important to the success of the school. Everything from responsible, understandable grant requests to that of tax returns and the ability to plan next year's budget well depends upon good data, managed in a warm, trustworthy manner. The management of the school's fiscal life, in a professional manner consistent with the vision and purpose of the school, is critical to the school's ability to provide its services to the community.

Development Director

As more and more schools realize the need to supplement their finances with gift income, for both operating and capital needs, the number of development officers in our schools has grown by leaps and bounds. Fortunate is the school that recognizes this eventuality before it becomes an emergency, because then the necessary groundwork can be laid before an actual appeal is required, greatly enhancing the possibility of success. A development officer who is put in the position of immediately having to generate gift income, without time to do the necessary groundwork, will have difficulty. He will initially be able to do only fundraising, not development, and there is a difference, even though they do go hand in hand.

The role of the development director is gloriously complex while being at the same time utterly simple: He must raise money, and in doing so, he must first raise friends. This is the difference between fundraising and development—the fundraiser, usually a special event or a one-time occasion, does not seek to develop a lasting, future-oriented relationship with the donor. The focus is on the financial support. In development, the focus is on the relationship, which may, or may not, lead to financial support in the future. It is not by chance that so many of the development officers in Waldorf schools are also responsible for public relations and even advertising, because much of their effort is in informing the community about the schools. This effort is not only for enrollment purposes, but also for general friend-raising.

A good analogy for the development director is a gardener. He must very gently and carefully sow any number of seeds, then periodically water and cultivate, until ultimately it becomes possible to gather in the harvest—provided the weather doesn't destroy his crop! We all know how devastating a school crisis in confidence, of one sort or another, can be.

Development officers, first and foremost, are advocates for the school. They must be articulate about the goals and objectives of the school, not only pedagogically, but also organizationally—site development plans, construction priorities, financial priorities—so that they can respond to the parents and the public. This implies a detailed working knowledge of the school, and the most successful development officers are those who are included in the working of the board and faculty, and not just the work of the development committee. It also implies that the school actually has a long-range plan, and knows what the needs it will be facing are and how these needs will be prioritized. Common are the development people who have had to struggle for this information. In his book *Designs for Fund-Raising*, Harold J. Seymour states the following:

> Getting down to the specifics, the purpose of any development office at whatever kind of institution should be simply to develop support by service and gifts. The direct role in the area in fund-raising itself is to promote all three legs of the fund-raising tripod—occasional capital campaigns, consistent annual giving by all elements of the constituency, and the promotion of deferred giving through bequests and living trusts. The indirect role in the area of public relations—because it is development's very lifeblood—is to sustain a critical awareness and a lively concern for the ways in which the institution deals with the arts and graces of appreciation, hospitality, responses to suggestions and criticisms, and all the other major processes of dealing with its constituency—past, present and future. Whatever the size or nature of the institution, purpose should never aim for less than this or attempt to do much more.[4]

This sums up, very well indeed, the focus for the work of the development office. However, what, exactly, is the school's constituency? This must include all past and present families, all friends of the school, all local businesses who do business with the school, and the local community. It is necessary for the development office to maintain a connection with each of these constituents—usually through mailings, news releases and on-campus events. One of the key constituent groups in need of such ongoing maintenance is the alumnae. Keeping in touch with them is a major element in the friend-raising efforts of the development office, and clearly demonstrates the long-term nature of this activity. Again, fortunate is the school that has maintained and updated its mailing lists since the beginning!

The development director must be able to inspire a cadre of volunteers, for the work cannot be accomplished by one person alone. Indeed, the whole community should

The Roles of the Administrator, Business Manager, and Development Director

feel that development is their concern, and that everything they say and do is reflective of the school community, especially with respect to public relations and advertising.

Perhaps the best way to illustrate the role of the development director is with the following quotation from John D. Rockefeller, Jr.:

> Some people have a less keen sense of their duty and responsibility than others. With them a little urging may be helpful. But with most people a convincing presentation of the facts and the need is far more effective. When a solicitor comes to you and lays on your heart the responsibility that rests so heavily on his; when his earnestness gives convincing evidence of how seriously interested he is; when he makes it clear that he knows you are no less anxious to do your duty in the matter than he is, that you are just as conscientious, that he feels sure all you need is to realize the importance of the enterprise and the urgency of the need in order to lead you to your full share in the meeting of it—he has made you his friend and has brought you to think of giving not as a duty but a privilege.[5]

Conclusion

In every successful Waldorf school, close attention is being paid to matters of communication, coordination, resource management, fiscal management, friend-raising and fundraising. How the schools organize these efforts may result in any number of different combinations of positions with any number of titles, but the bottom line is that the capable handling of the tasks and duties of administrator, business manager, and development director are essential to the well being of the school.

ENDNOTES

1. Rudolf Steiner, *Towards Social Renewal*, translated by Frank Thomas Smith, Rudolf Steiner Press, London, 1977, p. 12.
2. Ibid.
3. Ibid., pp. 13–14.
4. Harold J. Seymour, *Designs for Fund-Raising*, Fund Raising Institute, Ambler, PA, 1988, pp. 116–117.
5. Ibid., Appendix, p. 198.

DAVID ALSOP *served six years as a class teacher, eight years as a Waldorf school administrator, and three years working for AWSNA full time, all within the Sacramento Waldorf School community. During this time, he has had working meetings with the boards and faculties of no fewer than fifteen Waldorf schools on questions of administration, and he has been active as organizer or participant in numerous economic and organizational conferences.*

> Confidence is one of the golden words that must govern social life in the future. The other golden word is love, love of that which we have to do. And in the future, good deeds will be done out of love for humanity.
> – Rudolf Steiner

Chapter 6
ADMISSIONS AND PARENT EDUCATION
by Anniken Mitchell

One of the most exciting experiences in the life of a Waldorf school is to encounter the steady stream of children who find their way to the school, their class, and their teachers. The journey to the school seems to be through the most varied and interesting circumstances.

The process of Admissions is there as a helpful guide in making the choice of sending one's child to a Waldorf school as conscious as possible for the prospective parent, and for the school. A clear process also helps the teacher to receive the child into her class with knowledge and forethought so that the needs of the child can be met.

The circumstances and staff available in each school will determine who will carry out the different functions of the admissions process. However, what is important is that the overall procedure is covered with care and attention so that the class teacher and the full circle of colleagues can welcome the child into their care. It is not just the individual teacher but the faculty as a whole who together will carry the joys and difficulties that each destiny encounter brings to them.

Telephone Inquiries

After an initial exposure to the existence of the Waldorf school, prospective parents will in most cases make further inquiries over the telephone. This initial, direct contact with the school is of great importance. It will establish a "warmth" connection between the school and the prospective parent. Have concise, consistent, clear information available. Be prepared to answer briefly what Waldorf schools are all about, what grades you have, the cost, the length of the day, etc. Be interested, patient and friendly; establish a sense that the school is accessible and available for further exploration. Inform the parents of upcoming events at the school that might be of interest to them and invite them to call back if they have further questions. Keep a card file on all inquiries for further reference, follow-up calls, and the mailing list of school events. Include the name, address, telephone number, name and birth date of the child, what grade they are interested, and what year they are seeking admission. They should also be asked how they heard about the Waldorf school.

Information Packet

After the initial telephone contact, send out a packet including your school brochure, a letter detailing the admission's process with financial information, the latest school newsletter, a calendar of events and any other information on Waldorf education that might be helpful to prospective parents.

Informal Interview and Tour

If the initial contact and packet of information have piqued the interest of prospective parents, they will call back and at this point an informal interview and tour of the school can be arranged. This initial visit is best conducted without the child. This visit provides an opportunity for both prospective parents and the school to get a sense for each other. Topics to cover might be first to get a picture of how they heard of your school, and how much they already know about Waldorf education and what educational values and environment they hope to find for their child.

If parents are new to Waldorf education, the admissions person will explain briefly the history, educational philosophy, and aims of Waldorf education, covering topics such as the role of the class teacher, the threefold nature of the child and how it relates to the change in consciousness and is reflected in the curriculum. Also give a brief picture of the history of your own particular school, school organization, school community and parent participation. Allow for many questions; the best conversation will come up if you can find a common point of interest and can engage the prospective parent in a good discussion.

Also get a brief description of their child, his/her educational history, and family history. While touring the school is in progress, you have a great opportunity to talk about the pedagogical method in praxis, from grade to grade. The mood and social experience of the teachers and children at work speak volumes and make the visit to the school truly enjoyable and memorable for most visitors.

Application

At the conclusion of a mutually successful admissions interview, the prospective parents would send in their application along with school records and a non-refundable application fee. The application form should cover basic information, such as the child's name, birth date, sex, year and grade for admission, parents' names, address, phone (home and place of work) and schools previously attended. It is also helpful to know of siblings, their birth dates and school of attendance. It is wise to ask the parents, as part of the application process, to write a biography of their child, including developmental and health history and any unusual circumstances in the family history.

Upon receipt of the application and records, the admissions person will meet with the class teacher to give a picture of the child and family, and if the teacher wants to proceed with the process, the family will be invited back for an interview with the class teacher. The child will be invited to visit the classroom and be observed by the teacher (if the child is in a grade higher than the first grade).

Class Teacher Interview

Before the meeting with the prospective family, the teacher would have read through the application and school records, and familiarized him/herself with the general situation of the child. The interview will, in general, give a fuller picture of the child's developmental, health and educational history and a sense for the family life, history, and values. It will also give a clear picture of the child's relative skill level and allows for an evaluation of the child's spatial orientation and dominance. Record comments and observations. Share with the parents the areas of concern in one's own class and answer questions pertaining to curriculum and school life.

The format of the class teacher interview will have to reflect the age of the child. Most of the new children entering each year come through the kindergartens, which places a big workload and responsibility on the kindergarten teachers who work with these new families in preparation for a first grade commitment.

Some helpful guidelines for admission interviews for the different age groups are as follows:

Preschool and Kindergarten—

- Give a description of the child from birth to change of teeth according to the Waldorf theory of child development. Explain the importance of imitation, play, rhythm and physical environment for the young child, and how these elements are nurtured in the daily and weekly activities in the kindergarten.

- Get a full picture of the child's biography and social experience prior to the kindergarten.

- Engage the child in play and conversation to determine development in both areas.

- Have the child draw a picture.

First Grade—

Acceptance of kindergarten children into first grade should not be automatic, but require a new application form from all incoming families. This gives both the school and the parents a chance to look at the connection they have to each other and the readiness of the child for the first grade experience. Many schools do not yet have the first grade teacher available at that time of year to conduct all the admissions interviews. The kindergarten teachers along with one class teacher can meet with the children and prospective parents. In addition to the biographical and family information on the child ,the teachers will observe the child in relationship to:

- language development: What is the level of clarity in child's speech and thought patterns? Is the child able to engage in conversation with the teacher?

- physical coordination and spatial orientation: How does the child walk, what is the posture in standing and sitting, gestures in handling objects? How are the handshake and eye contact? Determine left/right dominance in eye, ear, hand, and foot. Can the child follow simple series of instructions, clap rhythms in sequence, hop, run, skip, and walk backward?

- artistic expression: Can the child draw a recognizable picture, and perhaps, a simple form drawing? Can the child sing, match a tone?

- other: How is the child's relationship to his/her parents and other adults? Can the child leave the parent to go with the teacher? Is the child free from wetting or soiling during the day?

Grade 2—

All the above.

- reading: able to recognize letters
- arithmetic: able to solve simple problems with the four processes
- writing: able to write simple words
- physical coordination: able to recognize left and right
- artistic expression: able to draw simple form drawings and line rhythms

Grade 3—

All the above.

- reading: able to do some reading—for fluidity and comprehension
- arithmetic: Some mastery over the times tables; can add with carrying, and subtract with borrowing
- writing: able to do simple writing, a short dictation
- physical coordination: able to jump rope, hopscotch, and rhythm exercises
- artistic expression: can do mirror form drawing

Grade 4—

All the above.

- reading: able to read a simple text and retell it, has some familiarity with parts of speech and punctuation
- arithmetic: able to carry in addition and multiplication, single digit division, mental arithmetic, familiarity with measurement, word problems
- writing: able to write a brief composition on a subject related to an experience they have had
- artistic expression: able to draw a picture of a balanced human being and a form drawing

Grades 5 & 6—

All of the above with more complex content

- reading: able to read fluidly with good expression; good comprehension of material read
- arithmetic: able to work with fractions using all four procedures
- writing: composition and dictation to include basic fourth/fifth grade words
- artistic expression: able to draw a picture of a balanced human being and a more complex form drawing

Grades 7 & 8—

Children entering the 7th and 8th grades require careful examination. They should be asked to demonstrate their abilities in reading, arithmetic, writing, physical coordination, and artistic expression as asked in the lower grades. The class teacher should evaluate carefully if the student can fit in with his/her class of children. The social balance of the class needs to be considered, and the teacher should be aware of what this new student will bring with him or her when he or she enters the class. Oftentimes a teacher will find a student who seems to fit in as if that child had always been there.

It is a good practice for the class teacher and a special subject teacher, especially competent in dealing with the middle school, participate together in the student evaluation, and that the parents' commitment to work with the school and continue with Waldorf education be affirmed.

If the student has not had foreign languages or work with musical instruments, extra tutorial support will be needed in the beginning to help the child in the transition period.

Admitting a High School Student

Prior to interviewing a high school candidate, the admissions person has the advantage of having school records, recommendations, an application form from the parents, and an application form from the student that should include an essay, a piece of artistic work and the student's views on many issues.

Usually the family will come together to an interview. The first part of the process could include a general presentation of the Waldorf high school and the expectations of your particular school. This should be delivered in an upbeat friendly manner interspersed with dialogue with both the parents and the student. Next, the interviewer could give the prospective student some reading material and ask him/her to wait outside the office for a short while.

Alone with the parents, the interviewer can probe more deeply into the student's background, gifts, difficulties, relationships with both peers and parents, with authority in general and finally reach an understanding about what the parents are looking for in their choice of high school. Then the parents are given reading material and asked to wait outside and the student is met alone. During this time the interviewer can ask frank questions about the student's personal interests, academic motivation, extracurricular pursuits, relationships with parents, peers and former teachers, and his/her view on drugs and alcohol. The interviewer should be very clear on explaining the school's policies and give the student the understanding that he/she is free to make choices. If the Waldorf school is the choice, then it is understood that a relationship of trust is established with regard to the school's rules. It is important with adolescents to empower them to want to make the right choice for themselves in cooperation with their parents.

Acceptance

After completion of the class teacher interview and classroom visit, the Admissions Director and class teacher will bring a description of the child to the college of teachers who, as a group, then accept the child into the school. A letter indicating acceptance or not will then be sent by the school to the parents. The acceptance letter should include an enrollment agreement, to be signed by the parent and returned to the school with a non-refundable deposit, which ensures that a place will be held for the child.

Enrollment Packet

In addition to the enrollment agreement, the full enrollment of the child should also include:

a. tuition and payment plans for the parent to choose and any other financial information relative to your school

b. health assessment form for their family doctor to fill out about the child

c. immunization waiver form if the parents do not wish the child to be immunized

d. emergency addresses and phone numbers in case of emergency

[All of the above must be returned to the office prior to the first day of school.]

e. parent handbook

Acceptance of Children with Special Needs

If during the class teacher assessment it becomes apparent that the child would require educational support beyond what the class teacher can offer, a second interview and assessment would take place with the school's care-group, who together with the school physician would outline the appropriate therapeutic and educational support for the child. If the school agrees that the child might benefit from this program, a conditional acceptance would be offered, with a trial period and reassessment of the child's progress after a period of time. The class teacher would confer with the care group, and keep written records of all agreements and expectations with the parents.

Re-enrollment

The other process in the life of admissions in a school is the yearly re-enrollment of the current student body for the following school year.

The timing of this process is closely linked with the setting of the budget and the determination of tuitions for the coming academic year. Class teachers can get a sense from their class parents during the mid-year parent/teacher conferences of what their intentions are for the following school year. This estimation will give the board of trustees a preliminary picture of what enrollment numbers might look like. However, it is always an act of faith to set a budget based on projected enrollment—the reality of each class's enrollment will not be certain until the first day of the new school year!

As soon as tuitions are set, a new enrollment agreement is sent out to all families, to be returned within 2–3 weeks along with a non-refundable deposit of around 8% of the full tuition costs. This deposit will secure a place for the child in the class and will give the school a picture of the commitment for the coming school year. The college and board should receive monthly updates on the enrollment picture, based on children re-enrolled and new applications received in each grade. Families applying for tuition assistance will be re-enrolled pending a satisfactory agreement being reached on tuition assistance, and a new agreement will be issued when the financial aid process has been completed.

Exit Interviews

In the life of the school, it is important to include an exit process, by which we strive towards parting with families with as much consciousness as we received them. This process is called the exit interview and is intended to bring clarity and conclusion to the relationship. It is a time to tie up loose ends and to cultivate positive feelings.

The parents will be informed in the cover letter with the new enrollment agreement that, if they are not re-enrolling their child, they should contact the class teacher personally and inform the school administration in writing. A letter will be sent by the school confirming receipt of such a notice and that a place will not be held for the child. Each family with a child leaving will be asked to meet with a designated faculty member for an exit interview. The college chairperson or another college member will also participate in the exit interview where there is a possibility of bad feelings or stormy questions around withdrawal.

The interviewer should record, in a friendly manner, the parents' views to include:

1. a brief history of the child's tenure at the school; the year entered, teachers, significant absences
2. How has the child progressed, where is he/she in comparison with peers, what are his/her strengths and weaknesses?
3. the family's relationship with the school, how they have experienced the school's strengths and weaknesses
4. their reason for leaving the school
5. their future plans for the student's education; where will he/she go and what kind of a school will he/she attend?

An outline of these and other questions should be given to the parents in advance and the notes of the interview should be kept as a record of the college, who must be informed of the interview.

New Parent Orientation

At the beginning of the new school year, all new parents are cordially invited to attend a parent orientation. This is an opportunity to get a better picture of what life as a parent in a Waldorf school is all about. Faculty and office staff give an overview of the organizational life of the school, who is in charge of what, where to bring questions and concerns and how to participate in the life of the school. Parent representatives would share information about the activities carried by the parent body such as the Christmas Fair, the Auction, and other social and fundraising events. After the children have been welcomed into their classes, it is also important to welcome the parents into the community of adults, who all make their contributions in one way or another to make the Waldorf school possible.

Parent Education and Outreach

In most cases when prospective parents bring their children to a Waldorf school ,it is out of a feeling that this educational approach is right for their child. An ongoing parent educational program serves the purpose of deepening their understanding of the educational aims of Waldorf education. Parents must be nourished and sustained in order to have the stamina to make it through many years of financial and moral support that they will give to their particular school.

The most immediate format available is the regularly scheduled **class evenings,** when the class teacher gives an overview of child development and the curriculum for that year. Special teachers are invited to these evenings to share examples of work done with the children in that class. It is also an opportunity for parents to get a taste of the artistic activities that the children engage in through exercises in painting, modeling, eurythmy, and speech.

Other occasions throughout the school year that help build a sense of joy and school community in the educational experience are: **class plays, school assemblies, musical evenings** and **all festival celebrations. Study groups, parenting workshops, anthroposophical core courses**, and a **lending library** are essentials for those parents who want to probe deeper.

In addition to these in-house events, a yearly schedule of public events, such as a **winter lecture series, workshops, open houses** and **exhibits,** serves a twofold purpose of both attracting new enrollment and interest in the school and offering the parent body rich and stimulating events throughout the year.

An **enrollment committee** consisting of both parents and teachers has a vital role in helping to organize the calendar of public events. A more informal way of introducing the school to prospective parents is to invite them to an **enrollment tea**, where a teacher and host family would be available to answer questions and share their experiences in a Waldorf school, both from the teachers' and the parents' perspective.

Organizations within the local community like the Lions, the Rotary, the real estate companies and the public libraries usually appreciate hosting a speaker and/or a display of the children's work. A well-planned program utilizing the teachers in a fair balanced manner can make your school known throughout your local community and help prospective parents become aware of Waldorf education as a strong and viable educational choice for their children.

Anniken Mitchell attended the Oslo Waldorf School in Norway as a child. She has lived in Wilton, NH, for the last 19 years where she has raised four children and served for seven years as the Director of Admissions at both a high school, High Mowing School, and an elementary school, the Pine Hill Waldorf School.

Chapter 7
COMMUNITY RELATIONS AND OUTREACH
by Cornelius Pietzner

Community relations defines a very broad area both operationally and conceptually. Because of this it may seem abstract, remote, unnecessary, ethereal and diversionary, and not relating to the "true" function of a school, especially a Waldorf school! Such an attitude is perilous, and will be ever more so as the American public awakens to the need for a deeper, more comprehensive and effective relationship with education altogether. It (the public) will demand greater participation in mainstream education and in those forms of education which have been proven over time to be successful and relevant to the needs of children and nations. Waldorf education and all its exponents will wish to respond to and encourage such a dialogue, such an involvement. This dialogue will include the area of community relations!

Every Waldorf school is an important member of the surrounding community. Each day the school receives important people from the community through its doors, and each afternoon it sends important members of the community back to their homes. This daily breathing relates a Waldorf school in the most direct fashion to the community it serves, through the children it serves, and through all the people who are closely connected to the children that a Waldorf school serves. The issue of community relations is important for every single Waldorf school. The issue of public relations for the school movement as such is a related but slightly different issue. The potential for the Waldorf school movement to become an active and contributing part of the larger issues within the educational environment of this country is both substantial and exciting.

Public or community relations is much more comprehensive than a narrow program of periodic interfacing with the media or surrounding locality. Indeed, a true public relations encompasses and relates to many of the other areas within the life of a school addressed in this book. In this sense, community relations is a fundamental component of every Waldorf school. It connects areas of admissions, parent and board relations, and fundraising.

Community Relations and Outreach

Community relations begins at home. In any service organization everybody is involved as a bearer of the message of the organization. The stronger the coordination among the bearers of the message, the more powerfully can the message usually be conveyed. Furthermore, the greater the message itself is believed by its bearers, the greater is its credibility.

Community relations need not be reactive. It can be a powerful, proactive expression of the impulse of Waldorf education and the specific impulses of a particular school in a particular location with particular strengths and unique challenges.

Community relations is as much an attitude as an activity. It is as much tolerance, interest, openness, confidence and sharing as it is a laundry list of school functions, open houses, enrollment teas, press releases and public service announcements. This attitude can perhaps best be approached by considering community relations as a dialogue, a conversation—which is mutual and two-way. Community relations is not a desperate push to project, at all costs, your message onto an unsuspecting, illiterate and hostile "real world." It is not merely generating and delivering public service announcements and developing recruitment brochures. It is not a single function for a "hired gun" or an endless random string of events. It is, much rather, an invitation to relate, to participate in the life and growth of your community and its educational realities and needs.

None of us, either as individuals or as organizations, exists in isolation. We need and want interaction, common cause and mutual involvement. Community relations, at its simplest, is the activity of avoiding isolation.

Reciprocity and mutual influence between the inner exigencies and outer conditions of a school is a critical issue for the effective integration of the Waldorf school in the community. A Waldorf school needs to have a reflection of its activity within the larger community. It needs a mirroring and a response. And while we are generally clear about our ideas (pedagogical, social, etc.), we are also tentative and often inartistic about their idiom. Thus to some extent, community relations can also be seen as the attempt to develop the appropriate idiom for our ideas. Occasionally, others do this much better for us, than we can do ourselves.

For example, several years ago, then Secretary of Education William Bennett issued a small booklet called *What Works in Education*.[1] It describes basic educational ideas. It uses "conventional" language. Much of what is contained in this booklet is a description for what Waldorf schools actually do or would advocate! However, very few people seemed to be aware of the publication of this booklet and its coincidence with some of the ideas of Waldorf education.

Returning to the element of dialogue or conversation, we come to the basic image of community relations, which is best conveyed through the lemniscate or figure-eight. In this magical flowing line, the inwardly turned gesture of an organism (school), achieves a crossing point by which it becomes available, displayed, public in an outward and generous posture.

The lemniscate demonstrates a profound harmony and equality from one surface to another. In like manner, the meditative work of the college and faculty, and the pedagogical work performed by the school community will have a relevance, connection and parallel that includes the larger community.

To summarize: Community relations is an attitude of participation, of being a contributing, part of a larger function. It is not an attitude of isolation, self-righteousness or missionary zeal. It involves everyone at the school—secretaries, faculty, all helpers—and can never be effectively delegated or remanded to a "PR coordinator" (just as an effective longer-term fundraising effort cannot be vested solely in a Development Coordinator).

Community relations is a dialogue, represented by the wonderful form of a lemniscate. It has both inner and outer surfaces—indeed one is the extension of the other. Community relations is comprehensive and permeates many facets of a school's general administrative involvements.

Community Relations:

1) Image of the lemniscate –   Dialogue ⧖ Relationships

2) Reciprocity/correspondence between inner & outer functions

3) Outer gesture also mutual, give-and-take

4) Idiom ⟵⟶ Ideas

5) An attitude of bridging

6) Everybody is involved

There are no fixed recipes for community relations, no prescriptions. Public relations is not a one-time, splashy happening. To assume an inflexible rigid "program" of events would be not to understand that each school is inserted uniquely into a unique community. Real involvement in the life and affairs of the community, at various levels through a diversity of means indicates real community relations. Interest, confidence, sensitivity, flexibility and perseverance are appropriate "ingredients" to undertake the joyous and fulfilling tasks of community relations.

Focusing the Effort

Any community relations effort will be best served by planning and forethought. There are different ways to consider your events. First and foremost, determine your goals and purpose. There are generally three broad areas which occasion "community relations":

1) Enrollment

Goal – to introduce parents (and their children) to your school and Waldorf education to increase the student population. This is an ongoing, annual task—albeit with different emphases.

2) Fundraising

Goal – to deepen existing donor relationships, to introduce and cultivate new prospects to the school and to Waldorf education; to share plans, ideas, goals with an identified constituency with the eventual goal of generating gift income. There will be different emphases depending on the actual situation, sources and nature of gift income.

3) Community Participation

Goal – to present your school and Waldorf education for professional participation in workshops, colloquia, conferences, discussions, etc., to a broad spectrum of your local, parent and professional community.

The audience and specific purposes of such events will vary greatly—from basic public lectures to weekend workshops and to larger scale conferences. The expected "return" is to be a contributing and participating member of the community and to foster a greater level of understanding and insight into the work of the school and Waldorf education as such.

Each of these three areas involves events and activities specifically suited to achieve its goal. The clearer one can be regarding the needs and purpose of the activity the more suited, and thus effective will it be. One can obscure and confuse the primary, "bottom line" intent of the activity through assumption and lack of categorization or planning.

If goals are neither clear nor articulated, they will not be met. Mixing up goals frequently leads to disappointment.

For Example: Area #1– Enrollment – Consider, and take note of, enrollment activity and inquiry cycles. When do inquiries come most frequently? From where, what part of town? What kind of people inquire and in what form? Compile some basic statistics as the "raw data" from which you will develop your recruitment and enrollment activities. You may find that serious inquiries (and interest) come most frequently from mid- to late August through October (Cycle #1), and again from March (Easter) through June (Cycle #2). November through February may be slack times regarding enrollment.

Focus and develop your enrollment activities during these cycles—with one major activity per month. Use the interim times (Nov Feb June July) to develop efficient, prompt, friendly and convincing responses to inquiries (phone calls, interviews, packets etc, see Chapter 6 Admissions). Utilize the evidence of your raw data to help you effectively plan this timing and focus of your activity.

For Example: Area #2 – Fundraising and Development – This is a complicated area, with numerous dimensions, needs and opportunities. A school may have four areas of income—two of major importance: tuitions and gift income. Of (usually) lesser significance are (unrelated) business income (gift shops, school stores, etc.) and endowments.

Fundraising and Development are ongoing responsibilities—with annual appeals, capital campaigns, and all the innumerable auctions, craft fairs, car washes, bake sales, holiday sales and so on that serve as community functions while raising urgently needed dollars.

Most charitable giving occurs towards Christmas/Hanukkah time. The annual appeal and events related to it will be scheduled during December. Very often the major bazaars, sales, craft fairs, etc., take place in late November or early December, complemented by a second major event in early to late Spring.

Thus we may generally observe community efforts related to Area #2 taking place in early winter and mid-spring. The preparatory activity in fundraising is critically related to the success of the solicitation. Again, timing is of major importance.

For Example: Area #3 – Community Participation – These events serve a variety of needs and connect your school to people, issues and concerns in a multitude of ways. Some are:

Community Relations and Outreach

- Lecture Series/Adult Education—for parents, the community, professionals, civic and social clubs

- Workshops/Professional Development – for Waldorf colleagues, interested educators, parents, etc.

- Conferences, colloquia, etc. – for professional development, research, etc.

One can observe that these and other events conspire to create their own annual calendar. Each focus area calls for outreach in a specific direction to a specific audience for a specific reason. Each has a different purpose and will be organized differently. Planning and evaluation are two critical components in making any event a success and might include a team or multi-disciplinary approach to achieve the broadest perspective.

The activity calendar slowly suggests its own natural rhythms, based on the statistics (raw data) or needs you will have identified in the planning stages. Identifying the primary goal will suggest an appropriate event in timing with cycles suggested by your own information and experience. As you begin the year, you may wish to project your activities according to the areas outlined above or add your own categories.

Aug, Sept, Oct	Nov, Dec	Jan, Feb	March, April	May, June, July
↓	↓	↓	↓	↓
Enrollment	Fundraising	Community	Fundraising	Enrollment
				Re-enrollment

Focusing the effort, regardless of the activity area, is a determination and refinement of your objectives. This may also be called developing a strategy or marketing plan. There are numerous, and sometimes conflicting approaches to this area. One approach and one of the simplest, recommends:[2]

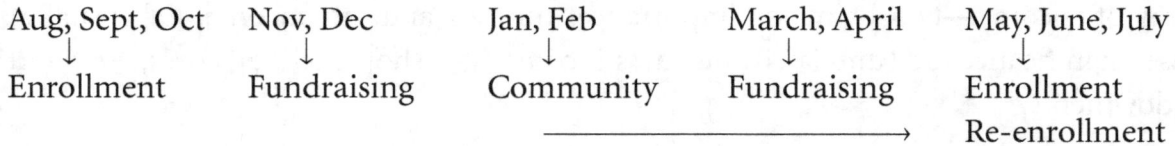

1) Select your market objectives
   ↓
   (What do you want to accomplish?)

2) Identify target market
   ↓
   (Who do you want to approach?)

3) Develop a marketing strategy & program
   ↓
   (How do you want to do it?)

The "market" may be comprised of different elements:

1) *Demographic* – what age range, social-economic status, etc., is your group?

2) *Geographic* – where is your market located?

3) *Behavioral* – what are relevant and supporting patterns, habits, interests, acquisitions, etc.? Think of a profile, or likely candidate.

4) *Volume* (usage) – what frequency or kind of involvement are you looking for? Parents, donors, volunteers, participants for events, board members? How often will you want their involvement?

Consider this a sketch which you can amend, alter or "flesh in" to suit your particular orientation. However, breaking down and analyzing your constituency by function, type or other characteristic may facilitate developing appropriate relations and achieving your school's goals.

In considering your constituency, you will also want to reflect on what you wish to offer—and how it may match your community's needs. Product, price, distribution and promotion are the four areas commonly considered in developing a marketing strategy. Although these terms reflect a business imprint, it can be helpful to apply a dissimilar and unusual paradigm to your considerations. All four areas are important for the healthy unfolding of a Waldorf school. Perhaps we rightly overemphasize "the product"—for without such an excellent one, what would we be working so hard for? Yet an excellent and unique "product" can languish and falter if its delivery and price are inconsistent, boorish and over-inflated.

Planning your annual calendar will help you to maximize the effectiveness of your activities. Naturally, there will be other events conflicting with your schedule—yet slowly you will notice and confirm a rhythm to your community relations work adjusted to the three major areas of outreach. Over time this will become a foundation for additional activity or variations appropriate to the biography and development of your school.

The Process of Community Relations

Community relations has technical aspects as well as procedural issues that may enhance the overall effort. The participants in the process of community relations are of immense importance. The process of developing events itself may reflect a sensitivity to a larger circle of people. Most people will respond positively to a genuine invitation to become involved in an activity. This allows your school to develop a critical support base—the volunteers.

Volunteers

Individuals, both parents and friends, may wish to contribute to your school in different ways. An often under-utilized and over-looked resource are people with talent in your community who can offer skills, time, involvement, enthusiasm, and will! No school can afford to neglect the invaluable role of the volunteer. The volunteer can carry a crucial function in the cycle of events that bridge the school to the community.

Volunteers will need explicit instructions, clear mandates and specific and real responsibilities, with reasonable time frames, realistic parameters of involvement, and reachable goals. They will need ongoing support, evaluation, encouragement and recognition. Frequently, the last two elements are not properly carried out. It is easy to use volunteers and expect great results without supplying them with the necessary tools to accomplish their tasks. Volunteers are donating real assets to your school and should be thanked and acknowledged. Volunteer development and, perhaps even more importantly, volunteer retention require commitment, consideration and time from your school community. These can be formal occasions which will confirm to the volunteer the value of his/her involvement with your organizational efforts and goals. An "Award Ceremony" or "Thank You Dinner" are two of many options.

I stress this component of volunteer development because too often I have seen an emphasis on the receiving end of things—expending considerable efforts on getting gifts, getting resources donated, getting volunteers, etc.—with an inadequate correspondence in the giving back end. We know that thanks and gratitude belong to receiving but somehow, with the numerous obligations and pressures, this aspect can be neglected. The result may be ineffective and unenthusiastic volunteers, or worse, a diminishing base of ongoing volunteer involvement.

The Goal

Focusing and narrowing the purpose and expectation of an event or activity is a primary task in helping you achieve your needs. This aspect is often ignored or assumed—the goal may appear obvious. Usually, if it does appear too obvious, it is too broad or ambitious. An Open House should not, for example, intend to explain everything about Waldorf education, display all the children's work over the years, boost enrollment by 100%, make the whole community ecstatic about your school, raise funds for your capital campaign, generate a series of media articles and introduce anthroposophy to everyone who signs the guest book! "Well, of course not!," we may say (though secretly hope this will all take place).

Determine why you do something and for whom it is intended. Wrestle with a few important priorities until they become clear. For instance, if you are expecting a visitor of some influence, try to determine what is enough and what will be too much for the visit. People do become overwhelmed—and your eminent visitor with the glazed eyes may have been overloaded with all the innumerable things he/she has been exposed to.

Sorting out, identifying and refining goals is exciting and necessary. It will suggest and help shape your activities.

- Do you want press or media exposure? If yes, what kind? How will you approach the matter? What angle might work? What are your back-ups?

- Do you want greater attendance at a public lecture? If yes, who do you want to come? What groups? How will you approach them? Will you go in person, call, or write to solicit their attendance? Will you speak to the group representative? What is your core group (of attendance)? Why do they come? Can they help you increase attendance? Who do they know? etc.

- Do you want to increase student enrollment? Why? What consequence will it have? (This is a slightly different question, but it can be answered in relationship to the community relations perspective). If yes, what data will you be working from to focus your efforts? Where is the data? If it isn't there how can you get it? What does it tell you?

These are all basic questions—but it is precisely these basic questions to which we so often presume the answers. Try and answer, straight forwardly and simply, these and other such questions. Write your answers down. Become clear about them—and they will help you prioritize and plan. Developing priorities will help shape your policies. Knowing your operational policies clearly will make your tasks more defined, more accessible.

These are all tasks which should precede the often frenetic schedule of events for your community. Just as an ounce of prevention is worth a pound of cure, a pound of planning is worth a ton of events!

Planning & Evaluation

The pre- and post-analysis of an event is as critical as the actual execution. Planning and evaluation are potentially community-building processes through the inclusion of volunteer and committee members in the discussions. By including a larger group, one fosters a sense of involvement and develops a vested interest in the outcome of the event. People want to feel a part of what they are doing. Asking for advice (and listening to it) can be tremendously upbuilding. Include different elements of the community in your planning and evaluation.

Take time to plan. Take additional time to evaluate. Make a (written) record of what went right and what when wrong. The evaluation should have different parts to it. Did you reach your stated financial, social, scheduling goals? This discussion should form a document which will be used as a planning tool and guide for subsequent events.

Community Relations and Outreach

Sufficient effort and commitment should be made to properly include the planning and evaluation components as a basic element of any community relations event.

Planning (and evaluation) should be applied not only to single events, or events in succession, but to the year itself. Having some forecast of the year's events and needs reduces the random scheduling of occasions. Indeed, planning in longer-term frameworks can be integrated into the long-range planning and development needs of your organization. Planning does not eliminate spontaneity. It is not a binding directive, but a road map or blueprint to help you achieve your goals. The process of planning may also help formulate and clarify your goals.

For example, assume a school has successfully developed eight grades. All is going well—the school is growing at an orderly rate. In two years' time, however, new buildings will need to be built on recently acquired land—to accommodate the growth in the student body and the increasing programmatic diversity. The question has been living silently for some time among faculty: "Should we move towards establishing a high school?" This question gradually comes into common discussion. It is a complicated, difficult question—with many different and differing perspectives. A process is determined by which this question will be addressed. This process is slated to last for 24 months. Part of the process must include current parents of students in all classes, but especially those in grades 4–8. Potential new parents will also need to be included.

This hypothetical situation will draw on many skills as it is a deep question of biography, development, organizational strengths—readiness. It is also a question of community process and community building. It will become a question of community relations. As the process evolves—a process lying at the very heart of the school and its unfolding life—the need for incorporating the community and involving individuals within it will become of paramount importance. Community activities will need to take place at the research, or early stages, of such a question. Thus one can see how planning can draw on and include the community in essential long-range issues of the school. The image of the lemniscate, once again, appears and we can experience the need for a mutually supportive modulation between inner questions and outer phenomena.

Every school can take steps and practice basic skills in developing their own community relations. Some steps are "action-oriented," some belong to the realm of planning—all require the attitude that your school needs the recognition and support of the community to thrive.

Some basic suggestions:[3]

- Develop effective graphics – consistent, unique, not overly complicated, compelling.

- Implement strategies for getting media coverage (include variations of all kinds of coverage).

- Train and support public speakers within your school community.

- Critique and develop a few individuals who will venture out into the community—as well as inviting audiences in.

- Gain the involvement of well-established, recognized people in the community (ask directly, with reasons why, explanations of what you need and wish to accomplish, and how you think they can help).

- Encourage special events; use milestones, individual accomplishments, awards, honors, etc. Use such events for media coverage.

- Develop a portfolio of photos that can be used for media and literature.

- Build your mailing list by category, and don't be afraid to edit and cut the list from time to time. Bloated lists are expensive, unwieldy and intimidating. Who wants to send monthly "Lecture Announcements" to 6000 people?

Each of these areas is important and possesses complex ingredients in your overall community relations work. They should be researched and studied in greater length than this chapter allows. There are many ingredients, many techniques to making community relations work effectively. Most of these can be learned and assimilated quite rapidly.

There are, naturally, deeper and more fundamental issues of community relations which are by no means of a technical or practical nature. Some of these areas will point to the general structure of the Waldorf school itself and may illuminate more profound elements within the school. For example, if the leadership and sense of overall vision and purpose is weak or confused, the community will sense this quickly and intuitively. Strong leadership doesn't mean one strong leader—but a clear, convincing message coming without equivocation is crucial.

A vibrant, realistic sense of vision and purpose—issues which are deeply related to the life and health of a school—will emanate into the community. This too is community relations. If the inner life of the school can carry the strength of enthusiasm, the light of clear insight and common purpose, and translate this in confidence and openness to the community at large, the message will be convincing and effective.

It is important to:

- Regularly define and refine your public relations activities and schedules.

- Be consistent, and persistent! Planted seeds will hopefully become fruit. Find effective methods and build on them.

- Vary your approach! This needn't be contradictory. There are numerous PR options. Explain, experiment—community relations takes many forms.

- Know your constituency. Identify your various groups, both existing and desired.

- Involve everyone! Community relations is not for the few—it belongs to everyone. Your whole school community is involved and responsible.

- Give it time to work! Community relations is a process; it will take time to build and solidify. Don't expect or press for results too early. All relationships are built over time, with multiple and varied exposure and opportunities.

The school community as an organism builds its own life-body and cycle over time.[4] This interweaving flow of activity which gives a school its true identity and makes your school what it is, belongs to the most intimate part of the organization's biography. Yet it is just this life-body—wherein, over time, the institutional memories will lie—which needs to flow out of the school and into the surrounding community. This is a precious activity—yet the community itself will give back to the life-body of the school. It is this giving back which achieves the crossing point in the lemniscate we have chosen as the image for community relations.

The school does not just impart, or give away. In giving to the public it develops mutual interaction and receives support, advice and recognition as a dialogue of ongoing involvement. This interaction brings new life and activity to your school. Good luck!

Endnotes

1. *What Works – Research about Teaching and Learning*, U.S. Department of Education, 1986.
2. Eugene M. Johnson, "Developing a Marketing Plan for a Non-Profit Organization," *Non Profit World Report*, Vol. 4, No. 5, pp. 28–30.
3. *Meridian Non Profit Strategist* (Vol. No. 11, Issue 4, Oct. 1990), interview with Los Angeles PR firm, Terzian & Assoc.

4. For further discussion of this theme, see *Extracts–The Economic Basis for Waldorf Education*, Vol. 2, Cornelius M. Pietzner, "Community & Public Relations," p.7, 1990, Threefold Educational Foundation; and *Handling Public Relations–A Guide for Waldorf Schools & Other Organizations* by Cornelius M. Pietzner, 1984, Sunbridge College Press; available from the author at Camphill Soltane, Box 300A, RD 1, Glenmoore, PA 19343 (215) 469-0933.

CORNELIUS PIETZNER *graduated from a Waldorf school, studied at Williams College, and spent a year in Norway and the Mideast studying the oil industry. He worked for three years at the Waldorf Institute as Director of Public Relations. He spent three years at Camphill Special Schools responsible for Development and Public Relations. In 1988 he founded Camphill Soltane and has been responsible for development, board, promotional and outreach activities.*

> Love is higher than opinion. If people love one another, the most varied opinions can be reconciled… This is one of the most important tasks for mankind today and in the future: that men should learn to love together and understand one another. If this human fellowship is not achieved, all talk of occult development is empty.
> — Rudolf Steiner

Chapter 8
EVALUATION
by David Mitchell

The administration of every Waldorf school has a professional responsibility for implementing some form of evaluation procedure. The purpose of evaluation is to affirm that you are doing what you say you want to do as an individual, as a student, or as an organization. Evaluation provides an objective statement that can lead to growth, increased confidence, and interpersonal sharing. This chapter will explore teacher evaluation and student evaluation.

Teacher Evaluation

To truly "e-valuate" (to draw out the "value" from) we must be able to work in complete consciousness out of colleagueship. Evaluation is meant to solve problems and provide for professional growth; it is not intended to place blame. However, it must be recognized that in human organizations intentions and actions rarely coincide exactly. There are always problems to be unraveled.

The manner in which a Waldorf school is governed represents a cultural deed through which the promise of renewal in society exists. Therefore, it is no surprise that Waldorf Teachers place such importance in expanding their level of competence. The teachers in the first Waldorf School "felt confidence in the 'power of ideas.'" There were no external guarantees."[1] The striving of the teacher is to constantly improve at our tasks. This is why evaluation is so important in a Waldorf school.

Assembled in the Society's blue room in Stuttgart in 1919, in the first building ever built exclusively for anthroposophical purposes, were twenty four individuals who had come together to listen to a pedagogical course by Dr. Rudolf Steiner. Dr. Johannes Tautz, the historian of the Waldorf school movement, reported that Steiner told the teachers that they were, "working on a mandate of the spiritual worlds." The courses lasted until 3 or 4am. He told them that "Waldorf teachers must become useful but conscious tools of the spiritual worlds. They must allow the impulse of the spiritual worlds to flow

Evaluation

through them. The work of running the school could only be done as a group. They must be colleagues together!" He affirmed that it is difficult to do this today. They were told to think away everything that is physical (body, etc.) of the other person. They were told to try to perceive only the striving, otherwise they would be overcome by the negative aspects of the other person, referred to as the Double. They were encouraged to cultivate the feeling that everyone knows something that they themselves don't know.[2]

Evaluation can serve a number of purposes. First, it can serve to help teachers to become as competent at their task as they are capable of becoming. Second, it can show all teachers a basis for knowing what is expected and what they can do to meet those expectations. Third, it can give the colleagues the means for having an overview of the entire school. Fourth, it can provide the means of identifying those individuals who are not able to meet the needs of the children at whose service the school is dedicated.

The first stage of evaluation is in the hiring process.

Hiring New Teachers

The college usually appoints an individual to be in charge of letting the Waldorf Teacher Training Institutes and other Waldorf schools know that positions in the school will be vacant in the next academic year. This person will also handle all correspondence between the school and candidates and subsequently will invite individuals to come for a visit. It is very important that schools phone for references to get candid statements. Letters are fine, but, if you really want to know the complete story about a person, speak with someone and ask questions!

Rudolf Steiner said: "The term *colleague* means to read together out of the open book of karma. If we are in conflict with someone, we will study his/her book of karma especially."[3]

Usually several candidates are brought before the college and discussed. Those candidates thought most likely to fit into that particular school will be invited for an interview. In some cases the school will underwrite all or a portion of the cost of the visit.

Each individual is usually hosted by the school for two or three days. During this time the candidate will visit classes and have individual discussions with faculty members. He or she will be acquainted with the pay scale and the faculty benefits. One individual would speak specifically about the person's spiritual path, and his/her commitment to anthroposophy would be asked about. A tour through the community would be given and the history of the school would be shared. Also, the difficulties that they might face in that particular community would be shared.

At the conclusion there would often be a tea or other social occasion with the faculty. The candidate would be invited to a faculty meeting where he would be asked to share his biography. He would be asked what he considers his strengths to be, what areas he will need to be helped with, what his special needs are, and whether he has any particular questions he would like to ask the faculty.

In most schools the candidate is asked to think about his/her experiences for a few days after the visit. Is the group of teachers that he met a group that he feels karmically connected with? Can he envision going into the future with them? He is then asked to write or phone the contact person and inform that person whether or not he would still like to be a candidate. If the reply is negative then he is candidly asked to respond why. This is then shared with the college. It is very important for the school to know how it is seen by people from the outside, so growth can take place.

If the candidate is an especially desired one, he may be asked to call the school if he has any other offers he is considering before making a final decision. This insures that the school maintains control and is not inadvertently handicapped in its decision-making process by a long list of candidates.

Once a candidate is confirmed by the consensus of the college, then some schools write a letter inviting the teacher to join the school. It is important that the decision to hire someone is made with full consensus because this makes everyone responsible for the success of the new teacher. In the hiring letter the school would write a detailed description of the position and other duties that would be expected, and the pay level/benefits, and a response in writing would be requested. This is considered a legal contract.

Some schools prefer to send a formal legal contract (see Appendix) to be signed. This contract would have a detailed description of the job being offered, rate of pay, and grounds for dismissal.

Hiring New Staff

In the case of a person being hired by the school for a non-teaching position, a complete job description would be written and the person would be informed whether he is responsible to the board of trustees, the college, the executive committee, or the administrator. A timely review of his work would be planned, say within the first three months of employment.

Evaluation

After the hiring of a staff member or a teacher is confirmed, an announcement would be made to the parents, and the candidate would be invited to a social gathering where they would be welcomed and introduced to the greater community.

New Teachers Load

The new teacher is usually given a minimum of extra responsibilities in the first year. His class load is as small as practical, and in the case of a first grade teacher, most of his time is spent with his own class. This extra time allows the new teacher to make contact with the parents and to put down roots in the community. The faculty extends itself to help make the transition as smooth as possible, and the college assigns the new teacher a mentor.

Mentoring

The more experienced Waldorf teachers have the responsibility to assist incoming teachers by becoming mentors. The new teacher might be a complete novice, right out of one of the training institutes, or an experienced teacher coming from another school. However, mentorship is most effective when a partnership is created—both individuals acknowledge that they can learn from each other and that they both are on a path of development.

The mentor would establish regularly scheduled, weekly meetings to discuss the new teacher's work, to answer questions, to be a friend, to explain school policy, and to try to anticipate areas where she might require help. This mentor should be sure to make early class visitations, and should be acquainted with the teacher's spouse and children. The mentor represents the new teacher to the college and gives reports as necessary. The mentor would also express any perceived need of the new teacher to the college.

Colleague Support

Some Waldorf schools have borrowed a good idea from the Quaker schools that is called the "buddy system." At the beginning of the academic year, each faculty member is paired off with a colleague to whom special attention and support are pledged.

This colleague acts as an individual "care group" for the other and vice versa. He or she would be attentive to those areas of concern that we need to know about before they become a crisis. A mutual understanding of helpfulness is encouraged between both parties, and one can represent the other to the colleagues in areas such as unforeseen economic hardship, etc., where it is better to have someone speak for you than to speak for yourself.

Ongoing Teacher Training

As previously discussed in Chapters 1 and 2 of this book, the college and faculty meetings are times of study and growth. These are times when we get to know one another and to exercise ourselves in artistic deepening.

Before the beginning of each academic year, many faculties set aside 3-4 days for professional days. During this time the new faculty for the school meets to take up practical business, to study, to do speech work and sing, to do modeling, painting, eurythmy and other artistic work together. All of this warms up the faculty prior to the arrival of the children. These meetings are also the time to do biographical sharing. For example, space can be set aside for each faculty member to speak for 10 minutes about some figure in their biography to whom they feel gratitude. Everyone would share on the same topic, spending about an hour a day each day, until everyone has had a turn. Other topics one might choose are: an event around the nine-year change that they recall, or a suffering and a joy from the past year—the possibilities are endless. I have found these exercises to be invaluable in getting to know my colleagues!

Other activities regularly included in faculty meetings that allow for evaluation are:

- **class reports** where teachers speak briefly about each child in their classes and give an overview on how they are meeting the challenges of the curriculum;

- **parent meetings** where the class teacher and a college member meet with the parents of a class to discuss the children and the activities of the class;

- **child studies** where a teacher will bring to the faculty a specific child to be discussed. The teacher would first present a detailed physical picture of the child, then move to his or her soul strengths and needs, building up a picture for the other teachers to share;

- **pedagogical presentations** where the teacher will metamorphose a prepared study that the faculty is undertaken and make it come alive;

- **special subject reports** where the language, handwork, manual arts, and gym teachers speak about their classes and program;

- **office reports** where the administrator or office personnel report to the faculty on their struggles, joys and work load.

The reports in faculty meeting allow for interaction from one's colleagues and provide space for ongoing evaluative discussion.

Evaluation

Finally, I have found it invaluable to have 5 minutes of open time at the closure of every faculty meeting during which anecdotes can be shared, followed by 5–10 minutes of meeting evaluation. During this time any colleague would be free to comment on anything that occurred in the meeting. Comments might be made on how the agenda was formed; if one was offended by something that was said; if someone felt that someone else had too much to say; if someone was grateful for something that someone said, etc. This is a time to let the steam off or to express appreciation. It is not a time for debate, and responses are not allowed. It is a time for colleagues to review their time together and to make any comments to the entire group. This can help to avoid backbiting outside the meeting and can insure that every issue involving colleagues is addressed in the proper forum—that is, with the fully assembled colleagues themselves.

Waldorf teachers have the foundation for working together in a still deeper way, based on the work done in the faculty meeting, as described above. As Waldorf teachers we must insure that the quality of our education continues to improve. It is easy to become professionally isolated—to be spun in our own cocoon. We have the possibility to generate interest in our colleagues and in what they are doing. We can become aware of the spiritual essence of each other! We can make time to get to know each other, as we make time to get to know the children. Peer and self-evaluation are the means by which we can accomplish this.

As schools expand and develop in maturity it is necessary to adopt policies that formalize a process of evaluation that may have been formerly haphazard or nonexistent.

Teacher Evaluation

As a school matures, the teachers will recognize the need for rhythmical teacher evaluations for three reasons: to help the school set its goals, to support individual development, and to uphold the quality of the school as a whole. The aim of evaluation is to confirm and acknowledge.

Many public schools use evaluation as the means of determining merit pay. (These evaluations have not always been viewed as constructive.) However, in the Waldorf schools, evaluation is used solely as the means to improve oneself and the quality of the school. In reading the pedagogical works of Rudolf Steiner, one recognizes that there is an objective, archetypal picture of the teacher toward which we are all working. It becomes specific when you enter the classroom and see how a teacher copes with the expectations that the school has set forth.

Self Evaluation

Most Waldorf schools have a self-evaluation procedure. This means that all teachers and staff members will evaluate themselves each year in both a written and an oral form. Usually the chairman of the college of teachers oversees the evaluation process which is an ongoing one. Every teacher would agree to following this procedure when they were hired. (See Appendix)

All teachers would appear yearly before the college and share how their classroom management and discipline are going. They would be asked to comment on their speech, self presence, authority, give-and-take and rapport with the children. They would also be asked to address their teaching methods, form, order and content of their lessons. The children's work would be spoken about, the achievement of the class, their care for materials, etc. The aesthetics and the hygiene in the classroom would also be referred to, as would the teacher's relationship with parents and colleagues. (See Appendix for sample forms)

Everyone in the college would be free to comment on these presentations in the spirit of mutual growth. Strengths would be affirmed and areas of concern would be noted. The one difficulty I have experienced is that it takes true courage to be honest and frank. This must be practiced. If the self-evaluation response from the colleagues is allowed to evolve to backslapping and unbridled praise, it will lose its effectiveness. The task is to be frank, honest, to use soul tact, and to speak with loving kindness.

Classroom Visitation

Every teacher in the school would be required, as part of their schedule, to make time to visit other teacher's classrooms, at least three times over the course of the academic year. A short report of each visit should be included in that person's personnel folder. It would also be encouraged that teachers attend conferences as well as visit other Waldorf schools.

Master Teacher Visits

Periodically the school would invite a recognized "master teacher" who would visit and observe classes. This person would be asked to evaluate the teachers and discuss their findings with them based on at least two visitations to each class. The master teacher would write a report (see Appendix) and pass it onto the teacher for him or her to read and sign. These records would be kept as part of the teacher's personnel files. The master teacher would be invited to the faculty meeting to give his or her impressions of the school to all the teachers.

Evaluation

Questions of Teacher Competence

The college of teachers is the forum for evaluating teacher competence. Problems in this regard should be directed to this body in the presence of the teacher concerned. An evaluative discussion would follow. Whether or not the concerned teacher remains for this discussion should be left to the free decision of all. Either the teacher may decide to leave, or a college member may ask that he leave; otherwise, he will be part of the discussion. A written record should be kept of recommendations and decisions, and if they were not present for the discussion, these should be communicated to the teacher within 24 hours by the mentor or the designated college member.

It is important not to let an evaluation instrument grow stale. Any evaluation system is only as effective as the evaluators and what they do with it.

In her book, *Teachers at Work*, Susan Johnson points out the following pitfalls of evaluation. Some teachers complained that "evaluators feel obliged to find areas for improvement," for nit-picking or "picking inconsequential problems." Others complained that evaluations were "infrequent and ritualistic." A middle school teacher complaining about evaluation said that he observed teachers keeping their best classes for the evaluation: "It's more like a staged production."[4]

Questions from Parents

Parents or teachers wanting to raise questions about a teacher's competence should address them to the college chairperson or to a college member, who will arrange for a discussion to take place. All parents should be informed through the parent handbook, or through normal school information channels, that they have this avenue for raising questions.

Dismissal of Colleagues

There may come a point in the process when it is understood that, for the sake of the children, a teacher cannot be retained. Hopefully, the processes above will have been successful, and the teacher in question will come to her own awareness that she must terminate her relationship with the school. If this is not the case, then a group of teachers should sit with the teacher and explain that the "confidence of the colleagueship" in her has eroded. Every possibility should be extended for the teacher to withdraw herself. This karmic responsibility is something we all take upon ourselves when we join the school.

If the teacher does not resign, then the college may have to dismiss her. If this is done and the above procedures have been followed, then there should exist a written record of evaluations stating the reasons and the failure of the individual to institute change. Severance pay should be decided and everything should be as clear and as factual as possible. It should be clearly expressed that the judgment is not being made that the individual is a "bad" person or incapable in other areas, but for the sake of the children, the relationship with the school has been judged unworkable. The board should be informed of the firing and a lawyer should be notified.

When the difficulties of firing a colleague were discussed at the first Waldorf school, one teacher commented that the teacher would be sure to cause trouble in the community, to which Rudolf Steiner replied: "In my opinion it is better that it suffers from without than from within!"[5]

One particular teacher was seen by Steiner as needing to be dismissed from the school. Speaking about it with the college he said,

> It is always a problem when a colleague works more out of personality than out of spiritual striving. ...[T]here is always trouble when someone ... brings a certain personal tone into the affairs of the school. (This individual) brings a personal tone into everything. He finds it difficult to get down to essentials. He would like to have succeeded in becoming a Waldorf teacher. He would like to be a poet. He would like the children to have confidence in him. The particular qualities he has make one sorry for him. We must see to it that we offer him something else instead. But he will always be difficult. For certain things that belong to the spirit of the School he will simply not understand at all, especially in the teaching of manual skills.
> It is very difficult to allow sympathy to play in where objectivity is essential. It is often misguided. I don't think he has it in him to find his way into the whole spirit of the school![6]

Care Group

Many schools have found that a committee of experienced and caring teachers can constitute a care group. The care group pays attention to relationships and hardships amongst the colleagues of a particular school. These individuals can take on specific problems and can meet with a teacher at home or at some other point outside the school. Usually the care group works under the auspices of the college of teachers and

Evaluation

reports directly to the college chairperson, although in some schools it is a the faculty chairperson who will bring a name to the college if someone is falling apart. In some schools the entire college serves as the "care group."

Evaluating the Children

Usually we are required by the state to keep academic records for the children. These records are to keep the parents informed of the child's progress and to be available to the next school in case the child transfers.

The Elementary Age Child

Waldorf school teachers are so active with their students that in the younger elementary grades a grading system is unnecessary. Rather, the teacher writes a flowing report to the parents about the child's progress, and a verse encapsulating the report is written to the child.

> A Waldorf elementary teacher stating joint spiritual and academic goals for education said: "We deal with the whole child—the spiritual, physical, and intellectual parts of the child, seeking to reunite these." In other words we as Waldorf teachers have a common goal.[7]

Standardized testing does not have a lot of use in Waldorf schools, and recent studies find that this might be just fine.

> … Edward Deci and others have demonstrated in a variety of experiments (Deci & Ryan), external accountability systems tend to undercut the intrinsic motivation of teachers and students alike and thus distort the learning process. In testing … the direct attention to low-level skills and facts … drives teachers and students alike to attend to (only) what is tested.[8]

Another study showed that

> … serious problems with so-called objective forms of testing can no longer be ignored. Many reduce learning to multiple choice test items that trivialize knowledge and learning. Many are written by educational test experts remote from classroom practice and students, and who are uneducated in the subject fields … The development of effective evaluations requires a recognition of the enormous potential and range of the human mind, a respect for

the diversity and complexity of human cultures, and a recognition of the limitations of current pencil-and-paper objective testing techniques for assessing such qualities and traits with much subtlety or precision.[9]

On the evaluation of children, Rudolf Steiner had the following to say,

> We could give two reports, one in the middle of the year as an interim report and another one at the end of the school year. As far as the powers-that-be permit it, just write general information about the pupils in these reports. Characterize the pupil, and mention a particular subject only if it is specifically outstanding. Be as positive as you can, and when the pupils come into the higher classes do not grade them more than absolutely necessary.[10]

The teacher will have constant contact with the parents through class evenings, home visits, the telephone, and during after-school pickup. Usually there is a parent interview conducted at mid-year where the child's progress in all aspects of his/her school life is discussed with the parent. Then at the end of the year there are written reports by all the teachers on each child.

In the middle school, grades 6–8, it is necessary to have more frequently written reports to keep the parents informed of where they can help to insure good habits or provide tutorial help. (See Appendix for example of a middle school science report form.)

It is very important that all evaluative reports are proofread by the school for grammar and spelling errors, and that each class teacher is aware of what the special lesson teachers will say so that the reports are consistent.

An example of evaluation for young children in a Waldorf school involves teacher observation. How can we observe the children better so that we can more adequately serve their needs? When we observe the children, we are actively involved in a process that has our interest. Later when we are contemplating a child in the solitude of our homes, we can summon up these observations as we build an objective picture of his/her being. The effort that we put into this activity calls upon the angel of the child to come to us with inspiration that can help us meet the child's particular needs.

The following are some questions we might ask ourselves to school our observations for pedagogical evaluation.[11]

Physiological:
- Is he/she large headed or small? What is the color of the hair? What is the pallor of the skin?
- What is the shape of his/her feet and hands?
- What is the shape of the ear? What is the spacing of the eyes? How is the body proportioned?
- Is the white moon in the fingernail distinguishable?

Movement:
- Is the child well-coordinated, or awkward?
- Does he/she walk on toes, heels or flat-footed? Do his/her feet turn inward or outward?

Warmth Organism:
- Are his/her hands moist, cool, warm?
- Is the child usually well dressed for the temperature? Any complaints of high fevers or headaches?
- How does he/she react to being touched?

Fluid Organism:
- What is his/her heart rhythm?
- Notice his/her speed, endurance, strength? Does he/she perspire a lot or a little?
- Does the child need to urinate frequently? Drink a great deal of water? Have a strong body odor?

Physical Breathing:
- Does the child breathe deeply or with shallow breaths? Through the nose or mouth?
- Is the out-breath or the in-breath more pronounced? What is the quality of his/her speech?
- Does he/she snore?

Soul Breathing:
- Is the child introverted or extroverted? Is he/she a cosmic or earthly child?
- Is the child fantasy-rich or fantasy-poor?
- How (and how often) does he/she laugh, cry? What are his/her sleeping, waking rhythms?

- Is his/her thinking focused or dreamy? How is the interaction with his/her peers?

School Work:
- What is the child's reaction to discipline? Is he/she artistic?
- Is he/she adept at remembering detail? Is he/she neat?
- What is the usual condition of his/her desk? How does he/she hold a pencil?
- What kind of attention span does he/she have? Does he/she establish eye contact?
- How does he/she sit in his/her chair?

Children in Need of Special Care

There exists in most Waldorf schools a care group which looks out specifically for those children who need extra help and attention. Ideally this group has within it an anthroposophical doctor, a curative eurythmist, a Bothmer gymnast, a curative painter, a Hauschka massage specialist, the school's reading/math tutor, and several class or specialty teachers. Of course, the budget defines (unfortunately) what we are able to provide, but no one can deny the desperate need that exists in most of our modern children for these therapies!

How can we observe that there might be a problem when we look at the children? There are four levels of medical complexity which travel inwardly beginning with the physical body, going to the etheric, the astral and finally the ego. Each has a corresponding therapy, and each is more complex to deal with.[12]

The first level of deformities can be observed in the *physical body*. The anthroposophical doctor might recommend such therapies as: modeling, Bothmer gym, Feldenkreis, rhythmic massage, lymphatic massage, or neuromuscular massage. Indications that the physical body, or home, of the child is not as harmonized as might be are:

>   Physical deformities
>   Posture problems
>   Poor circulation
>   Clumsiness or poor coordination
>   Dizziness
>   Disorientation
>   Nervousness
>   Poor attention span

Evaluation

The second level can be found in the *etheric body*. The anthroposophical doctor would use curative eurythmy as a therapy for the etheric body. Here we might observe the following:

> Poor circulation
> Spatial disorientation, including mixed dominance
> Bedwetting

The third level concerns the *astral body* which can be treated with curative painting, artistic therapy and music. These soul problems may include:

> Emotional problems
> Polarity problems (expansive behavior/hyperactivity or contracted
>   behavior/involution)
> Emotional transitions (life crisis, nine-year change
> Asthma (soul posture of rigidity often becomes asthma)
> Epilepsy (The soul and spirit dive down into the body and can't get out.
>   There is a feeling of being dammed up, which results in a seizure.)
> Problems with sleeping and waking (There are problems within the soul and
>   astral body; children could benefit from expansion and contraction
>   exercises

The fourth level involves the *ego*. This is the integrating level. The anthroposophical doctor might recommend intensive speech work and counseling. Recognized symptoms might be:

> Problems of self esteem/self image
> Juvenile diabetes (weakness of the ego)
> Problems with honesty or truth

The High School Student

The high school student needs individual and active evaluation. Besides the regular meetings with teachers and sponsors, the adolescent needs constant feedback from his/her teachers on progress. On the other hand, the high school teacher needs to be constantly evaluating his/her own teaching. Susan Moore Johnson writes that

> … a high school teacher who was head of peer evaluations in
> his school explained that when a teacher was slated for review, a
> committee would be formed, including the teacher's department
> head and two colleagues of his or her choosing. After the teacher

had completed a written self-assessment and the group had met to review the teacher's goals and concerns, each committee member observed one of that teacher's classes for an entire week. In addition students completed written evaluation of the teacher's work. Finally the committee reconvened to review the materials; report on their observations, and discuss opportunities for improvement.[13]

The teacher in a Waldorf high school can use evaluation as part of a threefold process with his/her students:

- to reinforce and solidify what the students have already learned,

- to stretch the students beyond what they have learned,

- to activate the students' ability to think analytically and synthetically and to use discrimination. The students should be trained to be able to view problems from different points of view.

The teacher could ask the question: "How will I know the students have achieved my predetermined goal for the class?" Some criteria should be set to determine if the student has performed adequately, keeping in mind that each student will respond out of his or her individuality. Therefore, when evaluation begins the teacher must make sure the expectations are appropriate for each individual student.

When devising your own personal evaluation, the following points could be considered:[14]

1. Do the students have the knowledge to recall the material covered in the class?

2. Do the students have the ability to comprehend and make use of the material which was covered? Can they communicate using points they have learned?

3. Can the students apply the ideas that they have learned to other situations in their lives?

4. Can the students analyze the knowledge that they have comprehended and applied and can they organize it into a totality?

5. Can the students synthesize the material? Can they take parts and pieces and formulate the whole?

6. Can the students discriminate or judge the value of the ideas they have learned, and can they communicate their relationship to those ideas in an independent manner?

Evaluation

Testing can solidify what the student has been taught. It should highlight the important aspects of a lesson and be a learning experience in itself. To be comprehensive and fair, evaluation must recognize the students' different learning styles, and it must draw upon both their left and right modes of thinking. Evaluations can be as varied as the lessons they test. Following are just a few general and specific ways of evaluating high school students.

In general (adaptable to virtually any subject) students are called to:

- make presentations to the class;

- write block books containing notes, essays, charts, maps, illustrations, etc.;

- answer unseen essay questions based upon preparatory questions given out ahead of time in a previous class period;

- take oral examinations;

- do independent projects related to the subject.

More specifically by course, the teacher can consider the following:

English
— Have students write a piece in the style of an author they have studied.
— Insert punctuation in an ambiguous passage.
— Complete sentences, saying whether the verb is transitive or intransitive.
— Recognize previously unseen passages from authors they have read.

Foreign Languages
— Have students write and perform skits, scenes from plays, puppet shows, etc., to show fluency.
— Spot the "deliberate errors" (testing recognition skills).
— Write down words and add their own synonyms (testing vocabulary).
— Do oral exercises "against the clock" (testing speed and fluency).

History
— Have the students "write a description in the day of _____."
— Describe a typical market scene in a given historical period.
— Write letters, diary entries, or newspaper articles set in the period being studied.
— Make written (and oral) portraits of a historical figure.

Science
- Write reports on the biographies of famous scientists, then reconstruct the report to give a short oral presentation to the class.
- Prepare projects for an extracurricular science fair.
- Imagine that they have been recognized as experts on a subject being studied. Give the students 20 minutes to develop questions for the producer of the radio show to use in an interview.
- After studying starches, sugars and cellulose in chemistry, give the students five unknown powders in the lab and have them identify them using tests of solubility, melting and boiling points, reaction to Fehling solution, Molisch reagent, iodine, etc.

Evaluating the School

It can be a great help for schools to have a vision into the future. This can be formalized through the writing of a Mission Statement and a five year plan. The Mission Statement is a concise statement about the goal of the school that all faculty help formulate. The five-year plan has three components: an economic forecast, a plan for the physical building of the school, and a pedagogical plan, showing development of the curricula offerings.

The Association of Waldorf School of North America has written A *Guide for Self-Study, Evaluation, and Accreditation for Waldorf Schools*. This vehicle is now being tested for suitability, so I will not go further into this subject. A copy of this guide can be obtained from AWSNA.

Conclusion

It is a challenge to teach and administer in today's world. There is much present today in our society which causes obstacles both in the children and in ourselves. What we need is to cultivate an inner joy, a sense of adventure, and a good sense of humor. What we are really doing is practicing new forms which will always be in process and will probably never be perfect. It is in our human striving that we make the forms come alive.

It is everyone's task to be responsible and wakeful. This is the challenge of today—and the goal of a good evaluation, for teachers, for our students and for our school!

Evaluation

ENDNOTES

1. Johannes Tautz, April 9, 1982, Spring Valley, NY, notes of David Mitchell.
2. Ibid.
3. Ibid.
4. Susan Moore Johnson, *Teachers at Work*, Basic Books, NY, 1990, pp. 270–275.
5. Rudolf Steiner, *Conferences, 1919-1920*, Volume 1, Steiner Schools Fellowship, 1986, p. 114.
6. Ibid., p. 112.
7. Op. cit., Johnson, p. 224.
8. Ann Lieberman, ed., *Building a Professional Culture in Schools*, Columbia Teachers College Press, NY, 1988, p. 18.
9. Beatrice and Ronald Gross, eds., *The Great School Debate, Which Way for American Education?*, Touchstone, NY, 1985, p. 382.
10. Op. cit., Steiner, p. 67.
11. For background information on the relevance of these questions, see the following: *Newsletter, Association for a Healing Education*, Volume 5, Winter 1991; *The Study of Man*, Rudolf Steiner, Anthroposophical Press, 1919; *The Bridge between Universal Spirituality and the Physical Constitution of Man*, Rudolf Steiner, Anthroposophical Press, 1920; *The Foot*, Norbert Glas, Anthroposophical Library; *The Ear*, Norbert Glas, Anthroposophical Library; *Curative Education*, Rudolf Steiner, Anthroposophical Press, 1924; *Occult Physiology*, Rudolf Steiner, Anthroposophical Press, 1911.
12. Acknowledgment to Dr. Thomas Cowan, school doctor at the Pine Hill Waldorf School, who has guided my colleagues and myself in this area.
13. Op. cit., Johnson, p. 275.
14. David Mitchell and Douglas Gerwin, *The Creative Learning Process: Advance Learning*, 1988, privately published work.

DAVID MITCHELL *has been both a Waldorf class teacher and a high school teacher. He was trained in evaluation by the New England Association of Schools and Colleges to jury private and public schools in the Northeast. He is currently very active in the Association of Waldorf School of North America and has served as an adjunct Professor at Antioch New England Graduate School of Education. He lives in Wilton, NH, with his wife and four children.*

Chapter 9
WORKING TOGETHER
by Cornelis Pieterse

When adults come together in a sustained working relationship, there is a constant flow of dialogue swinging between the extremes of affirmation, and conflict. This chapter was written to address those adults choosing to work together out of an inner connection and commitment to anthroposophy, most specifically in, but not restricted to, Waldorf schools. In most Waldorf schools, a college of teachers assumes the shared responsibility for the destiny of the school as well as the interpersonal relationships between the adults who staff the school.

The unique role of a college as a meditative group has been addressed in a previous chapter. However, any group of adults might benefit from an examination of the nature of conflict: how to recognize it, how to deal with it, and how to transform it.

Conflict is an integral and important part of all social interactions, whether this be within a group or between individuals. Every issue discussed has its polarity, and a healthy Waldorf school will learn how to use polarity in its faculty discussions to form the tripartite, or third viewpoint, to which all may recognize with consensus. Sometimes, however, the tripartite is not recognized and the polarity remains. This can result in conflict. We may then experience that conflict finds its way into discussions with particular intensity and persistence!

In working with conflict and trying to resolve it, we must be clear that there are no rules, models or easy steps to follow. Each situation is unique and demands our full attention and awareness so that we may come to an appropriate response. We are asked to create anew from our inner resources rather than what may be prescribed by social norm or authority. Often we may not know if our actions and solutions are correct for a given situation until we have tried, even experimentally, and then consciously evaluated the results.

New soul/spiritual capacities are slowly and tentatively surfacing in humanity! We may already experience that a colleague or school community member can offer a particular insight or intuition or can exercise a particular social skill that brings healing to a situation. Let's stay awake to what others can bring. We must also learn to recognize and trust our own intuitions and perceptions and have the courage to act out of them.

This chapter explores aspects of the nature of conflict and the role it plays within the structure and development of social life. We will examine our own relationship to conflict (including a few words on conflict and karma) and offer possible guidelines and techniques for working with conflict. We will conclude by describing some exercises that schools can employ to help work with conflict.

The Nature of Conflict

With a couple of possible exceptions, the nature of conflicts in a Waldorf school is essentially similar to what we might find in other organizations. We are living in a necessary phase of our ego development in which the strongest antisocial forces are at work. Name a shortcoming and I can find its echo living in my own being! We can all elaborate on our own, countless human qualities which stand in the way of a healthy social life: martyrdom, all kinds of fears and phobias, jealousies, prejudice, dogmatism, desire for power and influence—to name a few. We also have the basic human needs to be included, accepted, liked and recognized by others. These qualities are alive and well in most of us and therefore in our communities.

Rudolf Steiner pointed out that sympathy can be just as destructive as antipathy.[1] A sympathetic inclination toward a person can be blinding by recognizing what may be incorrect or even immoral in what was said or done. Seeking to affiliate only with colleagues with whom we are sympathetically inclined can result in cliques and power blocks which exacerbate conflict.

It is interesting to note that some conflicts have an icy-cold, below-the-surface, quality. These conflicts tend to run over a long period of time and often find no resolution at all. They are unspoken, invisible, but ever-present and could be described as cancerous in nature. Other types of conflicts explode in the heat of battle, are often short-lived, but tend to recur in definite patterns. (To familiarize yourself with your relationship to conflict, make a self-assessment of what type of conflict you tend to "favor," and what type of conflict seems to come to you from others.)

The nature of conflicts has an added dimension in Waldorf schools. We have been entrusted with the spiritual content and life-renewing stream of anthroposophy. This connection has given us access to a tremendous amount of knowledge about the spiritual world, human beings and their inner development, the two-fold nature of evil, temperaments, etc. To the extent that we allow this content of anthroposophy to be more assimilated by our intellect and less by our soul capacities of feeling- and will-life, it has the potential to remain a mere body of information. As such, it can be used to justify all kind of opinions and judgments against our fellow human beings, with the net result that it may gain us a position of power or superiority over them.

We need to mention these things not just to wallow in the negative qualities of man, but to acknowledge clearly that they are operative in conflict situations. If we hope to understand and work with conflict in a conscious way in our schools, it is imperative that we are awake to these ever-present antisocial forces. Standing fully within the age of the Consciousness Soul requires this awareness of us. On the one hand we must never lose sight of the fact that each human being is endowed with a higher Self accompanied by benevolent spiritual beings who continuously guide him. On the other hand, we all have a strong affinity to these antisocial forces and beings who seek to impair our evolution. If we are not awake, or if we try to ignore or deny the existence of these forces, then we make ourselves more vulnerable to their influence!

The weaknesses of the Waldorf movement are also its strengths! Rudolf Steiner was very deliberate in his intention to not have a headmaster or headmistress, or other hierarchical structures and orthodox social norms that people can fall back on. This fact brings with it a decision-making process that can be much more laborious, and during which human differences of opinion and conflict will more easily come to the surface. This, in turn, places a much greater responsibility on all of us to create social structures appropriate to our time and to our geographic and cultural backgrounds.

The following are some observations we can make about the psychology of conflict:

- The chance for a conflict to escalate is greater when we ignore or avoid the conflict.

- The more we are emotionally or materially dependent on another person(s), the greater the chance for conflict. In other words, conflict usually occurs within the context of interdependency.

- Two people in conflict often share those negative character traits which they perceive and then criticize in the other.

- Conflicts have their source in our feeling-life and can be driven and escalated only by means of hatred, fear and doubt. Pure concepts and thinking cannot create conflict. In the experience of the conflict, intellectual arguments are often thinly disguised emotions.

- Of all emotions, fear of the unknown and loss of control are possibly the most potent in creating and maintaining conflict.

Exercise: When you are in strong conflict with another person, find a quiet time during the day when you identify the main qualities he/she possesses that bring you into conflict with that person. Then, in an honest self-evaluation, assess what you have in common with that person.

Purpose: A greater understanding of yourself and the other, which will lead to greater acceptance of yourself and seeing, again, the humanity in the other

The Role of Conflict

At the end of Scene Ten of the Mystery Play, *The Soul's Awakening* by Rudolf Steiner, we find the dialogue between Lucifer and Benedictus (Johannes's spiritual teacher and guide) concerning who shall have dominion over Johannes's soul—Lucifer or Johannes himself?

> Benedictus: He will admire you but will not succumb to you.
> Lucifer: I mean to fight.
> Benedictus: And, fighting serve the gods.[2]

This dialogue may serve as an indication about the role of evil in life. While we should be careful not to automatically equate conflict with evil, conflict certainly has its origin in the dark and shadow sides of man. And, as in the case of evil, it plays an essential and, therefore, a potentially positive role in our own development and that of our institutions. It is often out of conflict, chaos or doubt that new impulses can enter our social creations.

In the unfolding of a meeting, all of us can confirm the experience that after a difficult moment—going through "the eye of the needle" by means of a confrontation—the meeting can reach a deeper level of significance. Once that happens, everyone knows it and is inspired by it. The meeting becomes more efficient without losing the necessary depth of deliberation. The analogy of a thunderstorm comes to mind, in which the flashes of lightning, the rolling of thunder, the threatening clouds and the driving rain will send us to seek shelter. Then, how fresh and light the world feels afterwards—something has been cleansed and renewed!

To recognize, allow for, and process the expression of conflict and differences among members of a group has many benefits. It provides a healthy diversity which will energize all members of a group. It allows for much greater individual and group learning and growth. A faculty, board or committee will gain greater flexibility and adaptability to meet the ever-increasing demands placed on a Waldorf school, the changing needs of the children, curriculum, community life, parent expectations and other social/spiritual questions. Through our differences a more meaningful unity and connection can arise—a sense of purpose. Individual contributions, pertaining to the life and performance of the group, are recognized as being essential to the success of the whole group.

Without conflict we would fall into blissful but dulling sleep. Among other things, conflict awakens us—it calls us to consciousness! What holds true for us as individuals holds true for groups and entire organizations as well.

If conflict awakens us, we may extrapolate that the more conscious we are as human beings, the less life's circumstances are truly experienced as conflicts. In other words, we still recognize the difficulties in life, but they are experienced as opportunities and gifts. As a lifelong process, we slowly gain a different inner relationship to what we used to call conflict.

> The gloom of the world is but a shadow.
> Behind it, yet within reach, is joy.
> There is radiance and glory in the darkness.
> Could we but see; and to see, we have only to look.
> I beseech you to look!
>
> Life is so generous a giver, but we,
> Judging its gifts by their outer covering,
> Cast them away as ugly or heavy or hard.
> Remove the covering and you find beneath it
> A living splendor, woven of love, by wisdom, with power.
>
> Welcome it, grasp it, and you touch
> The angel's hand that brings it to you.
> Everything we call a trial, a sorrow, a duty,
> Believe me, that angel's hand is there;
> That gift is there, and the wonder of an overshadowing presence.
> Our joys too: be not content with them as joys.
> They, too, conceal diviner gifts.   – Fra Giovanni (1386–1456)[3]

Conflict and Karma

Living with thoughts about karma and reincarnation may strengthen the main ingredient in all conflict resolution—our inner development!

When considering questions of self-development, karma and social life, we must first learn to live with apparent contradictions. On the one hand, conflict has a role to play in our interpersonal interactions; to be a modern human being means that we will meet conflict as individuals strive for consciousness. We must learn to accept it and embrace it. Neither reject nor fear conflict. We must learn to see and trust that everything that comes to us in due course has a purpose designed to further our individual and social development.

On the other hand, it is very important that we must never seek conflict or, even worse, create conflict on purpose! We must ask ourselves, "How can I best express myself?" We must also ask ourselves, "How do I best hear the concerns of others?"

Perhaps the central contribution by Rudolf Steiner to the spiritual legacy of mankind is his spiritual research into the questions of karma and reincarnation. Never before has any person articulated this spiritual reality so thoroughly and explicitly. From his works we can gain important insights that can shed a unique light on our topic.

Most events and people whom we meet in life, and the general circumstances in which we find ourselves, are a result of our own deeds and experiences in past incarnations. We know this to be called *individual karma*. One of the implications of this insight is the fact that the difficulties we encounter in other people and events do not find their cause in these people or events but, ultimately, in ourselves. When we blame our problems and conflicts on the people or circumstances (accidents, for instance), we point in the wrong direction. This is somewhat analogous to a young child who, after running into a chair, blames the chair for his pain.

We often hear ourselves say, "If only this person or this particular conflict were not part of our school, the school would be so much healthier and we could proceed with our tasks." There is a tendency in us to want to surgically remove a problem and to view it as extraneous to the flow of life rather than embrace it. I believe it is an illusion to think that the 'other person' is the problem. The events and people in our lives are brought to us by spiritual beings who work in close conjunction with our higher self. How often does it happen that we encounter the same patterns and the same kinds of people and conflicts? We are drawn like a magnet to those people who seem to present us with our issues and dilemmas. These people are mere vehicles for our growth and development on earth. As the child learns to orient himself spatially, congruent to his awareness of the separation of material objects and his own body, we need to orient ourselves in karmic laws. One of these laws tells us that all events coming toward us from without are intimately connected with our ego identity and its individual phase of development.

This consciousness needs to grow into a strong inner conviction that recognizes our inner relationship to the difficulties that come our way. As Johannes Tautz phrases it, "We ourselves have sought these difficulties. Man fashions his own destiny. The difficulties that he encounters are his own 'I' mirroring itself in his surroundings, in his social environments."[4]

Considering the unfolding of our destinies, we live within an amazing twofold dynamic. On one end of the pole is our daily waking consciousness. The world of the senses enters our consciousness and we are aware of how we think and feel about ourselves and others. In response we make decisions about, and we have preferences for, career, people, lifestyle, goals and values, etc. On the other end of the pole is our will-life that leads us through our limbs to events and people without our conscious participation and choosing.

As an exercise, we need to prepare ourselves so that when a person brings us a conflict, our inner reaction will be of great and genuine interest in that human being. Can we later recall all the details of that moment in the day: the room in which the conflict took place, the people present, colors, dress, mood, the seating arrangement and sequence of events? We must paint a picture before our soul of everything that was part of that moment. This effort allows us to cultivate an appreciation for the mystery of life and, according to Rudolf Steiner, orient ourselves toward a better understanding of our personal karma.[5]

What often is called "bad" or "old" karma between two people is, I think, a misunderstanding. Karma leads us to the moment of the encounter; then choices or new possibilities enter and weave into the relationship together with what is "given" and predetermined. To inwardly turn one's back from a long-standing conflict with another human being by judging this conflict to be "bad" karma is a subtle form of abdicating one's responsibility toward the present reality of the relationship. I believe that personal karma is not only designed to have us repay old "debt," but has within it fertile seeds for future possibilities and the call to develop new capacities of soul.

Next to personal karma, there also is *group, national* and *world karma*, and karma connected with the *different spiritual streams* which flow together under the umbrella of

Working Together

the anthroposophical movement and her daughter movements. Certain conflicts may have their root cause in the context of these larger streams. However, I believe that most conflicts have their strongest affinity to personal karma.

Elements and Objectives in Conflict Resolution

The following elements and prerequisites are not necessarily in order of priority or importance. All these objectives should live in our consciousness as we work with conflict. They are applicable whether you are a party in the conflict or if you serve as an outside facilitator.

There is not really a question of fully resolving a conflict. Some elements in conflict dissolve naturally while others may lead to the next level of challenges in the future. Our first objective in approaching conflict resolution must be to unlock a situation so that *movement* can happen in the fixed perceptions that people have of each other and of issues. If this movement can take place, conflict becomes a dynamic force for change and development.

The second condition is that the *process* of resolution is as important as the end result. It will be in the process that the necessary learning and social skill-building will occur. It is a common misconception that conflict resolution must result in having the parties smile at each other again and shake hands. While this objective can be an important step, the ultimate purpose of our work must be that paralyzing conflict can turn into creative differences and constructive diversity in our schools. Without diversity, our organizations and human relationships turn stale and stagnant. After all, there can be twelve legitimate points of view to each issue. How can these views be part of our deliberations without mutually excluding each other?

In resolving conflict, we must simultaneously work with two additional and seemingly opposing objectives. One very important goal is to create an atmosphere of *trust* among the parties; to have people look at each other with renewed eyes. Some of the exercises in this chapter are designed to accomplish this trust and to have each party "walk in the shoes" of the other. However, trust doesn't come from exercises. Rather it arises out of the work that we do together; it is born out of the activities and devotion that we experience with each other through working with the children! Still, without a basic level of trust, we cannot constructively work with conflict. The majority of our efforts will be spent building this foundation.

In the process of building trust between people, it is very easy to bypass our fourth objective. When we're making progress toward having people trust each other, it will be very tempting to think that now we have resolved the conflict. Often this is not the case. Most important is the pivotal rule that the conflict must be articulated and fully described. In other words, the conflict must become *perceptible*. Perceptible not only in its effects (because, most likely, this is painfully clear to all), but we must learn to phenomenologically describe the nature and chronology of the conflict. In a manner similar to a faculty's child study, we must describe and study the biography of a conflict. This process will have a very important benefit. By making perceptible what was hidden, we externalize and thereby objectify it! Invariably, the conflict loosens its destructive grip on the parties. In many cases, the process of bringing the conflict to our consciousness, by describing it, will be sufficient to allow for resolution.

The fifth condition is to have the *will to find a solution*! While conflict can inflict great misery on all parties (sometimes for long periods of time), people may still be reluctant to seek a resolution. There can be many reasons for this reluctance. Resolution brings with it the necessity for change and for more work on the part of all members in a group. It may, therefore, feel safer and more convenient to stay with the status quo of existing power structures.

When asked to facilitate conflict resolution, it is very important to assess how committed the parties are to finding a resolution. There are various ways to assess this commitment. We must pay attention to what people say or, more importantly, pay attention to their actions. What is the mood in a meeting? How genuine is the level of exchange and self-disclosure? How willing are the parties to commit to extra meeting time and allot the necessary material and human resources to the process? Individuals and groups can be ingenious in avoiding dealing with the issues at hand. It is important not to underestimate the elements that can stand in the way of conflict resolution.

Intimately connected with the will to find a resolution, is the sixth condition of *courage*. In working with conflict, inevitably we are confronted, not only with the shadow side of the other person, but also with our own. A precondition for working with conflict is that we don't place ourselves above the others in the conflict. Any sentiment that make us feel that another person's problem couldn't be our own works against the process of resolution. Honest and heart-felt humility joined by a certain fearlessness are all essential ingredients.

A seventh attitude is not to seek fault with a person or to find one party right or wrong in a situation. We must be *nonjudgmental* in all respects and in everything we do. Invariably, both (all) have played their part in the conflict. By drawing sides or pronouncing opinions and explanations, we invariably add to the conflict. We should be very careful to delineate between the processes of conflict resolution and that of evaluation. The latter aims for a decision or corrective action of some sort. The former, however, is purely designed to accommodate communication and further development.

The eighth requirement is to honor the *freedom* of the other human being. If we recognize that each conflict finds its origin within the souls of the individual parties to the conflict, then resolution must start with accepting our own responsibility in the conflict. We must know that no matter how obvious the shortcomings of the other may be, or how radically wrong his thinking is, I have the power to change only myself. No amount of effort on my part can make me change the other person or have him learn the lessons that I think life is teaching him. The idea of honoring the unequivocal freedom of the human being, so central to the impulse of anthroposophy, must permeate all our feelings and actions.

Two final guidelines are extremely important to remember and to apply whenever we can. One is that, when we are speaking of human interaction, colleagueship and, especially, difficult relationships—it is important that we learn to speak for our feelings and personal needs. It is a mystery and somewhat a contradiction to me that a movement, which excels in enriching the experience of childhood to many, many thousands of children, involves many adults who are so awkward and suspicious of expressing our feelings to each other. In our frailties and striving we bear witness to our humanity again! This brings us to the ninth requirement: *Speak from the heart* in anything you say. Conflict will evaporate when we make ourselves vulnerable to the each other, when we can confidently speak from our own strengths while allowing others to help us with our weaknesses.

The last condition concerns *group work*. In the vast majority of cases, a conflict between two members of a working group (for instance, a faculty), will adversely effect the workings of the entire group. This particular conflict will live in the consciousness and become the burden of the group. Additionally, almost without exception, other members of the group will find their alliances to the conflict and, subsequently, contribute to it. For these reasons (and others), resolution should always take place within the context of the full group! The benefit to this approach is simply that other members can become co-responsible for the process and, when resolution occurs, its redemptive influence will permeate the group and the entire organization. Please resist the temptation to have conflicts resolved in the corners (so-to-speak) of our organizations.

1. Conflict is intimately connected with our biographies.

2. Conflict must lead to further inner development.

3. We must embrace conflict, and not see it as extraneous to life.

4. We must dissolve frozen perceptions of ourselves, others and issues.

5. All our efforts must be to establish trust among human beings.

6. We must make the conflict perceptible in all of its aspects.

7. We must assess and engage the intangible soul forces of the Will, and have the courage to work with conflict.

8. In anything we do we must be nonjudgmental. Honoring the freedom of our fellow human beings must stand at the core of all our efforts.

9. We must learn to speak from our hearts and be in touch with our feelings and personal needs.

10. Most, if not all, conflict resolution must occur within the full circle of human beings who are affected by and contribute to the conflict.

Steps

The following outline of steps in conflict resolution, is much more a general guide than a rigid formula. When we facilitate or directly engage in confronting a conflict, our intuitions will guide us through the process. Very often, individual steps may have to be bypassed, or it may be sufficient to just cover a couple of these checkpoints. To better illustrate these steps, we will assume that the conflict has escalated substantially, effecting various individuals and different aspects of the organization.

Assessment & Commitment Stage

This first stage is important because it will lay a foundation and set a tone for the entire process. Primarily, we are considering three interrelated steps.

First, there must be an acknowledgment and identification of the problem or conflict, including the individuals who may be involved. Usually by this time, everyone is aware of the problem, and the need for finding a working solution becomes urgent. Second, some kind of an assessment is made about how the problem should be resolved. Decisions are made on how to approach the difficulties. It may be that just two individuals should get together and talk it out; or that existing channels of communication and/or procedures should be followed; or, a third party should be brought in (from within or outside the school community) to facilitate the process. Third, whatever the decision is, the main parties to the conflict must understand, agree and commit to the process! Without some basic form of agreement among the parties, resolving a conflict is practically impossible. In the latter case, a community might find itself, for the school's benefit, making an evaluative decision, some kind of arrangement that will allow for the continued running of the school. These decisions may run from binding arbitration, a negotiated settlement, or strict rules and probation, to asking an individual for his resignation. Any of these responses may be legitimate and necessary in certain cases, but it should be remembered that a conflict can easily metamorphose and shift to other areas and individuals in the school community.

Biographical & Descriptive Phase

As mentioned earlier, this phase is crucial. When special care has been exercised to make the conflict fully perceptible, some kind of resolution may already appear. In this phase, therefore, it is our aim to fully articulate what the conflict is and sketch its history. We map the conflict. While it is important to achieve clarity in describing the circumstances, do not overload the discussion with minute details, but, rather, learn to characterize the essence of the conflict. Sometimes this can be done with an image. In this process, it will become clear where the stories coincide and where they do not. If individuals strongly disagree on the course of events and nature of the conflict, we let these discrepancies stand. These discrepancies are part of the complexity of the conflict. Furthermore, at this stage we concentrate on bringing problems to light; not on solving them. It is a very necessary, often painful, moment in the process to have all parties (as a group) experience the severity of the conflict.

Perception-sharing & Mirroring Phase

This phase is truly the heart of the resolution process. Following and interlocking with phase two, phase three focuses on the actual interrelationships among people in the conflict. What are the perceptions that others hold of me? What is the impact of my behavior on others? Are my intentions consistent with my actions? Is what I say consistent with what I truly feel and think about others? (Ironically, many conflicts do not arise out of ill-conceived intentions but, rather, out of a failure to be honest and straight with others because we "don't want to hurt their feelings.")

The very definition of conflict is that perceptions we have of each other get fixed, stereotyped and distorted. Even the most caring and humane of us will discard data that contradicts the negative images we would want to hold of a person, and cling to those observations that confirm our preconceptions. Of course, what makes it more complicated is the fact that our perceptions and opinions of people are based not just on figments of the imagination; they all have a grain of truth in them! We could say that the purpose of this phase is twofold: One, to realign our soul forces of thinking, feeling and willing by means of perception-sharing so that our interactions with people can become three dimensional again; i.e., we learn to express what is truly living in us regarding our thoughts and feelings about a person. (The truth is often less painful than a sugar-coated criticism or innuendo.) Two, by using the mirroring or feedback process, we can gradually adjust our reality (self perception) with the reality that other people reflect back to us, thereby allowing the impact we have on others to be more consistent with our intentions.

Agreement & Contract Phase

If the conflict resolution resulted in the need to have certain forms of behavior and relationship change, then these changes must be clearly documented and agreed upon. For example, it may be that the parties agree to meet together on a weekly basis for the next three months in order to facilitate continued contact and communication. Or it may be agreed upon for each party to journal their inner work on the issues surrounding the conflict and exchange these journals with each other on a periodic basis. Or, it may be agreed upon to assign a speaking partner to each person. This colleague would function as an unbiased listener and advisor. There are numerous ways to accommodate further support for and communication with the parties that are in conflict. All these agreements must be ratified and periodically reviewed. None of these arrangements should run forever. They are merely outer support systems that have a temporary value to assist people in making necessary behavioral changes.

Systems & Organization Development Phase

In some cases, part of resolving the conflict requires that changes be made in the organizational structures of the school. It may be the formation of a new committee or changes in membership, or that amendment of certain procedures and policies. In extreme cases, it might even happen that the very foundation (vision & mission) of a school is being challenged or in need of revision. Individual development and organization development are reciprocal—the one effects the other. Rudolf Steiner indicated that any human creation reflects the consciousness of that human being and of the times, whether this is in art, science or our institutions.[6] I also believe that, in turn, our creations influence our consciousness.

As a rule, though, it would be a mistake to change the organizational structures first, before or as a substitute to working with the interpersonal conflict issues! Many organizations resort to making all kinds of system changes, only to find that these collapse because people still cannot work together. The old edict is true: Organizational structures are only as good as the people who work in them.

Review & Implementation Phase

When any decisions are made, then we should be clear who, what, when and how things are to be implemented. It is also important to maintain records outlining the conflict resolution process. Down the road there may be a need to refer to the proceedings for administrative and/or legal purposes. At all times, maintain a record of the agreements and decisions and read these back to the group before the meeting adjourns.

The review process is the most important learning tool that we have at our disposal in group and organization development. In it we look back on our creation and glean from it what worked well and what did not. Some of the guidelines regarding conflict resolution pertain to the review process as well. A properly conducted review neither judges nor intellectualizes. It merely describes and characterizes, in images, what transpired from a detached, but living, point of view. Do not fall into the trap of continuing your discussions and arguments. Make the review brief (7 minutes); just a couple of observations and descriptions will suffice. Stay with your personal learning and insights. Leave others free to discover their own diamonds in the sand. Ask open-ended questions such as: What worked best? When was the most difficult moment in the meeting? What image, fairy tale, weather or landscape did you associate with the meeting? How did you personally contribute to the meeting? Where was the golden moment of opportunity? If the meeting were a building under construction, what would it look like? By means of the review, we can learn from even the most difficult and frustrating meetings.

Exercises

What follows are a few exercises and process suggestions for conflict resolution and related trust-building/biography and mirroring/feedback exercises. In each exercise, any number of variations is possible.

Conflict

(1) Have opposing parties, in twos, sit across from each other and each draw a self portrait. When finished, each interprets his or her own picture for the other. Then, for 10 minutes, both articulate what new insights they have gained of the other in relation to the conflict.

(2) Have all parties draw, paint or model an image of the conflict. Then, conduct a general discussion about the nature of the conflict.

(3) Have each participant, silently for themselves, conduct an imaginary conversation with the other person in the conflict. The conversation should include a confrontation and what he would say and do in response. After 15 minutes, the participant writes down the essence of the conversation and shares this with the full group. The participant should identify helpful behavior and what was most difficult about the exercise. As an option, the full group could offer helpful feedback.

Trust Building and Biography

(1) Have half of the group blindfolded. The sighted people each take a person without sight and guide this person through the building or out through the garden/park/street. The sighted person gives a full account of all the obstacles on the way. Next, reverse the roles. Afterwards, the group shares insights and experiences.

(2) All biography exercises are essential for promoting trust. As a guideline, avoid long accounts of a person's life and history. Design specific questions to which people, one by one, then respond. It is important that people can have fun with the exercises.

- Describe your favorite room or place while you were a young child.
- What is your first memory, ever?
- Your first love?
- Describe the first time that you felt truly independent ("The world is my oyster.)

Mirroring/Feedback

This exercise allows individuals to speak and then hear how what they have said has been heard by the other. (For further explanation refer to the paragraphs on the Perception-Sharing and Mirroring Phase above.)

(1) When in a difficult phase of a discussion, have one person speak at a time, then afterward, another member of the group paraphrases what was spoken. Then proceed to next point.

(2) Assign two members of the group to sit outside the circle and have them, periodically, reflect to the group their observations and further process suggestions.

Sender:
- Whenever possible, seek permission from recipient.
- Address person directly.

- Use "I" statements only.
- Never speak for others or from hearsay, but from personal experience and how you were affected by the recipient.
- Use only very specific, concrete and recent examples.
- Do not editorialize, moralize or philosophize; just describe.

Recipient:
- Paraphrase feedback.
- Make sure you understand feedback or ask for clarification.
- Ask for examples and seek feedback from others to confirm or modify information.
- Never argue, defend your position or give reasons. Let what is mirrored live in you.
- You may speak to how you were affected by the exchange: confused, helped, relieved, angered, supported, etc.

For all participants:
- Share new insights and what you have learned.
- Remember that in the exchange, the value systems of both sender and recipient are operative; therefore, do not judge.
- Avoid extreme responses.

Process:
- Have sender give one statement at a time, after which recipient paraphrases and ask for clarification, if necessary.
- Repeat process once or twice more, if needed.
- Recipient may request feedback from others.
- Never have one person continuously sit in the "hot seat," but move the process on to other members of the group.

Conclusion

Our ability to work together as colleagues in Waldorf schools predicates a conscious awakeness to our relationships with one another in the social sphere. To be a "social" being is not granted to us as a birthright. Quite the opposite, we have to actively work towards it as part of our task in human evolution. It is hoped that this chapter may have shed some light on this path.

ENDNOTES

1. Rudolf Steiner, *The Challenge of Our Times*, Anthroposophic Press, NY, 1941, pp. 119–150.
2. Rudolf Steiner, *The Soul's Awakening*, G.P. Putnam & Sons, NY, 1920, p. 266.
3. Notes taken from a handout from the Waldorf Institute, Spring Valley, NY
4. Johannes Tautz, lecture in Spring Valley, April 9, 1982, notes of David Mitchell
5. Rudolf Steiner, *Karma Lectures, Vol I-VIII*, Steiner Press, London, 1956.
6. Rudolf Steiner, *Theory of Knowledge*, Anthroposophic Press, NY. 1940, pp. 100–118.

CORNELIS PIETERSE co-founded the Chicago Waldorf School, The Lukas Foundation (a social-therapeutic community), and Envision Associates (a consulting organization). He held various teaching and counseling positions in curative institutions in Europe and America. He was nine years at the High Mowing School in New Hampshire. For the last four years he has worked as a consultant and facilitator for corporations, Waldorf schools, and non-profit organizations.

Chapter 10
THE BOARD OF TRUSTEES
by Agaf Dancy

What functions does a board of trustees serve? Why have one? How should a board be related to the college of teachers and faculty in a Waldorf school? What are typical patterns of development, and frequently encountered difficulties? How can we improve communications, reduce potential conflict and misunderstanding? What should be a board's composition? Who should serve on one?

In this chapter we will explore these and related questions which surface time and again in Waldorf schools. Given the astonishing variety of people and organizational arrangements in the schools, it should be clear from the outset that there are no "right" answers. Each school must sort these things out in light of its own particular circumstances. Moreover, as a school grows and evolves, so will its board's functions and its relationship to the organism as a whole. For these reasons, those hoping to find in these pages a formula they can apply to their schools are likely to be disappointed. Although we will offer numerous suggestions along the way, our goal is not to present a static picture. Rather we hope to bring the issues into focus in a way that will contribute to more productive discussion among schools' faculties and boards, where the final responsibility rests.

What Functions Does a Board Serve?

Why have a board in the first place? If the school is "faculty run" is there any need for one? If so, what is its role, other than to rubber-stamp decisions of the faculty and college (if there is one)?

At one extreme are schools where the board is seen as a somewhat awkward appendage, maintained because articles of incorporation require that there be one. Its function is to serve as the school's legal face to the world, to provide official signatures and approve policy set elsewhere, but it has no real part in making policy or running the school. In effect, the faculty or college exercises the real powers which by law are assigned to the board.

For a board to be so completely disempowered is uncommon. Yet frequently one encounters, in the midst of a board-faculty conflict, indignation on the part of faculty members at the board's presumption to tell the faculty what to do. On the other side, among non-faculty board members, one encounters feelings of discomfort at being legally responsible for the school's actions while having little or no real voice in the decisions. Mindful of the fact that the legal authority (to hire, fire, and dispose of the school's assets, among other things) still rests with the board, some schools "protect" against the board's exercising this authority (and avoid potential conflicts with non-faculty board members) by filling all positions with faculty members or with anthroposophists who can be counted on to go along with the will of the faculty.

If all one wants of a board is to fill the legal shell, the above solution is reasonable. In most cases, however, schools are in fact asking their boards to serve other functions for which one needs the time and talent of non-faculty members. Fundraising and developing community connections are obvious tasks frequently asked of boards. Expert advice in legal or business matters is often sought by bringing on members with experience in those areas. The more talented, dynamic and committed to the life of the school these individuals are, however, the less likely they are to accept a role of rubber-stamping decisions made elsewhere. A tension can develop, a tug-of-war between board and faculty: Where does the buck finally stop?

At the other end of the spectrum are those schools, frequently in their infancy, where the board exercises the primary responsibility for school governance: hiring and firing teachers, setting salaries, deciding budgetary issues including what positions will be funded, thus what curriculum will be offered. This is often the case with schools just getting started. A parent group takes the initiative, forms a non-profit corporation and advertises for a teacher. The teachers, fresh from training (or with no training!), have their hands full mastering their classes. The parent-run board must carry the school's administration and financing and continue to evaluate the new teachers and the evolving pedagogical work for some time.

While there may be good reasons a school would tend at one time toward the purely faculty-run model or at another time to the board-run model, it seems the long-term health of a Waldorf school is best served if there is a balance, a sharing of responsibility between the board and the college/core faculty. One approach, frequently used, is to divide the responsibilities: the board deals with legal and financial matters; the college/core faculty with pedagogical concerns (including staffing issues).

The Board of Trustees

In the last analysis, there is no such thing as a pedagogical issue that doesn't have potential financial and legal implications, and there is no financial or legal decision that doesn't ultimately affect the pedagogy. There are inevitably areas of overlap: Can the school afford to make crafts a full-time position? How many hours of teaching will be compensated at full-time rates? What are the legal implications of the college's decision to deal with a complaint about corporal punishment in a certain way? There is a dynamic tension and the necessity for accommodation among the responsible groups.

Rather than viewing this tension as a problem, it can in fact be seen as an extremely valuable aspect of the life of a school. The board and the college/core faculty engage in a healthy dialogue in which each, by sharing different perspectives, keeps the other conscious.

The board can be pictured most usefully, not as a board of "directors," but as a board of "trustees." The board holds a trust. Its primary task, in this light, is to see that the school fulfills its mission, to keep it on course over the long haul. The college of teachers (or the core faculty, if there is no college) has the same responsibility. Both groups are ultimately responsible for all aspects of the school's life; the college/core faculty entrusts the board to carry the primary burden of financial and practical matters, while the board entrusts the college/core faculty to carry the primary pedagogical focus. Each is responsible for communicating and listening to the other in carrying out its primary trust. Some suggestions to facilitate this process of communicating and listening are presented later in this chapter. But more important than any specific technique is keeping alive the recognition that this shared trust exists, with the sense of mutual responsibility and mutual gratitude that it implies.

Phases in the Evolution of the Board-Faculty Relationship

As mentioned above, a frequent pattern in the life of a school is for it to start as an initiative of parents who form the corporation, become the founding board and hire the school's first teachers. At this point in a school's life, the teachers are generally happy for any and all help they can get, and the fact that the board is in charge of most of the school's affairs is not an issue. In fact, without constant involvement and tremendous sacrifices on the part of founding board members, most schools would have a hard time surviving their pioneering years.

As the school grows, it becomes impossible for everyone to do everything, as was done in the pioneering days. Hopefully, the faculty is growing stronger and taking on a greater share of the school's day-to-day administration (eventually with the help of a business manager or administrator), as well as taking primary responsibility for the integrity of the teaching in each class and in the school as a whole. Ideally, as a core of dedicated teachers forms, a transition is made to the forming of a college of teachers; even where this step is not taken, informal or formal structures evolve through which a core group begins to take the reins.

Often this is a time when problems crop up. Either the board is reluctant to let go, and a tug-of-war develops, or it backs out or is pushed out too soon, leaving overwhelmed and inexperienced teachers to struggle with things such as fundraising and financial planning for which they have neither the training nor the time. The ideal situation is one in which a gradual shift occurs towards a sharing of responsibilities as the college/core faculty becomes stronger. Obviously this requires maturity, tact and constant communication. The alternative, however, is that the board ends up in a power struggle with the faculty. Whichever group "wins," the school loses. Nearly as problematic for the school is the situation that emerges not from confrontation but from avoidance: Neither the board nor faculty feel they have the power to act, areas of responsibility are poorly defined, and no one knows "who's in charge."

Though less common, it can also happen in the life of a school that it finds itself with a weak or non-existent board (or one consisting of only faculty) and sets out to recruit new board members who can bring outside perspectives and exercise leadership in non-pedagogical areas. The issues are the same as above but in reverse, with the college/core faculty needing to make the transition to shared governance as the board becomes more capable.

In fact, it may happen during the full term of a school's life that at one time the board is stronger and more active, at another time the faculty carries more of the responsibility. Let us take as our starting point that both groups are in fact mutually responsible for all aspects of school life, trusting one another to assume the primary burden in one area or the other; then it stands to reason that if, for whatever cause, significant weakness exists in either the board or the college/core faculty, the other group will tend to step into the void. This could happen if there were a substantial loss of key faculty over a short period, requiring replacement with relatively inexperienced teachers; or, it could happen that for one reason or another, many key board members step down, leaving mostly faculty board members still serving. In such cases (and they do happen) it is appropriate for the health of the school that the stronger group assume some of the duties normally falling to the weaker group. What is most important, however, is that this be seen as a temporary situation, with the goal always to return to a condition of balanced sharing of responsibility.

The Composition of a Board

Who should sit on a board depends in part on what the school wants the board to do—and on whom the school is able to attract. Our discussion has been concerned mostly with the typical "working" board in which all members generally have duties as chairs or members of board committees and provide specialized advice to the board in areas of their expertise. There are, of course, also "advisory" boards which tend to meet one or two times a year over dinner, hear speeches about the work of the organization, and pull out their checkbooks. Their purpose is to give and raise money, or to lend prestige to the undertaking by virtue of associating their names with it. They might or might not have a "legal" existence via the organization's bylaws; if they do have more than ceremonial functions, these are generally handled by a smaller executive committee which actually governs. Such boards can be very useful to a school. However, the issues involved in recruiting, holding and getting the most out of such groups are very different from the ones typically faced by a working board for a Waldorf school, which are addressed here.

In the working Waldorf board, as in other non-profit boards, there is a mix of qualities one is hoping to assemble. There are various formulations of this, such as the "three Ws" of Wisdom, Wealth and Work. Board members should be people who bring at least one of the above with them: individuals who have a demonstrated involvement in the life of the school (on committees, fairs, etc.) and a willingness to work, those bringing specific wisdom in the form of special skills (lawyers, bankers, real estate brokers, etc.), and others with recognized stature and community standing, who lend the "Good Housekeeping Seal of Approval" and can help open doors to those with influence and wealth in the community.

Every school dreams of recruiting the local equivalent of the Chairman of General Motors or the wife of the head of the Kellogg Foundation. The reality, however, is that board formation is very much a bootstraps operation. Teachers poor as church mice and mothers working on the bazaar committee don't always have ready access to the Chair of General Motors. Rather, the initial pool of available talent consists of the parents of children in the school, the local anthroposophical community and the teachers. These are also, obviously, the groups who should form the core of any board, being most committed to and most knowledgeable about the school's mission and the impulses standing behind Waldorf education.

If major foundation chairs are not among them, so be it. However, it is possible for this initial group to begin a process of reaching out to others whom they know, who might then bring on others whom they know, and thus eventually attract individuals with high visibility and community standing. This is and should be a gradual process, as those recruited should truly become familiar with the school and committed to it before becoming part of a working board; they may, of course, be recruited for an advisory board using less strict standards.

Do all board members need to be anthroposophists? Or is it sufficient if they are just decent folk of good will? This question has been debated and answered in any number of different ways. Different circumstances may call for different answers. In general, though, it seems best not to tie the board's hands when it comes to recruiting qualified members. Clearly, not all the parents at the school are anthroposophists, nor necessarily are all those most involved and supportive of the school. What is necessary, though, is that all board members recognize the anthroposophical foundation of Waldorf education and do not have any problems with this reality.

How should membership be divided among parents, college/core faculty and community members? Again, there are no hard and fast answers. Still, as a general principle, it would be best not to overload the board with any one group, nor to underrepresent any of them. Each brings valuable insights and different perspectives to the work of the board. Especially important, as mentioned earlier, is that there be college members (or core faculty) who participate fully in the work of the board and who carry the board work back to the college and faculty. Many schools use as a rule of thumb the principle that one third membership each be drawn from the teachers, parents and friends in the community.

One of the concerns that often stands behind the above questions has to do with protecting the fundamental Waldorf impulse, of avoiding the prospect that a board majority may form which chooses to change the school's mission in significant ways. Such takeovers have occasionally happened. It is prudent, therefore, when setting up the bylaws, to build in mechanisms to prevent this.[*] A common approach is to establish an executive board of college/core faculty board members and additional anthroposophist board members. This "board within a board" would be self-perpetuating, and would have veto power over acts of the full board. Such an executive committee may be deemed unnecessary if the board itself is established as self-perpetuating and consists of no more than 12 to 15 members. The key to avoiding serious difficulties is to make the board self-perpetuating rather than elected by a general membership. Another important aspect to preserving continuity is to establish fixed terms (of 2 to 5 years) and to stagger their termination dates. Clearly, there should also be provision for replacement of board members who are consistently absent.

---

[*] See *Economic Explorations*, Mitchell and Alsop, AWSNA Economic Committee, Wilton, NH, 1988.

Avoiding Micromanagement and Other Pitfalls

As was indicated earlier, the primary task of the board is to see that the school fulfills its mission and to keep it on course over the long haul. The college or core faculty, as a governing organ, has the same responsibility, but with a pedagogical focus. Both groups, in fact, hold a trust.

One of the most common dangers for non-profit boards (and also for the college/core faculty) is overinvolvement with day-to-day affairs. This may come about as a result of a special interest a board member has in a particular area, or it may come as a kind of habit, or it may result from not having clearly defined levels of policy. The board (and the college) should be involved in the highest levels of policy; the board should concern itself with the big picture. It should avoid the temptation to meddle in the details of the administrator's job or the job of committees or individuals with a mandate. Its concern should be in setting basic plans and policies, and in evaluating the results of plans and policies that have been implemented. The actual implementation, and the subordinate policies and procedures required for implementation, the details of how a task is carried out, should be left to those charged with the responsibility. The effectiveness of their work can and should be subject to periodic review, but not to day-to-day scrutiny and interference.

A test of this is how frequently the board finds it necessary to meet. A board that is meeting more than 4 or 5 times a year in full session is either doing too much direct administering, or enjoys its social interaction. Such a board might do better to limit its official meetings and schedule more social events. A related test for a college or core faculty group is to ask what portion of its time is devoted to deepening the pedagogical work in the school, as opposed to time spent on immediate concerns. For both the board and college, the effective functioning of a committee or mandate structure is essential if they are not to be buried under the length of their agendas.

It should be noted, however, that both the board and college/core faculty will be involved in management at times of crisis. Such crises inevitably come in the life of a school. There are external threats, such as lawsuits over liability issues; and there are internal crises, such as the sudden loss or necessary dismissal of key faculty or staff, serious enrollment shortfalls, etc. In such cases, everyone gets involved and everyone pulls together. The important thing to keep in mind, however, is that once the crisis is passed, the board and college/core faculty should pull back. Normal operations should be restored as quickly as possible.

In addition to micromanagement, another common pitfall is the failure to properly educate new board members, especially about the significant differences in the way a Waldorf school's board works. In particular, the fact that school governance is a matter of shared responsibility between the board and the college/core faculty (assuming the school has matured to this point) is something that needs to be spelled out, ideally before a new member joins. Clear expectations and a delineation of the role of a board member, and of the board itself in relation to other bodies within the school, need to be communicated. One effective way to accomplish this is to prepare a handbook for board members (as there should be a handbook for faculty members). Among the things this handbook should contain is a well-written history of the school (kept up-to-date); a statement of the school's mission; and a statement of the school's vision of the future, in its most recent formulation. This should not simply be handed to an individual; someone should go over it with new board members as part of an initiation.

In many cases, of course, new board members are drawn from the ranks of those who have had an involvement with the school over time, as parents, helpers, and committee members. Such experience with the school is more valuable than any handbook; but the handbook is nevertheless an important resource, and useful when recruiting board members from the community who do not have long experience with the school.

Reducing Conflict and Misunderstanding by Improving Communication

Let us assume the presence of capable and dedicated college/core faculty members, equally capable and dedicated board members, and a general agreement that both groups will participate as partners in charting the school's course. Will all go well? What are the pitfalls that can trip up the most promising beginnings, and how do we avoid them?

Much has been said of the importance of gaining clarity about which group has primary responsibility for a given class of decisions, for example, that the board should have responsibility for general administrative functions, the college/core faculty for pedagogical matters. This has been extended, rightly, to defining and creating job descriptions or mandates for any number of specific areas of responsibility: faculty committees, board committees, faculty-board committees, mandate groups, etc. This is all necessary and can help to alleviate much frustration among those charged with the various responsibilities while freeing up the general faculty meetings (and board meetings) for dealing with the bigger issues rather than every niggling detail. Traditionally,

The Board of Trustees

Waldorf faculties get bogged down with everyone wanting to be in charge of everything, and the establishing of clear mandates is a necessary step in overcoming this problem.

But mandates alone are not enough. Necessary though they are, by themselves they can promote a tendency towards fragmentation and "turf battles" and can generate as much frustration as they are intended to relieve. This is because, in fact, very few of the big issues are cleanly defined and limited in scope. There are frequently areas of overlap. This is especially true, in the case of overlapping board and faculty responsibilities, and in matters affecting the budget. Many other areas are also of intense concern to both board and faculty, such as the presentation of the school's image to the public, compliance with governmental regulations concerning pedagogical matters such as qualifications of teachers, and legal issues arising out of discipline policies. If decisions on such issues are made by one group in isolation, without involving other concerned parties, all kinds of problems can arise. How can we avoid this and at the same time provide for effective division of responsibilities?

Most important, perhaps, is to cultivate a healthy attitude: the recognition that the college/core faculty does have a legitimate interest in many issues which have been entrusted to the board, and vice versa (this applies to committees, mandate groups, and administrators as well). In fact, as was stated earlier, both groups can be seen as co-responsible for the entire life of the school. Such an attitude can help to promote communication and cooperation among groups.

Second, the above attitude can be embodied in our procedures. Specifically, it should become routine to ask the following three questions about any issue which is to come before the board (or faculty, or committee, etc.):

1. Which group has primary responsibility to decide the issue or set policy in this area? (This requires that basic areas of responsibility have been clarified. It may be that the issue should be referred to another group to take up first.)

2. Which groups or individuals should have input in the decision? Who is affected by it or needs to be heard? (All individuals/groups identified should be given an opportunity to speak to the issue before any final decisions are made.)

3. Once a decision has been reached, who needs to be informed of it? How shall it be implemented? (Frequently we drop the ball at this stage, so happy that at last we've come to a decision that we forget it needs to be communicated and carried through.)

Frequently, the chairperson can ask the first two questions before placing an item on the agenda, thus saving the time of the full group in taking up issues that belong elsewhere or that need others present to discuss effectively. The secretary can perhaps be responsible for asking the third question, before the item is closed. But all members should train themselves to ask these questions in relation to every agenda item.

Third, our structures should facilitate communication. In this respect it is essential that there be a reasonable proportion of board members drawn from the college (or faculty core group if there is no college). It is important that these faculty board members see their role in the board as full trustees, not simply as watchdogs for the faculty. Moreover, through them the board is represented in the college/core faculty. Their role in fostering communication and an appreciation for the concerns of each group by the other is essential.

Fourth, we need to make a commitment to fostering a sense of community and common purpose between the board and college/core faculty. People need time to get to know one another, to enjoy one another, to trust one another. The groups need time to explore and build up a common vision of the school's mission and its future. An annual retreat of the college/core faculty and board should not be seen as a luxury, but as essential. Other, informal opportunities for interaction should be built into the schedule: times to have dinner together or to share in an artistic experience, for instance.

Rather than considering these things to be frills, we should recognize how essential they are. All of us who are involved deeply in the life of a Waldorf school are called upon to make great sacrifices; all are overworked and overextended. If we are to carry on, we need to experience, along with the work, a joy in striving together, a joy in the process. We need to know that we are not alone, to experience the deepening of colleagueship, the possibility of friendship, of human concern for one another. When these qualities are fostered, our meetings become something we can actually look forward to. Creative energies are freed, and there is a quickening of our vision of the possibilities in the work we do together. It is out of this experience, first and foremost, that we will find the spiritual forces to create the future together.

AGAF DANCY *has been a class teacher, taking a class from first through the eighth grade. He served for many years on the Board of The Rudolf Steiner School of Ann Arbor. Currently he is Director of the Waldorf Teacher Development Association in the Ann Arbor area and serves on the AWSNA Board of Trustees as treasurer.*

APPENDIX

Chapter 1

    Sample Agenda 147
    Faculty Chairperson's Job Description 149

Chapter 3

    Request for Information Form..................................... 150
    Emergency & Class Information List............................... 151
    Class Trip Form 152
    Class Meetings 153
    Weekly Bulletin – Chicago 154-157
    Monthly Parent Newsletter – Pine Hill 158-169
    Faculty Newsletter 170-180
    Sample Flyer... 181
    Life in the Kindergarten 182-187

Chapter 4

    Definition of School Groups – Committee Descriptions 188-190
    Committee List from Chicago Waldorf School...................... 191-193
    Faculty Committee Distribution 194
    Mandate Form.. 195

Chapter 5

    Sample Administrator Job Description............................ 196-197
    Sample Business Manager Job Description........................ 198-199
    Sample Development Officer Job Description 200

Appendix

Chapter 6

Sample Admissions Director Job Description	201-202
Admissions Process	203
Admissions Procedures for New Parents/Exit Interviews	204-205
Admissions Procedures for Class Teachers	206
Sample Elementary School Applications	207-210
Sample High School Parent Application	211
Sample High School Student Application	212-216
Sample High School English Recommendation	217-218
Sample High School Math Recommendation	219-220
Request for Records	221
Enrollment Procedures	222
Tuition Protection Plan	223
Overdue Tuition Policy	224

Chapter 8

Sample Hiring Letter	225
Sample Teacher Contract	226-227
Sample Teacher Evaluation Policy	228-229
Evaluation Criteria for Teachers	230-231
Peer Evaluation Agreement Letter	232
In-House Evaluation Form	233-234
Middle School Course Evaluation	235
High School Student Progress Report	236

Chapter 10

Board of Trustees Committee List	237
Sample Legal Description of Board	238-242

Sample Faculty Meeting Agenda

December 19, 1991

Snack and Clean-up: Sherry, Lorey, Yvonne
Next Meeting: Merilly, Anniken, David
Place: 4th Grade Classroom
Chair: Arthur

If you are not able to attend the faculty meeting or will miss any portion of it, it is your responsibility to notify the faculty chairperson prior to the meeting. Please be prompt.

Verse	1:30pm

1. Who is not here?
    Minutes
    College Report
    Board Report
    Administrative Report and Preview
	1:35–2:00

2. Last minute announcements about Pageant	2:00–2:10
3. Advent singing	2:10–2:25
4. Advent reading – Stephen	2:25–3:00
5. Child study (John S. from 5th grade)	3:00–4:00
6. Wrap-up from Christmas Fair	4:00–4:15

7. Closure:
    Open time
    Meeting evaluation
	4:15–4:45

SNACK	4:45–5:15
8. College Study	5:15–6:00
9. College Meeting (College members – see Agenda in envelope in your mailboxes.)	6:00–7:45

Meeting evaluation and ending by 7:45pm.

Appendix – Chapter 1

Note: Please submit to Catherine any business items which need to be listed at the bottom of the faculty agenda.

    A. Check early duty chart for February.
    B. The Christmas party will be at the Auers on Dec 23 @ 7:30pm.
    C. All middle school report descriptions are due in the office by Dec 20.
    D. Place all abandoned clothing in the bin in the hall before the break.
    E. Snack preparation must not keep faculty from being on time to the faculty meeting!

Appendix – Chapter 1

Sample Faculty Chairperson Job Description

APPOINTED BY: College of teachers
TERM: Two years, with annual review at Easter by the college

GENERAL DESCRIPTION: The faculty chairperson is the external representative of the school. S/he stands before the full faculty, the parents and the children as the official spokesperson in all public gatherings and is the primary contact between the school and the community.

AREAS OF RESPONSIBILITY:

(1) Official school representative "figurehead" who presides/represents the school in public meetings.

(2) Responsible for resolution of parent-teacher difficulties.

(3) Carries overview of kindergarten, lower school and middle school meetings.

(4) Oversees class evenings (plans calendar and is aware of class issues)

(5) Is the embodiment of "Corporality Chair" for personnel and for children (makes sure school is clean!). Ensures timely arrival, participation in school activities for personnel.

(6) Is a member of the Executive Committee and helps plan weekly faculty agenda. Is responsible for, or delegates chairing of faculty meeting.

(7) Serves as AWSNA delegate, if possible.

(8) Serves as a member of the board and college.

(9) Acts as host for all school visitors.

(10) Is the liaison between the Pedagogical Coordinator and the Executive Committee.

(11) Serves a two-year term and rotates in alternate years with the college chair at Easter.

(12) Two hours/week administrative hours are scheduled along with time for Executive Committee.

ACCOUNTABILITY: The faculty chairperson is accountable to the college.

Appendix – Chapter 3

Sample Request for Information

REQUEST FOR INFORMATION
COMMUNICATION

Caller's Name: _____

City _____

State _____ Zip _____ Other _____

Home Phone: _____ Business Phone _____

Child's Name _____ Sex _____

Birth date _____

Entering Grade _____

Comments:

How did caller hear about the Waldorf school?

[ ] Friend
[ ] Newspaper
[ ] Phone book
[ ] Radio

FOLLOW-UP

Information sent by: _____

Date mailed: _____

Follow-up phone call by: _____ Date called _____

Comments:

Teacher interview scheduled?   [ ]Yes   [ ]No

Teacher _____ Date/time of interview: _____

Enrolled?   [ ]Yes   [ ]No   Date _____

Entered on computer mailing list? [ ]Yes   [ ]No

Appendix – Chapter 3

Pine Hill Waldorf School
Wilton, New Hampshire 03086
(603) 654-6003
EMERGENCY AND CLASS LIST INFORMATION 1991 - 1992

Student(s) Last Name(s)	First Name(s)	Date of Birth	Grade
_____	_____	_____	_____
	_____	_____	_____
	_____	_____	_____

Mother's Name & Address

_____
Name
_____
Address
_____
Address
_____
City   State   Zip
Phone (   ) _____

Father's Home Address (if different)

_____
Name
_____
Address
_____
Address
_____
City   State   Zip
Phone (   ) _____

Mother's Business Address

_____
Address
_____
Address
_____
City   State   Zip
Business Phone (   ) _____

Father's Business Address

_____
Address
_____
Address
_____
City   State   Zip
Business Phone (   ) _____

Please indicate below the names and telephone numbers of three friends or relatives who could be called upon to come and care for your child in case you cannot be reached:

1. _____   _____

2. _____   _____

3. _____   _____

The nearest emergency care facility is Milford Medical Center, 130 Nashua St. If you prefer a different hospital, please indicate below:

Emergency Care Facility _____

Address _____   Phone _____

Doctor to be Notified (**must be filled out**) _____

Address _____   Phone _____

Name of Insurance Company _____   Policy No. _____

Date of Last Tetanus Immunization _____

ATTENTION: ALLERGIES OR OTHER INSTRUCTIONS:
_____
_____

If my child is accidentally injured or taken seriously ill during the school day, I give my permission for him/her to be transported to and treated at an emergency care facility. I understand that there may be fees involved, for which I will be responsible.

_____   _____
Signature of Parent or Guardian   Date

Appendix – Chapter 3

CLASS TRIPS AND OUTINGS

Grade _____

Destination _____ Phone No. _____

_____

Departure Date _____ Time _____ Place _____

Return Date _____ Time _____ Place _____

(Will call school at (time) _____ if there is a change in the approximate time of return.)

Transportation

School Van _____ Driver _____

Private Vehicles:

   Drivers _____

   _____

   _____

Supervision

Parents _____ _____

Teachers _____ _____

Things to bring: snack
                      lunch
                      rain gear
                      hat, coat, sweater
                      bathing suit
                      spending money
                      other

PERMISSION SLIP NEEDED BY _____ **MONEY BY** _____

****

_____ has my permission

to go to _____ on _____

SIGNATURE OF PARENT OR GUARDIAN   **DATE**

Appendix – Chapter 3

Class Meetings

At least three meetings a year should be scheduled.

Another teacher should be present.

Notify office of your choice of dates, referring to Events Calendar located in office. Class meeting times and dates should be put on Events Calendar by secretary. They will then be listed in the "Tuesday" newsletter.

Write a letter to your parents, inviting them to each meeting far enough in advance, indicating your agenda.

Have a scribe take notes which can be shared with absent parents.

Suggested form of meetings:

- Artistic activity: painting, modeling, form drawing, eurythmy, etc.
- Curriculum discussion, child development, main lesson work, special teacher reports, related themes—festivals, toys, TV, form of faculty meetings, etc.
- Questions and business
- Allow time for sharing
- Building up a picture of the class
- Social concerns
- Discussion of themes above

"In curriculum discussions the teacher is the authority. In questions of child raising, TV, home life, etc., teachers and parents are on an equal footing, working towards common insights." (from our workshop with C. Schaeffer)

Provide times for parent socializing during the year.
    Potlucks
    Class plays, musical evenings with refreshments afterwards

Emergency phone number: Class teacher will install emergency phone (located in office supply closet) in the classroom during the class meeting. Telephone number 654-2662.

The teacher retains responsibility for building security during the class meetings.

Appendix – Chapter 3

CHICAGO WALDORF SCHOOL
Weekly Bulletin
Wednesday, September 18, 1991

GROWTH + INNOVATION = A FULL CALENDAR! As the Special Events Committee set the calendar for the 1991-92 school year, they worked thoughtfully to schedule festivals, parent evenings, committee meetings, workshops, parent-teacher forums and many other important activities, making every effort to avoid conflicts. If you have a problem with scheduling at any time this year, please let the Committee know. Thanks for your support! Sheree Moratto, Chair 312/764-9243.

Our first guest speaker this year is **Dorit Winter**, director of the San Francisco extension teacher training program of the Rudolf Steiner College. On Mon., Sept. 23 at 7:30 p.m. in the Marshfield gym, she will speak on **Adolescence: Change and Challenge**. All parents and friends of the school are invited. A $5 donation is requested and refreshments will be served.

The invitations are in the mail! Please mark your calendars and plan to attend this fall's **PARENT TEACHER FORUM** meetings. The first takes place Sat., Sept. 28 in the Faculty Room at Diversey from 8:30 a.m. to noon and will feature an open and lively discussion on **Families and the Pop Culture**.

Plans for the November PTF meeting will be discussed Thurs., Oct. 17 at 7:30 p.m. at Dara Salk's, 2559 W. Cullom. (Note change of date from Oct. 10.) Planning meetings are open to all. Any questions? Talk to Ron Richardson or Joan Merlo, 312/549-5270.

The fall festival of Michaelmas, with its image of the knightly St. Michael overcoming the dragon with his sword of light, is a time for courage, resolve and intentional activity. At the Chicago Waldorf School grade school students will celebrate Michaelmas on Mon., Sept. 30 with a day of yard work, cleaning and fixing-up at the school and Wrightwood Park. Parents are needed that morning to help with the various projects. If you can volunteer, please call Marita in the school office. Faculty coordinator is Susan Newberry, class teacher of Grade 2. On Sept. 30 children should wear work clothes and bring gardening gloves, if you have them. Class teachers or room parents will contact you for needed tools and equipment.

DON'T KNOW **WHAT TO BAKE** FOR THE UPCOMING **BAKE SALE AT THE EVANSTON FARMERS' MARKET?** Old standards--brownies, quick breads, any kind of cookie--more sophisticated items like pies, fancy cakes, yeast breads--all sell well. And there's always interest in the items that don't find their way onto most bake sale tables--whole grain, honey-sweetened goodies, sugar- or dairy- or wheat-free treats. Along with <u>lots</u> of bakers, we need help to price on Fri., Oct. 4 and to staff the table on Sat., Oct. 5. If you can help, please call Ilene Warfield eves. at 708/328-3212. **THANKS!**

VOLUNTEER OPPORTUNITIES GALORE! The **SCHOOL LIBRARY** can use help with many small but important tasks. If you could stay for 1/2 hour after dropping your child off, or come 1/2 hour before dismissal, librarian Becky Haase will be delighted to work with you.

See attached flyer for the **MUSIC INFORMATION EVENING!**

Our 1992 **CALENDAR** is on sale in the Four Seasons Shop. Now in its 3rd year, the calendar, illustrated with children's paintings, is a wonderful gift for families, friends and business associates. You can help make the calendar a successful fundraiser this year and in the future. Assistance is needed with mailing, retail and wholesale sales, bookkeeping, computer work, typesetting and art. If you have a few--or many--hours to give, let us hear from you now. And if you'd like to be involved in making long-range plans, work will begin in January on the 1993 calendar. The four members of the calendar committee would eagerly welcome your companionship in this endeavor. Call Melanie Hopp at 312/973-2582.

As the seasons change and warmer clothes are unpacked, donate the summer clothes you won't need next year and the winter things you discover your children have outgrown to the **RUMMAGE SALE**, scheduled for Oct. 21-24. Bring donations to the Paren Room at Diversey Oct. 15-18. Watch the Bulletin for more information.

PARKING NOTICE for our Chicago location...during the two weeks from Mon., Sept. 23 to Fri., Oct. 4, the large parking lot south of the Diversey building will be used by others. You will need to park on Marshfield or Diversey during those weeks.

DATES TO REMEMBER
Thurs., Sept. 19, **GRADE TWO PARENT EVENING,** 7:30 p.m., Mr. Richardson's room, Diversey.
Mon. Sept. 23, 5 p.m., **ANNUAL FUND SOLICITORS**, Faculty Room.
Mon., Sept. 23, **ADOLESCENCE: CHANGE AND CHALLENGE**, lecture by Dorit Winter, 7:30 p.m., Marshfield gym.
Tue., Sept. 24, **MUSIC INFORMATION EVENING**, 7:30 p.m., Music Room, Marshfield.
Sat., Sept. 28, **PARENT TEACHER FORUM**, 8:30 a.m.-noon, Faculty Room, Diversey.
Mon., Sept. 30, **ROOM PARENTS COMMITTEE,** 7:30 p.m. Diversey
Tues., Oct. 1, **GRADE 8 PARENT EVENING**, 7:30 p.m., Marshfield.
Tues., Oct. 1, **EVANSTON KINDERGARTEN PARENTS EVENING**, 7;30 p.m.
Wed., Oct. 2, **ORIENTATION MORNING**, 10 a.m.-noon, Diversey.
Wed., Oct. 2, **GRADE SEVEN PARENT EVENING,** 7:30 p.m. Marshfield
Thurs., Oct. 3, **CHICAGO KINDERGARTEN PARENTS EVENING,** 7:30 p.m. Diversey

CLASSIFIED

WANTED--2nd hand exercise bike. Call Susan 312/728-6505.

FOR SALE--Childcraft Crib'n'bed, white, $100. Gerry auto booster seat, 30-60#, almost new, $50. Want to buy: low dresser for children's room. Suzanne Shelton-Foley, 312/764-2252.

(Sorry--we're out of room! Our other classified ads will appear in next week's Bulletin)

Appendix – Chapter 3

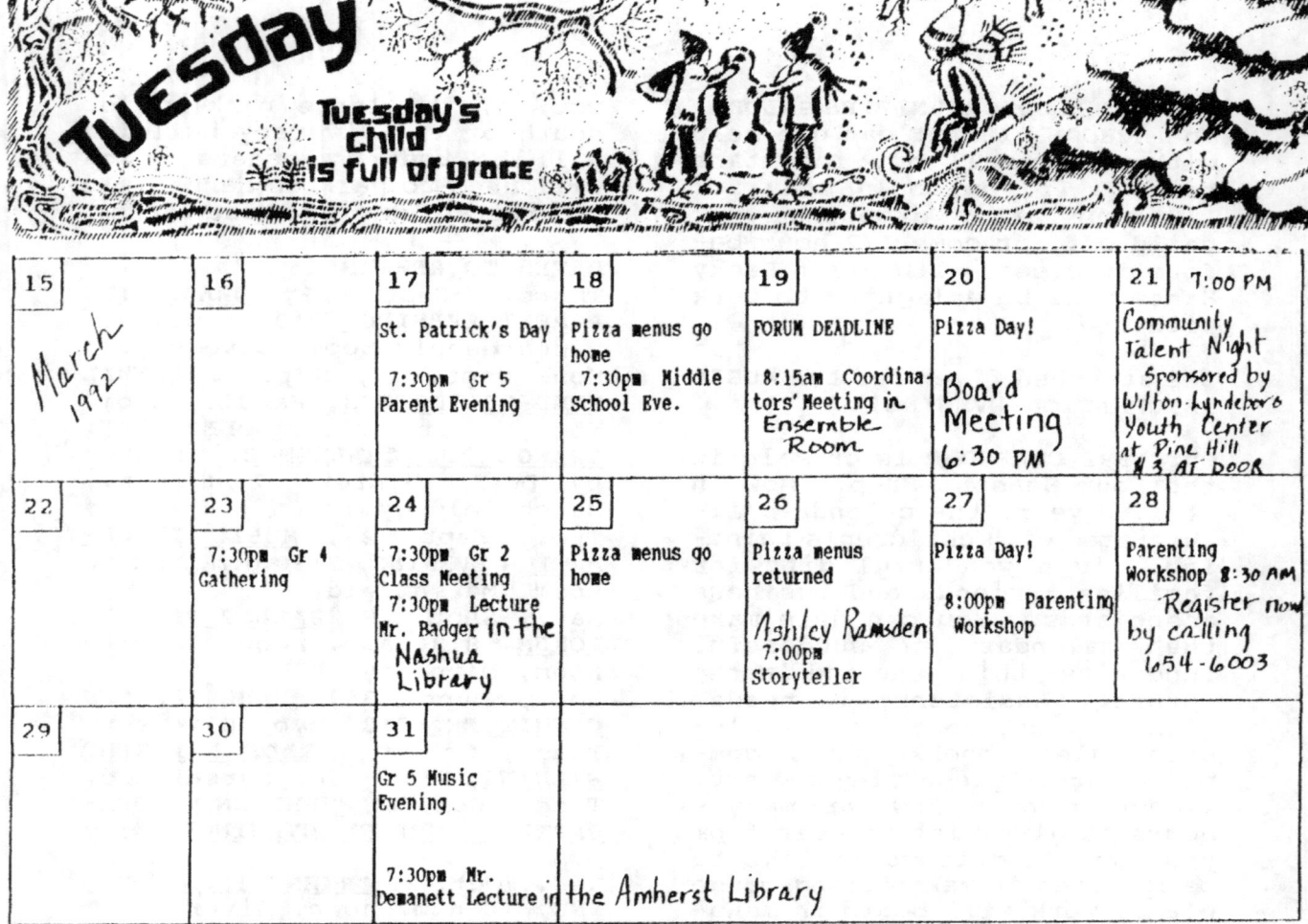

```
DON'T MISS
THE MIDDLE SCHOOL PERFORMING SCIENCES AND ARTS
EVENING
7:30 IN THE AUDITORIUM    WEDNESDAY, MARCH 18
```
Rise above mud season and come to an evening of physics,
comedy, movement, and music with presentations by:
```
        Grade 6    Physics Symphony
        Grade 7    The Ballad of the Glove and Lions
                   A Dramatic Poem of the French Renaissance
        Grade 8    Eurythmy - Spell of the Yukon
                   Soaring - A Fantasy by Schumann
                   The Pirate
        Middle School Chorus - selections
```
Parents of the lower grades are encouraged to attend to see
some of the work of our junior high school and experience
what is to come. Everyone is welcome!

FORUM DEADLINE is Thursday, March 19, to be distributed 3/31.

ENROLLMENT AGREEMENTS, registration fees, emergency and class
list information are due on April 1st.

REMINDER to please return your questionnaires for the Long
Range Planning Committee at High Mowing to the Pine Hill
office. If you have misplaced yours, please pick up another
one in the office. If you have any questions, please see
Catherine Weld.

REGISTER NOW by calling 654-6003 for the Parenting Workshop on Saturday, March 28. Choose "Growing with Young Children" or "Fathering - What are our children asking from us?" or "Sex, Drugs and Rock'n Roll."

The Board Meetings at Pine Hill are open to all who wish to come. The next meeting is Friday, March 20 at 6:30 pm. The agenda will include a presentation by Martin Novom on the role of Development in non-profit institutions followed by a Board discussion from 7:30-8:30. Reports from the following committees will be given--Finance, Building, College and Long Range Planning. There will also be follow up on Georg Locher's visit. The first half hour of the Board meetings are available for parents who would like to discuss specific issues; this must be scheduled with Catherine Weld two weeks in advance. Board agendas and minutes are posted on the bulletin board outside the office.

PIZZA PIECES - Friday is another raffle day. Remember, the raffle is now only $.50 a chance; not much for 4 free lunches. Thank you for your support. 8th grade.

TISTOU OF THE GREEN THUMBS, One Boy's Attempt to Influence World Peace...Don't miss this unforgettable evening with **Ashley Ramsden**, a masterful storyteller, in the Pine Hill Auditorium, Thursday, March 26 at 7:00 p.m. Children 8 years and older invited. Tickets sold at the door--adults, $5 and children, $3.

THE POT OF GOLD is all ready for spring with grass growing and lots of Easter surprises. We also have many new gifts for a wide range of ages--from wooden swords to wooden dinosaur bones, from friendly Waldorf dolls to strange Egyptian hieroglyphs.

Appendix – Chapter 3

Vol XVI, No 5   Pine Hill Waldorf School Wilton, New Hampshire 03086   January 1992
The Forum is a Pine Hill parent publication

Stopping By Woods On A Snowy Evening · Robert Frost

Whose woods these are I think I know.
His house is in the village, though;
He will not see me stopping here
To watch his woods fill up with snow.
My little horse must think it queer
To stop without a farmhouse near
Between the woods and frozen lake
The darkest evening of the year.
He gives his harness bells a shake
To ask if there is some mistake.
The only other sound's the sweep
Of easy wind and downy flake.
The woods are lovely, dark, and deep,
   But I have promises to keep,
      And miles to go before I sleep,
         And miles to go before I sleep.

The function of *The Forum* is to provide information and articles which relate to Waldorf education, parenting, or to the life of the Pine Hill Waldorf School. Articles that express opinions are individual opinions and are not necessarily a reflection on policies or beliefs of the faculty and school. All articles must be signed with an individual's name. Any article that is submitted without a name will not be printed. More detailed submission requirements can be found on the last page of this issue.

Janet Hymowitz,
*   Parent BodyChairperson '91-'92*
Susan Roitman, Editor
Judith Limondin, Ken Neidorf, Margaret and Rob
*   Rushton, Becki Sherman, Elizabeth*
*   Auer, Production*
Jean Davidson, Distribution

This month we have a beautiful cover by Jan Grossman. If we don't get any snow, you can paste it in your window ... and think snow!

The emphasis on the Middle School has expanded this month. As a first grade parent, I am glad for the glimpses into the future, and more than ever grateful for the Waldorf approach to education.

Our faculty has been wonderful in providing articles, but we would also like to see more from parents in the Forum. What are your opinions, questions, talents to contribute? As I have said before, think about what you like to do - and see if it fits an article for the Forum! Thank you.

Susan Roitman, Editor
654-5404

CHRISTMAS FAIR THANK YOU

I would like to extend a most appreciative "THANK YOU" to the many talented bakers who contributed to the Christmas Fair's dessert cafe. Not only were they delicious (I admit I tried a few!) but they were beautiful as well. Many of you were also busy contributing to other areas and so I thank you for all your efforts. Our two overflowing buffet tables were completely sold out! Yum! Thank you as well to the performers who entertained the eaters and gave a very special touch to the cafe.

A final thank you to the people who helped serve our customers (and had the self-control not to eat all the goodies!), especially to Sam and Maria Rosario who worked non-stop setting up, serving, and cleaning up. It was a pleasure working with all of you.

    - Lyra Bessey Engel

PARENT LENDING LIBRARY

There is a small collection of books in the school store for parents to borrow. The focus of this little library is to aid parenting. Please help expand the collection by contributing books you may have outgrown. Examples of specific subjects are: Waldorf Education, child development, health, festivals, crafts, anthroposophy, family life. Please bring your books to the Pot of Gold - and see what's already in our collection. It's a valuable, handy resource - and it's free!!!

AFTER SCHOOL CARE

The need for an after-school care program at Pine Hill has become an increasing concern both for families who are currently part of the school, and for prospective enrollment. This past fall, coordinators in each grade did an informal survey about after-school care. Childcare on Thursday afternoons as well as daily care until 6 pm was met with a positive response from a number of families. The possibility of having such a program at Pine Hill has been discussed with the Executive Committee. In order for an after-school care program to evolve at Pine Hill, a person and/or group of persons interested in formulating a proposal and initiating an approved program is needed. If you are interested in working on starting an after-school program, please contact Janet Hymowitz @ 654-6095, or Catherine Weld @ 654-6003.

    - Janet Hymowitz

Appendix – Chapter 3

VOLUNTEERING

My Pine Hill volunteer career began nine years ago. I was a new mother at the time, faced with many long and lonely days. I already knew a few Pine Hill parents, neighbors and other members of the Wilton Coop. Two of them, Priscilla Durrell and Cindy DiSalvo, invited me to join them in their work for the Christmas Fair, a relatively new Pine Hill Parent Group endeavor. I thought that they were being generous in their friendliness towards me. Little did I realize that I had a much desired skill. I could knit. Once a knitter of sweaters, I was soon to become a knitter of gnomes! For the next five years I gladly joined the annual knitted gnome workshops and each year someone would ask, "which class are you in?" and my response was always the same, "Oh, I'm not in the school yet."

Finally, Zachary entered kindergarten in 1987 and I felt that I had at last arrived. A few months passed and I was still feeling quite new in my status of being a Pine Hill parent when I received an invitation to join the group of parents soliciting donations for the Capital Campaign. I was surprised to be called upon so soon but was told, "We've been waiting for you - you didn't think you could get away with just knitting a few gnomes did you?" Once my foot was in the door, the path of tasks and jobs I have chosen has taken me in many directions. Along the way, I am still knitting gnomes.
- Janet Hymowitz

LONG-RANGE PLANNING
SHAPING OUR FUTURE

A biodynamic farm with a greenhouse, perhaps a windmill... a gymnasium... studio space for resident artists... joint field trips with other schools... a large deck joining the school building with the playground... extended day care... revenues derived from donation, not tuition... more socio-economic diversity...

Which of these are part of Pine Hill's future?

A long-range planning process for Pine Hill is now underway, and its horizon stretches into the next century. The planning process is led by the Board, and long-range planning committee. It will integrate the plans, hopes, and dreams of parents, faculty, and the board. Members of this planning committee include Mike Anderson, Laurie Birdsall, Steve Morgan, Catherine Weld, and Roger Wellington.

The long range planning group has already held brainstorming sessions with the faculty, the Board of Trustees, and now a group of parents. The next steps are to send a written questionaire to all the parents and ask detailed input from the Finance, Development, Building, and Enrollment committees, and The College of Teachers. The long-range planning committee hopes to complete its work in May. According to Roger Wellington, "This is the first time Pine Hill has planned for a 5-10 year span. We've reached a point where our enrollment is stable and we now feel that we can lift our heads up from the emergencies that have preoccupied us and look toward the future."

On January 8th, twenty-five parents met to share their individual visions for Pine Hill's future. These ideas will be one of the sources of input to the planning process. Other ideas in addition to those that began this article included "more use of the land by the community....more of a campus...a preschool...mothers and toddlers gathering here...a Pine Hill bus....paving the driveway..." and many more. These ideas came from a free-flowing, creative reflection and discussion led by Roger Wellington.

At the end of this "brainstorm," Roger pointed out that some of the ideas related to our wish to express ourselves as a community, while others were more focused on the school's plant and programs. Roger also noted after the meeting that a new mission statement for Pine Hill is being developed by the College of Teachers and the ideas that come from all the reflections and discussions at various meetings will be melded together in light of that mission. This mission will clarify Pine Hill's identity as a "K-8 school" in relation to other purposes.

Part of the January 8th parent's meeting was also devoted to reflecting on Pine Hill's strengths and weaknesses, and then surfacing suggestions for projects and actions to achieve the visionary ideas. The spirit and devotion of Pine Hill parents, our ability to come together, and the dedication of our faculty were identified by many in the room as principle strengths, as well as Steiner's gift...that we are floating in a larger pond, a movement, that is Waldorf education. Parents also wrestled with Pine Hill's relationship with the Waldorf education movement, and its relationship to our community and to American Society. The manifestation of "being special" as a weakness (isolation, sameness) as well as a strength (a center of educational excellence) was considered.

At one point, Roger challenged the parents to think about "how we would spend $500,000 if we had it." Although there were some suggestions that we could use such funds to complete and expand the physical plant and grounds, the discussion quickly focused on ways such a gift could be used as "seed money" to build an endowment, reduce tuitions, or allow experiments in alternative tuition financing. One refreshing idea was to "give it all to the Waldorf movement to educate more Waldorf teachers," which stimulated further discussion of Pine Hill's contribution to the world at large.

All of this rich and varied discussion will feed into the planning process as "raw data". At the same time, this parent meeting served a larger purpose. The invitation to first reflect on a large scale and broad scope... and then to share deeply felt values and dreams...was seized by parents to create a marvellous dialogue. I felt privileged to participate in this dialogue, and I believe that the self-and-other learnings we gained will stimulate positive developments at Pine Hill and in our larger communities.

- David Roitman

AUTHORITY AND THE TEN/ELEVEN YEAR OLD - THE SHINING HOUR OF CHILDHOOD

In his many lectures on education Rudolf Steiner speaks about the need for the teacher to be the authority in the classroom. This refers specifically to the teaching of children between seven and fourteen years of age. One can also view this as the journey a teacher and group of children make together (ideally) from first through eighth grade. Exactly what kind of authority are we talking about here? And what do we mean by authority?

With reference to the teacher as the authority in the classroom, two schools of thought come to mind. There is the traditional, conservative school of thought which implies the teacher is the unquestioned authority. This authority is either a natural gift of the teacher, or it comes in by way of rules, regulations and punishments. Second, there is an accelerated school of thought according to which the teacher stands in relief to the class as a whole as an objective, impartial counselor who will offer advice when it is needed.

By the first method the children are taught by the teacher. According to the second, the children are left more to themselves and are often guided in such a way that they learn from each other. If the first method is carried to extremes, the children may become oppressed, their free expression checked, imagination curtailed and creative ideas stifled. If the second approach runs to extremes the creative ideas and imagination of the children run rampant and lack the informative forces which would give them true grit, substance and inner structure. While excellent discipline may be the result of the first technique and chaos the bed-fellow of the other, one is left with the nagging question of to which of these two particular schools of thought do we in a Waldorf School belong? I believe it is correct to say we strive not to fall into the extremes of either one or the other.

In general children have a genuine need to place their whole-hearted trust in one or more adult human beings. This seems to be especially true of the child between six and nine, or ten years old. The child looks up to the adult with the greatest confidence; s/he feels protection and security. For the child this adult is a vessel of truth, goodness and all that is right in the world.

At about the age of ten or eleven years old this feeling of unquestioning trust in the adult begins to change and shift. Trust is still there at the core but something new enters into this pure feeling of trust, something that comes from the realm of thinking. S/he begins to look at the adult with a somewhat more critical eye. S/he begins to judge or question the deeds and actions of the adult. During this process of testing, which is not at all fully conscious, s/he has - or his/her higher being has - no greater hope and wish than that the trusted adult friend may pass the test successfully. S/he does not want to lose him/her.

In the classroom the child becomes more and more conscious of what the teacher can do and in what arenas the teacher fails and doesn't measure up. The child's sense of whether the teacher is fair or not becomes even stronger. But what really counts the most for the ten and eleven year old is whether the teacher is honestly and deeply interested in him/her and loves him/her just as much as s/he loves Sylvester or Gloria. If the teacher is able to create and maintain an atmosphere of confidence which stems from genuine interest in the well-being and development of each and every child in the classroom, then a natural wholesome form of authority is established.

It is now possible to see the emergence of another, or third, school of thought concerning authority which lies between the aforementioned two. Between the teacher teaching the child, regardless of whether the child wants it or not, and the other approach of the child being left more to him/herself, there is the third perspective - the child WANTS to be taught by the teacher. When Rudolf Steiner speaks of the teacher as an authority in the classroom, he means an authority that is created from within through interest, wonder, enthusiasm and love, not an authority created from without through laws and regulations.

For the ten and eleven year old child is not yet interested primarily in what the teacher knows. S/he will gladly forgive the teacher if a mistake is made in arithmetic. Of course if the teacher makes a mistake every day in arithmetic?!! Yikes!!!! Confidence erodes and a critical attitude replaces trust.

This ten/eleven year old stage and relationship with authority can be a real shining hour in the life of the child and teacher. It is also the beginning of a period of transition which will continue through middle school into high school. The teacher's task is to make as conscious an effort as possible to train the children for a new kind of authority. This is an authority which does not come from an individual, but from knowledge itself. The earlier sense of security brought about by trust in an adult human being has laid the groundwork for this new trust in knowledge.

There are many wonderful changes in the life of the ten/eleven year old. Like Odysseus of the Greek Mythologies the ten/eleven year old is ready to dip his/her oars into the waters of life, and the curriculum which the teacher is able to present during the Fifth grade year is rich and imaginative. The stimulation of these capacities in the children, combined with the interest, wonder and enthusiasm which these curriculum studies evoke and the creatively crafted presentation of the material by the teacher, reveals the roots of authority.

The teacher can be that abiding friend who does not trick, abandon or deceive. It is from this quality of authority that children enjoy and learn.

- Merrill Badger
Fifth grade teacher

LIFE IN THE MIDDLE

"8th Grade"

"The turquoise sea laps the brilliant white shore as the palms sway in the tropical breeze off the Indian Ocean." I would highly recommend a trip to the Kenya coast during a New Hampshire winter. The 8th grade ended 1991 with just such an "excursion." One's notions of reality are altered by the tremendous differences in our environments and cultures, and the amazing diversity of African life itself. The final day of our geography block was spent listening to Zulu music while fashioning water jars from clay. In spite of themselves, one by one the students began to join in the chanting of unfamiliar sounds.

Upon our return from Christmas the 8th grade entered into study of several phenomena that are easily taken for granted: water, air, and weather. This block in physical science is aimed at understanding the quality and properties of these most basic of substances as well as how they work to create weather. Through simple demonstrations in the classroom the students are guided to discovering the properties of water and air and how these properties are applied to practical problems in the world. For instance, the fact that in a fluid pressure increases with depth, is used to produce hydroelectric power. Our block will end with a week devoted to understanding weather, to the extent that it is possible. The 8th graders have returned from Christmas break full of energy and themselves. The balance of the year holds many exciting prospects for us. This time will probably pass too quickly!

- Stephen Fox

"7th Grade"
from Geometry to Geology to Geography

From the Theorem of Pythagoras and the mysterious relationship of pi to the parts of a circle, we passed on in January to a geology and geography of the circling globe. After examining the three layers of our planet (crust, mantle, core), we learned how the new science of plate tectonics has recently introduced revolutionary perspectives on its constitution. Hardly a cold rock hanging in space, the earth is being revealed as a warm, animate organism whose layers undergo more radical patterns of change than we ever imagined.

The continents not only float, drift, join and divide, but the earth's plates and ocean floors also submerge and re-emerge. Geology and geography become incredible detective thrillers involving scattered clues and demanding a new kind of imagination to grasp complicated change. How can it be that South America and Africa not only fit together like a jigsaw puzzle but also share matching rock formations? Did Siberia really come crashing into Europe and force up the Ural Mountains? Was Italy really a piece of Africa that collided with Europe and bulged up the Alps?

Having studied North and South America in the Sixth Grade, the jump to a specific focus on Europe and Africa is not as radical, if one thinks how the continents may have been somehow more intimately related in the past. The question of whether Europe and Asia are both continents or one big Eurasia becomes a more interesting one.

From the larger perspective of the whole earth and the formation of its 6 (or 7!) continents, we then examined comparatively the geography of Europe and Africa: topography, climate, peoples, customs, resources, etc. How are the character of peoples related to the parts of the continent on which they have settled? the lowland Dutch, the mountain Swiss, the island British, the Mediterranean Italians. Or what is it like to grow up in an African tribe in the savannahs of the Sudan or the rain forests of Nigeria? Map-making, drawing, fact finding research projects, folk tales, music, and exotic cooking help us to appreciate the virtues of a rich variety of different peoples and customs on the earth. Viva la difference!

- Arthur Auer

French News
"Bonne Année"

The sixth graders are plunging into a medieval mood in French class. They are hearing the dramatic story of the martyr, Saint Denis of Paris. This moving story is told in simple language, a basis for practicing all the language skills.

The seventh graders are approaching the performance date for the story of Joan of Arc. This play will be done both in English and in French and has been a full language immersion experience. They also have received their first textbook in French, a popular supplement to our usual fare!

The eighth graders have risen to the occasion of performing a Moliere comedy with their usual flair and exuberance. There are many deliciously ridiculous moments in the play - the wheezing, sneezing hypochondriac running to the exit with his bedpan - the wide eyed younger sister being spanked over papa's knees, then playing dead and causing him to sob in anguish - the doting wife, hypocritically waiting to snatch his fortune - the awkward scholarly suitor with memorized love speeches. Most importantly of all, though, it is performed entirely in French! Hats off to the 8th graders!

- Lorey Johnson

Reading Assignments

Over Christmas vacation the sixth, seventh and eighth grade students were given reading assignments. Sixth and Seventh grades had free choices and eighth graders were to choose a book, whether it be historical novel or biography or fictional account, set within the last hundred years or so. All selections were subject to Mrs. Birdsall's approval, of course. From the over fifty reviews submitted, we share with you reviews of the books which received one of our two highest ratings, "excellent" or "the best" (Please note: Books rated "poor", "fair", or "good" do not appear in this Forum. For your further reference, a complete listing is posted in each of the three classrooms.) If you are looking for a stimulating, well-written book to curl up with on a cold winter's evening, don't hesitate to ask one of our middle schoolers.

- Laura Birdsall

1. Alice in Wonderland - L. Carrol.
Raina "excellent"
Alice followed a white rabbit into wonderland where everything was nonsense. Alice couldn't see why the Mad Hatter and the March Hare never stopped their tea party because the Hatter's watch stopped at 6:00, or how the Cheshire Cat could disappear but have his smile remain, or how a baby could turn into a pig right before her eyes. Alice's adventures just got wilder and wilder and wilder!

2. Julie of the Wolves - J.C. George.
Emily "the best"
Amarog was the name of a wolf. He was the leader of a wolf pack. Miyax, an Eskimo girl, had run away. She depended on this wolf pack to give her food and keep her away from danger. They did so, and Miyax became very good friends with them. She named each little pup and adult, but she called Amarog, the leader of the pack, her adopted father.

3. Flaming Arrows - W. O'Steel
Nathaniel "excellent"
Chad woke with a scare, and he heard the scout at the door telling his father that Indians were going to attack. Chad and his family and all the other people that lived in the settlement fled to the fort. When they got there, they went down to get some water, but the Indians held them off so they were all without water. All the people in the fort were thirsty, and they didn't know how they could fight the Indians. Early one morning guns shot and arrows flew. And if you want to know what happens, I recommend you read the book.

4. Freedom Crossing - M.G. Clark.
Maya "excellent"
Laura is a fifteen year old stubborn girl who has just come back from Virginia to live with her father. Well, she was stubborn until she overheard her brother talking to a friend about the slave he had and was trying to free into Canada. She realizes that her brother and father work in the Underground Railroad and are trying to free a boy slave into Canada.

5. The Horse That Had Everything - B.B. Wildes
Katie "the best"
When Rick heard about the new foal down the road, he became very excited. Because the foal was born with an off leg and his owner had no use for him, Rick got to keep him! The foal, whom Rick named San, became very good friends with Rick, and they even went swimming together. After Rick managed to make San's leg better, he decided to race him. But the racing didn't work out, so San moved back in with Rick and they were happy from then on.

6. The Secret Of The Indian - L.R. Banks
John "excellent"
Omni was sure lucky to have that magic key and the plastic figures. It was awesome how Patrick and Omni could travel through time and go back to the

time when cowboys were around. I would have liked to be Omni and Patrick.

7. The Return of the Indian - L.R. Banks
Nahod   "the best"
This book is about a boy named Omni and how he brought a plastic Indian to life and helped his tribe to win a war. This is one of the best books I've ever read.

8. Luck Everlasting - N. Babbit
Abby   "excellent"
Luck everlasting was a touching story about a family preserved for ever. This may sound like a blessing, but it was more like a burden to the Tuck family. Never growing older or changing made them so sick of being the way they were that they would have done anything to be changed again.

9. The Kid Comes Back - J. Lunes
Christopher R.   "excellent"
Roy was a very good baseball player when he hurt his leg. I don't think the Dodgers could have won the pennant without him.

10. Man O'War - W. Farley
Carrie   "the best"
Man O'War was the best, most beautiful, fiery, majestic and graceful race horse the American turf ever knew. He traveled from race track to race track most of his life and was very calm on long rides that were mostly by train. His owner was Mr. Riddle, his trainer was Louis Feustel and his jockeys were Clyde Gordon, Harry Vititoe, Johnny Loftus, Clarence Hummer and Earl Sande. Man O'War entered twenty one races, and to the amazement of all people he won twenty of them and broke all race track records in which he ran a mile and an eighth in the blazing speed of 1:49:2! Man O'War's incredibly long life was full of excitement, love, sickness, thrilling and treacherous races and much more until the day of his death. And even to this day he is remembered as a hero, a wonder of all wonders!

11. The Yearling - M.K. Rawlings
Lee   "excellent"
Once there was a boy named Tody, who was helpful, dependable and strong. While hunting in the woods one day, he found a little buck fawn. He begged his parents for it, and they let him keep it as long as he kept it out of mischief. The fawn grew to be a yearling and began damaging the family crops. Would Tody be able to keep the yearling?

12. Guardians Of The Fall Stones - M. Caldecott
Morgan   "the best"
The priests of the Sun were well advanced in understanding the forces of the Earth and the power of the Earth which could be gathered in great stone circles that were located in many small communities of Bronze Age Britain. The sacred stones trilogy is about a girl whose ultimate wish is to increase the understanding and love throughout each small village of Britain.

13. Hatchet - G. Paulson
Vide   "excellent"
The book Hatchet is about a thirteen year old boy whose name is Brian and how he survives in a big forest with a bear and a moose for company. How long can Brian survive in the wilderness?

14. Calico Captive - E.G. Speare
Piper   "the best"
Miriam Johnson was an intelligent, beautiful and unusually determined pioneer girl. Miriam would would not have survived a day in Indian captivity had she not had her determination and her pride.

15. Gone With The Wind - M. Mitchell
Elizabeth   "the best"
Before the Civil War began, Scarlett O'Hara was a rich and spoiled girl who never had to worry about where her next meal would come from. But after the war began, her family was stricken by poverty. Throughout the war and everywhere she went, Scarlett kept meeting Rhett Butler. Little did she know that this was not merely coincidental.

16. <u>The Bridges at Toko-Ri</u> - Mitchener
Orin   "the best"
Former Navy pilot Harry Brubacker was a lawyer and had a wife and two kids when he was yanked back into service to fly in the navy. He was put on the aircraft carrier "Savo" under Admiral Tarrant. To bomb the bridges at Toko-Ri was considered one of the hardest missions in WWII, and soon he and seven other pilots would be flying that mission.

17. <u>Anne Frank - The Diary of a Young Girl</u> - A. Frank
Stephen   "excellent"
Anne Frank, a young Jewish girl, was forced into hiding with the beginning of WWII. Her simple diary reflects on the problems of her years in hiding as she slowly matures. Perhaps more importantly, though, Anne brings to light the horrors of the Holocaust in an incredibly sincere and moving way.

18. <u>The Right Stuff</u> - T. Wolfe
Andrew   "excellent"
American military test pilots climbed the pyramid of excellency, the ones that had the "right stuff" lived and made it to the top while the others crashed and died. This book follows the lives of some interesting pilots with the "right stuff" These were chosen to test-fly rockets into space. It was an excellent book.

19. <u>All's Quiet On The Western Front</u> - Remarque
David   "excellent"
This is an exciting book about a young soldier who joins the German army during WWI. He thinks it will be glorious and exciting but finds that it is not all he had hoped. The battles were gruesome and bloody. And he saw his four best friends die with much suffering.

20. <u>Jubilee</u> - M. Walker
Mandy   "excellent"
When Vyry was seven her mother died and she became a slave in the Big House. Vyry was a slave because her mother was black, but Vyry's skin was as white as her father's who was master of the Big House. Vyry became a strong woman. She lived through the pain of slavery and finally received her freedom at the end of the war. Even then she found her troubles were not over, but with a strong will and belief in God, she managed to make a new life for herself.

"The following article by David Mitchell will be continued in the next several Forums as it is quite long. You may wish to save the issues to have the entire article."
-Susan Roitman, Editor

DEVELOPING COMPASSION AND UNDERSTANDING FOR ADOLESCENCE

Our children have several little "ego births" as they grow to adulthood. The one year old overcomes gravity and develops coordination. The two year old begins to communicate with formal speech patterns. Three year olds speak of themselves in the first person singular. Also, this is the time that earthly memory begins. The four, five and six year old, live with their will in imitation. As the inner organs form, the body increases its coordination. The brain reaches nearly full size at seven. Around seven is also the age when the baby teeth fall out and are replaced by the adult teeth. The waist begins to take a maturer form at this time as well, thus bounding the rhythmic system. The American Indian had children reach their arm over their head to see if they could touch their opposite ear lobe. This becomes possible around the age of seven and was an indication that a new type of learning could take place. Usually by seven the arm has grown proportionately into the harmony of the Golden Mean, making this suddenly possible.

Around the age of nine we begin to notice specific changes in our children which can be a premature glimpse of what we will meet when they enter adolescence. We may notice for the first time that the child begins to experience the soul in a new way. They begin to feel loneliness, detachment, and fear. They feel naked, abandoned by the mother's protective sheath, alone in the world. Gesell referred to this time as "the emergence of self-motivation". Neurophysiolgists say that the age of nine is the age where one can start to carry tasks. Psychologists say that this is the time when "the tail of the snake" is experienced in the child's organism. This means that the ego is penetrating the metabolic system and the child can begin to complain frequently of headaches, stomach aches and nausea. It can be a strenuous time for the child!

Fortunately, this phase does not last very long. The child stabilizes and moves into what is referred to as the most harmonious period of childhood. The 11th year is the year that statistics state has the lowest mortality rate. This is the same in all countries throughout the world. However, two hundred years ago the most stable period was 12 years of age; like everything else, this too has become accelerated.

This peacefulness and harmony lasts until the onset of puberty. Puberty is the pinnacle of childhood. The word comes from the Latin "pubescere" which means "to be covered with hair". This is one of the outer signs that our child is entering that period known as adolescence. This word "adolescence" has only been around in English since the 15th century. The root of the word "al-ere" means to be "in need of nourishment". Understanding this can increase our compassion. It refers to a transition phase between childhood and adult-maturity where major biological and psychological changes are taking place.

At this time the children lose the Greek-like graceful relationship to their body. This frequently brings about a desire to revolt or to express anger. The children desire to, and must, throw off authority in order to develop self discipline. They must begin again! Parents and teachers must allow them to do this. In a Waldorf School they can come to the point where they don't like their class teacher. The class teacher must be secure enough not to take this personally!

The child usually reaches puberty at the end of the 6th grade. The Middle School has been referred to as "education's step child." It is commonly called the "graveyard of teachers", the "purgatory for parents" and is a "journey through a dark passage" for the children themselves. It can be a difficult time. This is why it is so very important for parents and teachers to understand what is happening to the child. The children must go through this phase. They must be rebellious and difficult and it is far better that we allow them to do this in their early teenage years rather than have to watch them suffer through it when they are in their 30's.

At this age the teacher must create substance in the material that is taught. It is a time where the children need real challenges, the teacher needs patience, a sense of humor, and a strong recollection of who the child really is, based on who they were seen to be in early childhood. Above all, the teacher needs to hold up the highest expectations that each child can attain, despite their complaints.

The teenagers in the 6, 7, 8th grade come to school wanting to train their thinking. Parents and the teachers, and other adults around them, become the whetstones for the sharpening of their intellect. They often make heroes out of sports stars, rock stars, and movie stars or have an infatuation or crush on horses, skateboarding, or fantasy games like Dungeons and Dragons. This is a time when the child can develop a crush or infatuation. It can be a sports figure, a singer, an actor or actress, or it could be horseback riding, skateboarding or whatever. This crush helps the child to forget all the bad things and the pain that they are experiencing and it involves their energy.

- to be continued -
- David Mitchell

COMMUNITY BULLETIN

PINE HILL WINTER CONCERT
The Pine Hill Winter Concert will be held Sunday, January 26, at 1:00pm. The middle school orchestra and recorder ensemble will perform selections from Tchaikovsky, Bach, Haydn, and more - featuring solos, duets, and trios. With Bonnie Achterhof directing this is sure to be a rewarding musical experience. Bring your friends and support this wonderful musical event!

BROOKLINE OPEN STAGE
Are you a local musician eager to share your tunes, meet other musicians, learn new songs, and generally enjoy an evening of good fun and

entertainment? Or are you just looking for an excuse to get out of the house and listen to some spirited live music?

Either way you're invited to come to Brookline's first Open Stage on Sunday evening, January 26, at the upstairs meeting hall at the Daniels Academy (right next to the fire station) in lovely downtown Brookline. Warm up a cold winter's night in a musical atmosphere that promises to be relaxed, friendly and informal, where everyone who wants to will have a chance to try out their favorite songs on a supportive and forgiving audience.

So mark those calendars now, dust off that old guitar or banjo, loosen up those vocal cords and plan to come join us. Coffee will be served and a small donation will be requested to cover costs.

For more information contact Basil Harris at 673-7911.   P.S. Time: 7:30 pm - 10 pm

HOUSING NEEDED

The ALL NEW ENGLAND MUSIC FESTIVAL will take place at Conval High School in Peterborough this year. Over 400 high school musicians will work under the directorship of an outstanding conductor and present two concerts on Saturday, March 14. We are looking for families to host one or more students in their homes. On Thursday, March 12, and Friday, March 13. If you can help please call Janet Koerber @ 924-7930.

SUMMER TRIP TO FRANCE

I am offering a two week trip to France next summer, June 25th - July 9th. The cost of the trip will be $1800.00 per person, including all transportation, lodging, three meals per day, and entertainment. We will spend four days in Paris, five days in the Loire Valley, and five days in the Western Pyrenees. The trip will be shaped according to the age group that I bring, for example, if the group is composed of adolescents, there would be more bicycling, longer hikes, and more evening entertainment. We will visit Notre Dame de Parie, Le Tour Eiffel, Chartres, Versailles, and a few Loire castles. In the southern section of France, we will visit the French Atlantic coast (gorgeous beaches), medieval forts and churches, and tiny Basque villages.

Interested? Call me and plan to come to a more informative gathering in my home on Saturday evening, January 25th, at 7:30 PM. RSVP.
- Lorey Johnson

PINE HILL PUBLIC LECTURE SERIES

February 12th   "Education is an Art"
A lecture by George Locher, head of the Waldorf teacher training at Emerson College, England. 7:30pm at The Pine Hill Waldorf School.

March 3rd   "Between Form and Freedom - Meeting the Needs of the Young Adolescent"
A lecture by Arthur Auer, Pine Hill class teacher. 7:30pm at the Milford Public Library.

March 10th   "Enthusiasm For Learning"
Basic skills, habits and attitudes in grades 1, 2 and 3 in The Waldorf School. A presentation by Pine Hill Teachers. 7:30pm at The Pine Hill Waldorf School.

March 24th   "Television: Your Child's Friend or Foe"
A lecture by Merrill Badger, Pine Hill class teacher. 7:30pm at The Nashua Public Library.

March 27th/28th   "Mothering, Fathering - Parenting, The Joys and Challenges of Raising Children in a Complex World"
A weekend workshop with Rev. Sanford Miller and members of the Pine Hill faculty.

March 31st   "Loving to Learn - What Makes a Waldorf School Different?"
A lecture by Dennis Demanett, Pine Hill class teacher. 7:30pm at the Amherst Town Library.

April 5th   OPEN HOUSE - A Celebration of Waldorf Education
1-4pm at The Pine Hill Waldorf School

All events listed may be subject to change: please call the Pine Hill
office (654-6003) to confirm.

Appendix – Chapter 3

FOR SALE
14 foot Starcraft aluminum boat with folding seat, oars, trailer, 7.5 Mercury Motor, anchor, seat cushions, canvas cover, other extras - $1,800 or BO
Sears Craftsman 10 inch construction, radial arm saw with an assortment of new blades, legs, and table - $350 or BO
Jonsereds 451EV 3.5 cu. inch chain saw with gas cans, new extra chains - $225 or BO
Girls, Murray-ESCORT, 10 speed bicycle with lock & kickstand - $30 or BO
McCulloch 85-SX Eager Beaver String trimmer/Brush Cutter, gasoline tank incl. - $85 or BO
Sears Craftsman 315.796610 -14 inch hedge trimmer, double insulated - $30 or BO
Jøtul, #602 cast iron, Norwegian, s-draft, air-tight Woodstove - $215 or BO
Sears Deluxe Ergometer Exercise Cycle #267.291221 - $55 or BO
Small Student roll top antique desk, needs refinishing - $45 or BO
      Contact David & Anniken Mitchell, 654-6382
DESIGN SERVICES AVAILABLE Logos, letterheads, brochures, illustrations, etc. Elizabeth Auer 654-6315
STONEHOUSE PRESS would like to be your printer. We are a full service Print Shop. We are known for our Quality, Competitive Prices, and Prompt, Personal Service. During the month of January 1992, mention this ad and receive 10% off your in-house printing order (all orders up to $1,000.00). Call Rob or Betsy Earle at 673-8383. Our hours are: Mon-Fri from 8:30-5:00. Remember, quotes are always FREE!
CREATIVE JEWELRY AVAILABLE from local silver/goldsmith. Custom design and repair work available. Call Sussy Ely at 654-5310
MEAT AVAILABLE Chemical-free beef and pork available at our farm. Raised with tender, loving care. Call Ron Lucas in Greenfield @ 547-3395.
SHEEP SKINS Large and small sizes, all colors. $45-75. Call Maggie Sauvain in Greenfield @ 547-3395.
CHILDREN'S TIGHTS Swiss (non-itchy) wool-silk blend children's tights for sale at Pot of Gold. Reduced to $12!
JOB WANTED 4th grade girl needs after-school care in *your* home one day a week. 8th grader or parent living near the school would be ideal. Call Joan Giese @ 429-0769.
CARPENTER AVAILABLE I am experienced in all phases of carpentry - from repairing sills to siding, roofing, and interior work. Also custom design. Am able to do total jobs, start to finish. Call Ron Lucas in Greenfield @ 547-3395.
ARTISTIC THERAPY introductory class featuring the healing qualities of color. Feb 1 - March 7, Saturday 3-4:30 at the Aurum Center. For further information, call Carla Mattioli, M.A., instructor, @ (413) 549-6208 or (603) 924-7401. Please register by January 26.
PSYCHOTHERAPY Fredrica Chapman R.N., M.S., C.S., psychotherapy for women. Working with dreams, illness resolution, relationships, self-expression, spirituality, and past-life regression therapy. Sliding scale. Temple, NH (603) 878-3000.
FOR RENT Lovely, sunny 3 bedroom apartment available in Lyndeborough Center. Call Lise @ 654-5048
FOR RENT Unique, open concept, 2 bedroom house on 23 acres available immediately. Great mountain view, plus 2 minutes from Pine Hill. $775 per month - includes electricity. Call John or Sarah Griffith @ 654-2806
FOR RENT Summer house right on Casco Bay, Maine to rent. Sleeps 6, with outhouse but has running hot and cold water and modern kitchen. Plenty of clam digging at low tide, good for boating at high. $375 per week. Call John Griffith @ 654-2806

Appendix – Chapter 3

Sample Faculty Newsletter

MAN'S ABODE

The earth and heavens are our great home.
The floor's the ground; the roof's a starry dome.
We share this house with all mankind.
A more beautiful dwelling we'll never find,

Unless we look at man as well.
God gave us a body in which to dwell.
The roof of our head protects us inside,
The walls of our skin are a place to reside.

Through the windows of our eyes
We see the world and starry skies.
On pillars of legs our house stands upright.
Inside it's all warm and glowing with light.

Poem written for the
Third Grade

Appendix – Chapter 3

Some thoughts on the time from Michaelmas through Christmas

The continuing drama of our life is set against the scenery of the four seasons. Beneath the canopy of the stars in the heavens the earth moves in orbit around the blazing sun. Winter sloshes and blows into Spring; Spring sprouts into Summer; Summer skips into Autumn, and Autumn sprints into Winter. In ages past these turning points were always represented by a festival. In pagan times there were fires and sacrifices. Worship was focussed upon deities of nature. After the birth of Christ came the Christian Festivals of Christmas, Easter, Saint John's Tide and Michaelmas. There are great cosmic mysteries hidden within the outer celebrations of these days. In the community of Waldorf Schools that circle the world much emphasis is placed on the healthy celebration of festivals. Doctor Franz Winkler in his book MAN: THE BRIDGE BETWEEN TWO WORLDS wrote the following:

> "Regularly recurring occasions for joy have been celebrated for ages as the most powerful healers and protectors of the human soul. . .
> The great religious festivals, if celebrated correctly, are the child's safest guide on his dangerous journey into adulthood. It is they which gently lead his inner perception from the world of the fairy tale into the world of adult religion. It is they which bring purely qualitative faculties, such as joy and gratitude, into proper relation with pleasure derived from material gifts. And it is they which weave magic bonds of love around a family, and thus prevent the estrangement between parents and children, so often at the root of juvenile delinquency."

In our modern times we pay scant attention to the significance of the stars and the movement of the planets. Our festivals are for the most part materialistic. Where amongst all the hustle and bustle of Christmas. . . amongst all the induced selfish feelings and self-indulgence often found in present coveting and present giving . . . amongst the magnified unhappiness experienced by the lonely and underprivileged at this time of year - where amongst all of this can we still trace the origin of Christianity? What do all our glass display windows, candy canes, blinking lights and tinsel have to do with the teachings of Christ? Is this recognition of Christmas the best we can do after nearly 2,000 years? Our capacity for imagination and festivity have been hardened. In an article in THE SATURDAY REVIEW Harvey Cox wrote the following:

> "In recent centuries something has happened that has undercut man's ability for festivity and fantasy. In Western civilization, we have placed enormous emphasis on man as "the worker" (Luther and Marx) and man as "the thinker" (Aquinas and Descartes). Man's intuitive and imaginative faculties have atrophied . . . . .

> The religious man is one who grasps his own life within a larger historical and cosmic setting. He sees himself as part of a greater whole, a longer story in which he plays a part. Song, ritual and vision link a man to this story. But without real festive occasions, and without the nurture of fantasy, a man's spirit shrinks. He becomes something less than a man, a gnat with neither origin nor destiny."

If we can accept the need to understand and cultivate the festivals, then we can now take a look at some of the inner and outer aspects of that period of time from September through the first week in January.

Let us consider the importance of light in our lives. In September the heat of July and August is diminishing. The daytime sky is brilliant in its rich blue. The air is so clear that when you are on a mountain top you feel as if you could see forever. The sun has completed its nourishing work and is on its decending curve towards Winter Solstice on December 21st, the darkest showers and shooting stars fill the nighttime sky with bursts of darting light. It is almost as if they were fireworks celebrating the supremacy that night is winning over day.

Here in New Hampshire the leaves are ablaze in a rainbow funeral when Michaelmas comes to us on September 29th. As they flutter to the ground the sky seems to expand above us and our souls search out into the heavens. The musky earth smell of leaves piled to mountainous heights by children who throw themselves into them is one of the last smells of nature before the earth is hardened by frost-making winds. Inside of man our blood begins to thicken and our thinking becomes more crystalline. Through these experiences one can begin to come closer to the mystery of Michael and his work in the world.

October is the gift of September. Warm weather can revisit us unexpectedly. It rarely gets too cold and the forests reveal unequalled beauty. Our activities become accelerated. There is always so much to do around our country homes.

Then comes November. The sunlight becomes veiled by leaden clouds. The trees in the forest are shrouded in gray. The leaves on the ground begin to lose their shape, and their color is one of organic decay. The earth has given up the last of her stored heat. The cold of the nights lingers even longer into the morning. The soil in our gardens must be turned and tilled so that it can receive the bounty of the winter's nights and be fructified. All New England gardeners know that the ground will be more fruitful in the spring relative to the degree of hardness to which it has been frozen in the winter.

During this time we turn our house lights on earlier and earlier, as the sun speeds toward the western sky. Our outer activities begin to tail off. If we look deeply into nature we can perceive the softly pulsing unrest of a new dawning. Next year's buds are prepared and sealed against the winter's blast. There is a stillness within the earth. That which will be the seed and silent root of all life in the next season lies in preparation. Man begins to be more reflective and there can be periods of emotional and psychological trial.

Then on November 11th we have the festival of Saint Martin. This date is the exact midpoint between Michaelmas and Christmas. Saint Martin's Day is mostly celebrated in Germany where it is customary to make a paper lantern and march through the dark, singing a song to Saint Martin. This year Saint Martin's Day coincided with the November full moon. As our little parade of neighborhood children sang and wound their way along the dirt road which connects our homes here in South Lyndeborough with lanterns swinging from sticks and a faint twinkle of a candle burning within, we were all greatly moved by the power of the enormous full moon in the dark November night.

As November turns into December, darkness becomes victorious over the light of the sun. So on the first Sunday in Advent, which is often called Candiemas, we celebrate our Advent Garden with crystals, a spiral of evergreen and a tall singular candle in the center which shares its light with the smaller candles of the children. With the warmth of the sun not sustaining us, man must find a light within himself, so, as an image we light the candle of hope. Into Advent season we bring expectancy and joy toward the Child of Bethlehem who was born on December 25th. The outer mood of Advent, however, is often chaotic. We can easily become pulled, overburdened, jostled by life. Everything outward seems to distract us from experiencing the true inner mood and quiet of Christmas. Perhaps, though, this is a blessing because it means that we must try ever more diligently and be much more conscious of overcoming the obstacles that we put in our path to block us from experiencing the true meaning of Christmas.

The darkness and chill of December nights draws us indoors. With us we carry the fruits of Michaelmas. The azure sky becomes the blue of Mary's dress in our creche scenes. The red of the apple becomes her dress. The brown of Joseph's cloak reminds us of our turned garden. The light of the candle recaptures the autumn sun. The green of the forest is brought inside in the form of Christmas trees, laurel wreaths, holly, and mistletoe. The brightest of the autumn stars is set atop our Christmas tree. The outer facts of Michaelmas move inward and become meaningful symbols at Christmas time.

Outside, the invisible working of the heavens is taking place. We may have the experience now that darkness surrounds us and our outer eye becomes blinded so that the inner eye of our soul may begin to see more clearly. The summer light can deceive our heart into imagining that the material outer world is the place of reality where all our human needs can be met, but in the night of Advent the heart becomes wiser and knows that this is not always so. Other realities can awaken if we allow the space. At this time, we can recognize that the imagination and inspiration from above - the light - is truly life and holds within it the power of new birth. It is in the darkness of midnight that Christmas comes to us.

Appendix – Chapter 3

Hal Borland writes in <u>THIS HILL, THIS VALLEY</u> the following:

> "As far back as the race memories and ancient legends of mankind run, the Winter solstice has been a time of questioning and wonder, followed by rediscovery of basic certainties. To see the daylight steadily shorten and the nights lengthen and deepen with cold was to feel the approach of doom. To see the sun stand still and then wing north once more was, and still is, to know that the cold gray of Winter must pass, that hope and belief are neither futile nor foolish.
>
> Hope is easy and belief is simple in a warm, green world. Winter is the time when man most needs the securities of unshaken certainty, whether it is the Winter of the soul or the harsh Winter of the year. And as surely as the Winter solstice brings some understanding of his universe, the spiritual solstice brings to man some understanding of himself. He seeks securities, and the more he must know that there are no securities anywhere, but only the old ones rediscovered.
>
> So comes the time for rediscovery. For though I may define security in a dozen different ways, the ultimate definition leads to the inner man, to myself. There must lie that certainty which gives life its meaning; and there also lies doubt, the depth of cold and darkness. I must know Winter if I am to know Spring and Summer."

In every season of the year our senses have the backdrop of nature to take pleasure from. In the depths of Winter, however, when nature is bare before us we must look to moral sources in order to find the strength and courage to see us through.

In <u>CHRISTMAS: A FESTIVAL OF INSPIRATION</u> Rudolf Steiner writes:

> . . ."The Christmas Festival is a festival of harmony with the whole cosmos, a festival of the realization of grace. It is a festival that can again and again bring home the thought: No matter how doubtful everything around us may appear, however much the bitterest doubts may enter into faith, however much the worst disappointments may mingle with the most aspiring hopes, however much all that is good around us in life may totter, there is something in human nature and essence that only needs to be brought vitally, spiritually, before the soul, which reveals to us perpetually that we are descended from the powers of good, from the forces of light, from the forces of truth."

Appendix – Chapter 3

As the year draws to a close Christmas is like a gate through which we must pass to reach the new year. Christmas day commemorates the birth of that child who in all innocence appeared on earth to become the vessel for the One who was to sacrifice Himself to redeem man from the sin of paradise. He was born in a stable in poverty and miserable circumstances. The purity of His heart is a message to all "men of good will", as the carol says irrespective of our social station if we can discover the deeper meaning of this within our hearts, new doors will open for us.

The Christmas Festival does not end on Christmas Day. We have what are called the Twelve Holy Nights. During this time, if we are truly awake, we might discover the way in which we can meet any outer circumstance in a spiritually true way through a deepening of our capacity for love.

The Twelve Holy Nights reaches its conclusion on January 6th which is called Three Kings Day and this is the other gateway which leads us out into the days of the new year. It was on this day that the Jesus child was visited by the three wise men, or priest-kings, who knew much about destiny, the past, and the future.

Once an Italian priest named Fra Giovanni, who lived from 1385-1456, was asked how a layman of the fifteenth century could cope with the difficult times that stretch from Michaelmas to Three Kings Day. He gave the following advice:

> "The gloom of the world is but a shadow.
>   Behind it, yet within reach, is joy.
>   There is a radiance and glory in the darkness,
>   Could we but see; and to see, we have only to look.
>   I beseech you to look!
>
> Life is so generous a giver, but we,
>   Judging its gifts by their covering,
>   Cast them away as ugly, or heavy, or hard.
>   Remove the covering and you will find beneath it
>   A living splendor, woven of love, by wisdom, with power.
>
> Welcome it, grasp it, and you touch
>   The angel's hand that brings it to you.
>   Everything we call a trial, a sorrow, or a duty,
>   Believe me, that angel's hand is there:
>   The gift is there, and the wonder of an overshadowing presence.
>
> Our joys too: be not content with them as joys.
> They, too, conceal diviner gifts.
>
>   And so at this time, I greet you.
>   Not quite as the world sends greetings,
>   But with profound esteem
>   And with the prayer that for you, now and forever,
>   The day breaks and the shadows flee away."

David Mitchell

Appendix – Chapter 3

Nature Spirits

(The information for this article was taken from Marjorie Spock's "Fairy Worlds and Workers")

The little child speaks of, and seems to know the fairy and elf world. In Ireland people speak and write about the Sheogs, Leprecauns, and Cluricauns, and there are some who know the customs of the Earth Folk very well. Our American Indians were intimately related to the Great Mother Earth, all creatures, the four elements, and the four directions. Can we say that all of this is only a figment of the imagination, or can it bring us to a place of questions? Why does this knowledge of nature beings and spirits appear in a variety of places? What experiences could these people have had to write and speak in such detail about nature spirits? Where, and when do we find this kind of consciousness? Is there a world behind the scenes?

It was one of Rudolf Steiner's deep convictions that fairyland should be a concern of the scientist as well as the poet. He spoke of the need to recognize the work of the fairies, for their work is part of the earth's prospering.

Nature spirits live in the "Land of Life", wherever vital processes are going on. It is important to realize that they react to their environment with either love or loathing.

Gnomes are earth-bound creatures who live below the surface of the earth and tend to the development of plant roots. They work all through the year bringing minerals to roots, and wielding magnetic forces to draw them down in the earth.

Undines, or water spirits, combine with and seep into everything about them. Theirs is a process of eternal change, and they are great transformers. Undines are all flowing motion, and it is they who draw sap up the trunks of trees, and stems of plants to join forces with the light. They work in the realm of rhythm.

Sylphs are the spirits of the light-filled air, who work in the atmosphere - they are lissome beings of light and air. Sylphs work closely with the undines using the magic power of rhythm. Sylphs and undines weave the fabric of the weather.

Fire spirits are the fairy race closest to the cosmic source of things. They bring warmth on their wings to our planet. They imbue this warmth with life. Pollen dust is the material way they carry warmth to its destination. Bees and insects help them in their work of pollination. Fire spirits are the generative force serving Nature. Seeds carry the signature of the Fire spirits. These Spirits bring the seeds to earth for gnomes to nourish.

Fairies have needs which we must satisfy if they are to work well. We must take care, when we speak of them, to do it lovingly. Elementals are the living soul of Nature. Our whole world lives in soul and body because of the presence of the Little People in it.

Liveliness of spirit will take one through the door to fairy land. To feel life is the key to making an acquaintance with the Little People. If we can attune ourselves to motion, as expressive gesture, we may learn to read the soul behind it.

"In olden times men knew a thing or two we have forgotten. They saw and worshipped Nature as a goddess. There was no question in their minds but that the living world was fairy country, where dwelt an infinitude of lesser spirits over whom she reigned. Natural events were regarded as their acts, performed in her service. And from every tree, every cloud, every spring, every flower these beings spoke with a voice to which the people hearkened. For wisdom is the breath of life in Nature, the exhalation of the goddess, and it was this wisdom that they sought in listening.

So it was from the Little People that men of earlier times learned such things as the secrets of the healing powers of plants, the properties of metals, the care of fields and flocks and crops and children, life's wise management." (Marjorie Spock "Fairy Worlds and Workers" 1980

Jean MacKay

Indian Harvest Song

Mother Earth, to you we're singing
Listen to our song.
Thanks for golden harvest bringing,
Listen as we sing to you
Songs of rain and sunshine.

On the trail where we are going
Ever shall we sing
When the winter comes with snowing
Still our hearts will sing to you
Songs of rain and sunshine.

Appendix – Chapter 3

Thoughts from the Alan Howard Seminar

From the first evening, those who came together to hear Alan Howard found they were to participate in the building up of a rather vast picture. We began each evening with an introduction of one of the following: painting, beeswax, form drawing, recorder playing, singing or eurythmy. This seemed to be refreshing to those who might have arrived weary from a working day. Then we gathered into a circle. It was as if at that moment, we were embarking on a journey in a little ship together.

During the first few minutes we engaged in an exploration of the thought world. The philosophical ideas brought to color and vitality by Rudolf Steiner were allowed to glow through the prism of Alan Howard's clear presentation. Man's spiritual endowment as well as his physical existence was described as having had, from the beginning of time, a lighting up and a dimming down. Awareness of this was described by Wordsworth in his "Ode on the Intimations of Immortality" from which Alan quoted.

It was as though we were taken to a land where an aurora borealis of ideas was reflected in thought forms, as if our heads were an icy northland.

Farther along our journey led to a vantage point from which we could attain the picture of man's lofty heritage. A common view of human deeds as seeds of destiny, ideas and actions formed itself. We were called upon to think how people whom we have encountered in life have given us special moments of help. It could be recognized that the unfolding of destiny can be a path that is not only binding but also freeing. Through Alan Howard's skilled words, we could transform the color and crystalline quality of the thought world's landscape. I like to think our next explorations brought us to a more plant-like realm...a garden where colors became flower images. The content of our talks centered on rhythms in nature and in man. Insofar as a seed can become a living plant with forces within it to become a tree, so our thoughts grew up and out into branches touching concepts such as reincarnation and the great power of Christianity. Christianity itself could be compared to a central tree whose tap root reaches down into the wellspring of new human destiny.

We encompassed the unique way the children in a Waldorf school are perceived as evolving human spirits existing and developing through life stages. New times demand we recognize they bring gifts and hinderances to their lives which need to be met with artistic, imaginative, spiritual perceptions. Rudolf Steiner has made such ideas accessible and understandable for those who wish to teach, and for those who are parents. A strong quality permeated our conversations at this point. It could be called a sense for the place of the moral as a truly manifested love for work, and for others. We heard a description of how this is nurtured in a Waldorf school. From an experience of our heads we had come to a realization of the heart.

If we proceed further in this seminar-journey metaphor we next found a panorama before us of the sympathies, antipathies, moods and temperaments which contribute to the variations in human personality. Sanguine, melancholic, choleric, phlegmatic types can be observed, usually in combinations with one dominant. Teaching or just being with others can be made more harmonious through the ability to recognize the types of temperaments. When we attempt to work with the temperament of another, instead of in polarity to it, more can be achieved. We can recognize our imbalances and strive to recover a unifying equilibrium. This is part of the Waldorf school's process with the children.

As the curriculum was reviewed we found that there is an approach to the sciences in Waldorf education which includes objective presentation of plants, animals, substances, but first in more of a story form...as nature stories, as word portraits of the Fables and the saints, etc. These stories then evolve into a more consciousness-evoking presentation of zoology, biology, chemistry, physiology and so on in the upper classes. All, however, is related to the human being. An attempt is made to build up the capacity to feel with depth, the beauty and wonder of the plant, animal and mineral worlds. There is an awakening to the fact that these phenomena exist in partial form in human beings as well. Appreciation can help correct tendencies (so prevalent in our times) to master technology and nature without caring for the consequences. With these ideas brought so well into focus by Alan Howard, I could also envision vast plains, crossed with herds of each species, arced above with flocks of magnificent fowl. The earth beneath our feet is laced with crystals and the veins of gold, silver, copper, etc. With all of these treasures at hand, what must we try to become in order to be a blessing to this nature rather than the means to its destruction? We are given the possibilities to be creators, kings, over the physical environment. Do we not need to build a spiritual environment within ourselves where life can flourish, not death? Our questions really came to this point.

In the final sessions we heard of the themes which can inspire us to strive for the best in each of us. The truly human aspect of our lives can flourish when we live in helpful social-mutual interaction. Man, through understanding of others, enhances possibilities for inner freedom, rights to equality in treatment and artistic excellence. Social Questions taken up by Rudolf Steiner were sketched out. These are goals for future workings in these social ways. In the classroom and in all aspects of life we need one another's gifts, talents and appreciation to lift us. In our arms, hands, legs, feet, lie the forces of will to embark on a further path - a kind of Silk Route to each other.

As we sat together on our final evening it seemed to me that we had gone out to the universe and returned with gratitude for each other and what we had learned together.

Danilla Rettig

Appendix – Chapter 3

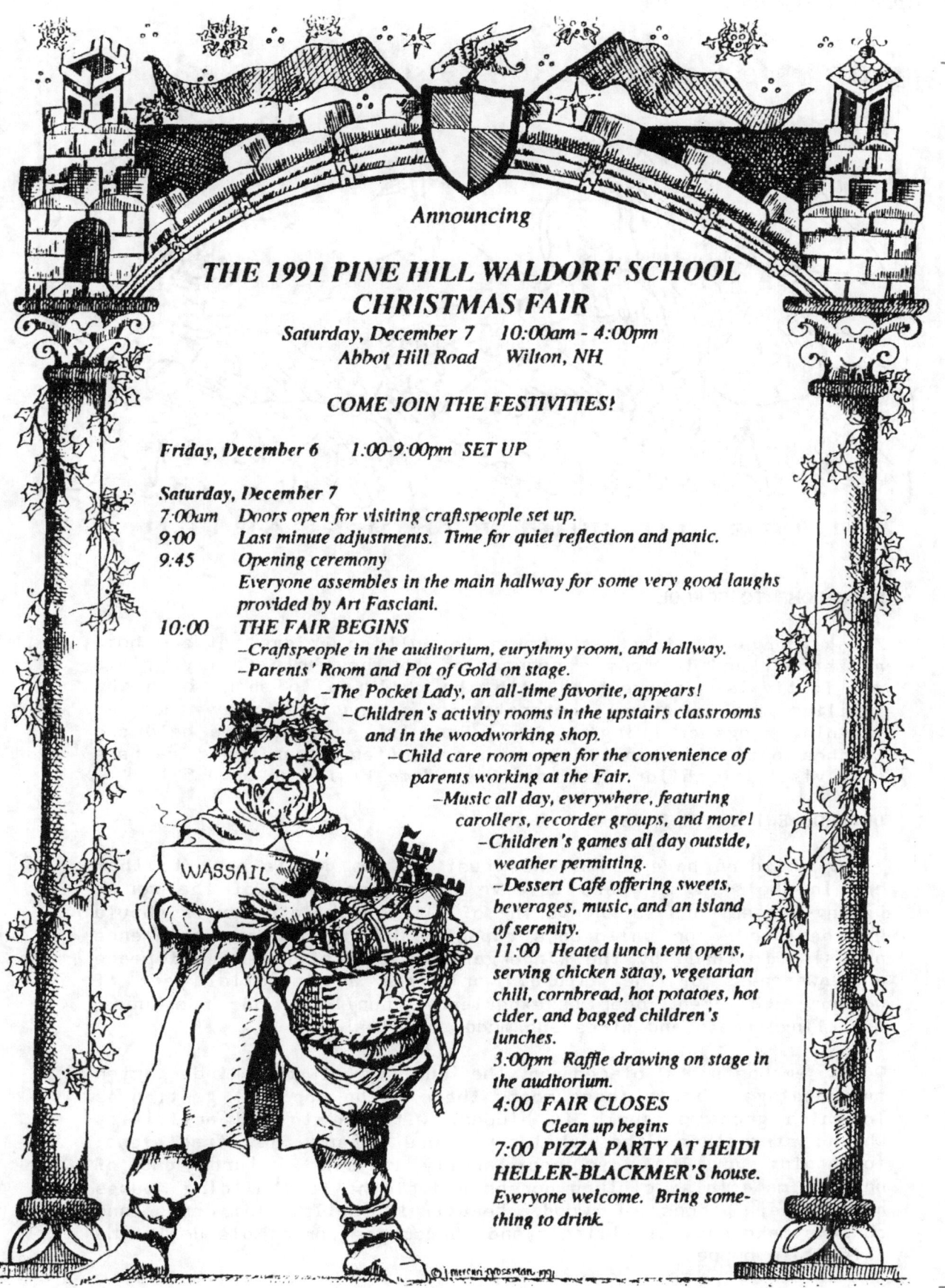

Announcing

THE 1991 PINE HILL WALDORF SCHOOL CHRISTMAS FAIR

Saturday, December 7   10:00am - 4:00pm
Abbot Hill Road   Wilton, NH.

COME JOIN THE FESTIVITIES!

Friday, December 6   1:00-9:00pm SET UP

Saturday, December 7

- 7:00am Doors open for visiting craftspeople set up.
- 9:00 Last minute adjustments. Time for quiet reflection and panic.
- 9:45 Opening ceremony
Everyone assembles in the main hallway for some very good laughs provided by Art Fasciani.
- 10:00 THE FAIR BEGINS
  – Craftspeople in the auditorium, eurythmy room, and hallway.
  – Parents' Room and Pot of Gold on stage.
  – The Pocket Lady, an all-time favorite, appears!
  – Children's activity rooms in the upstairs classrooms and in the woodworking shop.
  – Child care room open for the convenience of parents working at the Fair.
  – Music all day, everywhere, featuring carollers, recorder groups, and more!
  – Children's games all day outside, weather permitting.
  – Dessert Café offering sweets, beverages, music, and an island of serenity.
- 11:00 Heated lunch tent opens, serving chicken satay, vegetarian chili, cornbread, hot potatoes, hot cider, and bagged children's lunches.
- 3:00pm Raffle drawing on stage in the auditorium.
- 4:00 FAIR CLOSES
Clean up begins
- 7:00 PIZZA PARTY AT HEIDI HELLER-BLACKMER'S house. Everyone welcome. Bring something to drink.

Appendix – Chapter 3

from Michael Hall, Forest Row, Sussex, England

LIFE IN THE KINDERGARTEN

FROM HOME TO SCHOOL

The kindergarten teachers strive to build a bridge between home and school and to form a connection to the whole family; plays and festivals are prepared with the children to share with the families and parents co-operate in a practical way such as learning songs or bringing food. Parents' evenings are held and lunches and other social events are often organised. Teachers also visit the children at home [see *Home Visits* on page 51].

DEVELOPMENT UP TO 7 YEARS

Young children have faith and trust in the people near to them and in their first years believe in the goodness of the world. During these years the nurturing of all the child's senses should be cherished. The children's capacity for wonder and reverence are also fostered by the kindergarten. Both stillness and peace and awareness of the natural world are an essential part of wonder. Children deeply experience sunlight and darkness, sparkling frosts and fires and muddy puddles!

Great emphasis is placed on the quality of the kindergarten surroundings. Within these rooms there is an apparent gentleness in which great strength is hidden, with warmth and activities which strengthen the children more than the traditional toughening up. The toys are largely unformed, sturdy and of natural materials; clothes horses and cloths for building houses and ships; pieces of wood, beautiful shells, fir-cones and conkers make magical villages and landscapes for simple dolls and fairy-tale puppets.

ACTIVITIES

In the daily creative play time the children often re-enact what they have experienced. They may also enjoy water colour painting, eurythmy, singing games, baking bread for morning break, beeswax modelling and drawing, handwork, candle dipping, woodwork, gardening, outside sand and water play and going for walks. All of these activities are helpful in the development of the body, the senses and social life.

Break is also an important social occasion and a time to be grateful: a grace is included. The children benefit from being in the mixed age groups which are from 4 to 6 or 7. Older ones helping and caring for the younger ones gain a valuable and concerned awareness for each other. The older children's activities also include singing songs and playing games in a foreign language and in some classes they play the lyre.

RHYTHM

Because the activity and learning processes of the young child are largely unconscious, it is essential that we give a strong framework of rhythm, routine and repetition both at home and in the kindergarten. At home regular bedtimes, shared meals, restful moments and enjoyable walks help bring about peace and harmony for the whole family.

Beyond this there are the rhythms of the week, season and year. At kindergarten the weekly rhythm brings its day for baking, eurythmy and each of the other activities, so that each day has its own character. The seasonal rhythms are closely connected to the celebration of the Christian festivals around which the whole kindergarten year revolves.

FESTIVALS

Each kindergarten teacher brings these Festivals to the children as a picture, and so nourishes the body, soul and spirit. At Easter, for example, when the seemingly dead and wintry world springs to life again, the teacher does not speak of crucifixion and resurrection but tells stories of transformation such as *The Frog Prince*, *Snow White and Rose Red* or of a butterfly, and brings songs and poems.

The celebration of a Festival is the culmination of some weeks of anticipation and preparation, after which this picture slowly fades and the preparations for the next begin. We celebrate Christmas, Epiphany, Easter, Ascension, Whitsun, St John's, Michaelmas, Martinmas, Advent and St Nicholas. We also enjoy Maypole dancing and some teachers celebrate Candlemas on February 2nd.

The children love the activities involved in the preparations: finding twigs, flowers or nuts; seasonal and festive baking, painting Easter eggs, making lanterns or candles. All these help decorate the room.

BIRTHDAYS

These are celebrated as individual festivals, helping to create for the child a picture of his own life. There will be cards and gifts made by the children and the teacher, a new crown, candles, and a special story which in some classes is the story of the child's own life, created with the help of the parents.

IMITATION

Young children are intimately linked with the way in which other people think, feel and act. Their capacity for imitation is one of the keys to the work within the kindergarten. It is therefore important to provide a setting which is worthy of imitation. All the poems, songs, stories, singing games and plays the children do by imitating the teacher and then through repetition in their own play.

DISCIPLINE

Because of the often unconscious, dreamy quality of children under seven the use of authority is generally best avoided in these years. This does not mean the children may do as they like! For instance, where there has been a mishap such as a broken cup, the breaking is in itself shock enough to prevent a recurrence and it is more helpful to the child to clean it up nicely than to face extra remonstration. Discipline is more effective where the adults' ingenuity and imagination have been called into play.

STORIES

Simple fairy tales and those from the animal and elemental worlds are told, speaking to children in pictures they can understand. These stories are told, not read, for in this way the teacher can enter into the tale with the children in a deeper way. They are repeated word for word several times, and told in an undramatic way without drawing on the children's feelings.

THE MEDIA AND TOYS

As the development of the senses is so important at this age, television is particularly damaging to children under seven as the images are absorbed unconsciously and may interfere with their play and also that of others. The children's overworked imaginations make it difficult for them to receive the stories without emotion so that they can become unnecessarily distressed. Equally unsatisfying to the child's soul are seemingly fascinating mechanical and electronic toys. Teachers are happy to discuss alternatives to the media and gladly help with suggestions for play.

GENERAL INFORMATION

Children may enter in the Autumn and Spring terms in which they become 4, or in the summer term at 5. They begin with three mornings a week: Monday, Wednesday and Friday. This is generally increased to five mornings when they are 5 or over. Slippers and boots are needed every day, and rain and winter-wear as appropriate. Adults should accompany their children to and from the kindergarten; the children are not allowed to run down to the car park on their own without prior arrangement and we appeal to parents not to drive up to the kindergarten. Please inform your teacher if your child is going home with another adult. Parents are also requested not to let their children climb in the rhododendrons near the car park. Lastly, please let your kindergarten teacher know as soon as possible if your child is unwell.

Appendix – Chapter 3

HOME RHYTHMS

There are all kinds of ways in which we can actively support our children's development and the work that their teachers do with them at school.

One of the fundamental elements of Waldorf education is rhythm. The children experience this strongly in Kindergarten and from class 1 onwards in the main lessons, while the celebration of the festivals gives a rhythm that is basic to the whole school.

We can support all of this by giving our children a strong feeling of rhythm at home as they grow up, for if we examine our own lives we see that rhythm plays an important role. We sleep and wake, we breathe in and out, and we pass through the seasons again and again. We soon feel the detrimental effect of any disturbance to these rhythms: if our breathing is interfered with we panic and we lose our security. If we are deprived of sleep we feel disorientated in the world.

And so it is for our children. If their daily life is chaotic, where for example their mealtimes are irregular or they are looked after by lots of different people, they are more likely to become jumpy and unsettled as a result of having to adjust continuously to new situations.

For both children and adults modern life is lacking in rhythm. We are no longer affected, for example, by natural rhythms: when it grows dark we put on a light and when it is cold we put on the heating rather than go out and chop wood. We can have lettuce and strawberries for Christmas, go shopping any time, go swimming in the winter and have hot baths whenever we like. And gone are many of the jobs which involve repeated rhythmical activity, so that children rarely watch cows being milked, butter churned or wool being spun.

For us as parents it is therefore really vital to try to build rhythm into our children's lives wherever we can -- through regular mealtimes and story times, often repeating the same story. We can help them develop a strong feeling for the days of the week and the weekend; we can do seasonal things with them, such as decorating eggs at Easter, going for walks, planting bulbs in the Autumn. Having a special corner at home for treasures found on walks, twigs and flowers, shells and stones or seasonal pictures can be enriching and fun. Lighting a candle before a meal or at bedtime, saying a simple grace or a bedtime prayer helps children to find their place in the day. With older children it is helpful for example to do their music practice at the same time each day, to have a regular homework or reading time, a set bedtime and a particular job or task to carry out daily at a certain time.

And so through such experiences a real feeling of security is built up in the children so that they can move through the complex world in which they live feeling more confident and at ease, while they have greater forces available to them for the development of all their capacities. In bringing a flexible and creative rhythm into daily living, our children have a gift for their entire lives.

Appendix – Chapter 4

Definition of School Groups

Pedagogical Groups

Lower school, middle school, kindergarten teachers: Each group meets bimonthly to discuss pedagogical concerns specific to their particular grade level. All class teachers and special teachers of that grade level attend.

College of Teachers

The college consists of teachers who have made a strong commitment to the destiny of the school. College members are responsible for the spiritual-cultural life of the whole school and to that which furthers the education of the children, teacher education and growth, and parent education and involvement.

Enrollment Committee

The main function of the enrollment committee is to help Pine Hill School improve its visibility in the community through public outreach programs such as open houses, public talks, teas, exhibits, and advertising.

Adult Education

The goal of the adult education committee is to strengthen and promote understanding of Waldorf education both for our own parent body and prospective parents through lectures, workshops, and class evenings.

Legal/Business Groups

The board of trustees is responsible for all financial and legal activities, including capital fundraising, financial management, long-range planning, and setting and maintaining the annual operating budget. The board consists of four college members and between seven and eleven parent/community members. The college members are determined by the college, and a nominating committee presents of slate of nominees to the board.

Finance Committee

As a board committee, the finance committee monitors the financial health of the school. Using input from the college of teachers and other board committees, it develops and administers the school's budgets and financial policies and oversees efforts to plan adequately for the school's growth and development.

Tuition Aid Committee

The tuition aid committee is formally a subcommittee of the finance committee but functions as a largely independent ad hoc group that meets from mid April to early

June. Its task is to review tuition aid applications in confidence and allocate fairly the funds budgeted for aid by the board.

Compensation Committee

The compensation committee was created in the fall of 1991 as a joint college-board committee. Salaries and benefits for faculty and staff are discussed, proposals agreed upon, and recommendations are made to the full board of trustees. It has developed a five-year plan for teacher salaries.

Development Committee

The development committee is a committee of the trustees composed of trustees and non-trustees. Development Officer, Liz Morgan, coordinates the responsibilities of this committee, which include the annual foundation, research and grant writing, events, publicity, and the capital campaign.

Auditorium Committee

The auditorium committee oversees the outside and special event use of the Pine Hill auditorium, eurythmy room and classrooms. Processing paperwork, communicating with renters, exploring and presenting programs that enrich the cultural life of the students and community are all functions of this committee.

Safety Committee

The safety committee oversees the buildings and grounds of Pine Hill in terms of potential hazards. Parents and teachers can bring their concerns to this committee. Past actions include posting No Hunting signs, inspecting playground equipment and recommending removal of the Ark, and requesting rules for skateboarding, first aid procedures, etc.

Class Coordinators

Class coordinators support class teachers and serve as the liaisons between parents and class teachers. The coordinator invites communications from parents by cultivating a relationship with them. He/she communicates parental concerns and interests to the class teacher.

Christmas Fair

Traditionally, the Christmas Fair has been the largest fundraising event for the school. It is a day of delicious food, beautiful crafts, tiny toys, children, magic, music and friends!

Auction

A spring auction is held, during which goods and services offered by parents and teachers are auctioned as a fundraiser; skits are often presented by the faculty.

Pot of Gold Store

The Pot of Gold is our school store and was started by parents in the summer of 1990. Items available include toys and games, crafts and school supplies, candles and festival-related gifts, adult and children's books.

Forum

The *Forum* is the parents' monthly publication and includes articles, essays, prose, poetry, opinions and letters. It is sent home with the children and mailed to any non-parents who request it.

Ski Program

The ski program is organized and run by one or more parent volunteers. The children participate in cross country or alpine skiing on Thursday afternoons.

Appendix – Chapter 4

Committees

from the Chicago Waldorf School

    Room Parents Committee
    Finance Committee
    Development Committee
    Annual Fund Solicitation Committee
    Special Events Committee
    Holiday Fair Committee
    May Fair Committee
    Site Search Committee
    Long Range Plan Steering Committee
    Ad Hoc committee to organize parent-teacher organization

Room Parents Committee includes all room parents (2 or more for each early childhood and grade school class). People are asked by teachers to serve as room parents and usually do so for two years at a time, though this is flexible. The group meets five times a year to consider questions of school-wide interest. Room parents meet independently with their individual class teachers.

Finance Committee is a committee of the board of trustees. Its members are appointed by the board for indefinite terms. The committee meets monthly to consider issues of budgeting and financing.

Development Committee membership is open to anyone interested, and people may be recruited to join by current members, who include chairs or representatives of the Annual Fund and Special Events committees as well as board members, college members, the Development Coordinator and others. The committee is presently seeking new members including representatives of the Room Parents and Parent Teacher Organization. It meets monthly.

Annual Fund Solicitation Committee includes a small "core" group whose task is to plan the Annual Fund campaign, and a broader group including all the volunteer solicitors who visit members of the community to solicit gifts. This year 18 parents of current students and alumni served on the committee. The committee meets none to ten times a year, with meetings concentrated in the fall when training and evaluation sessions for the campaign are conducted. Current members recruit others to join them on two-person solicitation teams.

Appendix – Chapter 4

Special Events Committee meets monthly to plan and coordinate special events in the school community. Its members include chairs of major events, such as the Holiday Fair and May Fair, and others interested in organizing various community activities. The group plays an important role in scheduling, organizing and evaluating events. Membership is open and present members often recruit new members.

The Holiday Fair and May Fair Committees include the various chairs of subcommittees involved in different aspects of these annual events. Planning meetings occur several months in advance of the event, but work is most concentrated near the time of each event. Members are recruited through the usual channels—person-to-person, through the *Weekly Bulletin*, through information gleaned from the annual Parent Service Survey on which people are asked to indicate their volunteer interests.

Site Search Committee meets periodically to discuss possible locations for the school. (We lease our facilities and are looking for a permanent home and/or a more satisfactory interim location.) Individual members work outside the meetings to investigate possible sites. Membership is open.

Long Range Plan Steering Committee has met periodically during the past year to shepherd the process of developing and disseminating our Five-Year Plan. Its six members were invited to serve by the college and board. It will self-destruct after the plan is adopted.

The Ad Hoc Committee, working to form a parent-teacher organization formed from interested parents and teachers, attended a community development weekend workshop led by Chris Schaefer. They have met regularly over the past four months to discuss concerns and possible ways of working. It is expected that a more formalized structure will emerge as the parent-teacher group takes shape.

Most committees seem to form around a need or concern and to consist of people who are interested in the particular area of endeavor and willing to commit themselves to working on it. There is a general pattern of setting policies by consensus, usually in response to a question that is raised by something that happens. Committees evaluate their own work regularly and change their approach as seems appropriate.

Terms of office vary. In the Development, Annual Fund, and Special Events committees, the chairs have each served for two years and new people are coming on as chairs for two-year terms. The ideal for leadership of individual events is that there should be two co-chairs for each event, a "veteran" and a newer person who is learning the ropes and will be next year's veteran. This does not always work out in practice.

Leadership roles are generally available to people who actively seek them, and volunteer (parent) leaders, teachers, and staff members (particularly the Administrative Chairman and Development Coordinator) may identify potential leaders and recruit them for particular jobs.

As in most volunteer organizations, efficiency is not necessarily the highest goal of committee work. The social process of working together is extremely important, and the self-reinforcing cycle of commitment and the investment of time, creativity and resources is not always the most efficient way to operate. However, the work of committees is made easier through organized leadership, carefully worked out agendas, good communications (including minutes), attention to evaluation, and recognition and appreciation of volunteers.

Rhythmic scheduling, well in advance, of meetings and other activities is also important. (We try to set up our calendar for the entire upcoming school year in the spring and include regular committee meetings.) A feeling of warmth and hospitality makes committee members more comfortable and fosters the kinds of social relationships that enable people to work effectively together. Refreshments help! And providing the necessary staff support is vital.

I would not say that we have an articulated mandate system, although we may be working toward it in some areas. I would describe our structure as a more fluid one, dominated by the pragmatic concerns of getting various jobs done and by the availability of people willing to take them on.

Appendix – Chapter 4

FACULTY COMMITTEE DISTRIBUTION
Note: This shows faculty only, parent names are not listed.

BOARD OF TRUSTEES
- David
- Laurie
- Arthur
- Catherine

FINANCE COMMITTEE
- Roger
- Marc
- Lorey

TUITION AID COMMITTEE
- Lorey
- Anniken

COMPENSATION
- Arthur
- Pat

DEVELOPMENT COMMITTEE
- Liz
- Catherine
- David

CAPITAL CAMPAIGN
- Catherine
- Liz
- David
- Marc

LONG RANGE PLANNING
- Dennis
- Roger

FACULTY CHAIRPERSON
- Laurie

CLERK OF FACULTY MEETING
- Merrily

MIDDLE SCHOOL CHAIRPERSON
- Arthur

LOWER SCHOOL CHAIRPERSON
- Merrily

CORPORALITY COMMITTEE
- Laurie Pat Catherine

FACULTY ROOM ORGANIZER
- Linda

PLANTS
- Laurie

SAFETY COMMITTEE
- Marc David

MONTHLY ASSEMBLIES
- Merrill

COLLEGE CHAIRPERSON
- Rena

CLERK OF COLLEGE
- Judith

EXECUTIVE COMMITTEE
- Rena Laurie Catherine

ENROLLMENT COMMITTEE
- Anniken Dennis

ANTHROPOSOPHICAL SOCIETY LIAISON
- David

SCHOOL DOCTOR LIAISON
- Merrily

MUSIC COORDINATOR
- Bonnie

ASSEMBLY HALL SCHEDULER
- Anniken

COSTUMES
- Lorey

ADVENT GARDEN COORDINATOR
- Sherry

LIBRARY COORDINATOR
- Stephen

FRONT ENTANCE MAINTAINER
- Lisa

GROUNDS
- Stephen

FAIR LIAISON
- Merrill

HALLWAY DECORATION
- Anniken

ADULT EDUCATION
- David Yvonne

PEDAGOGICAL COORDINATOR
- Dennis

REMEDIAL GROUP
- Merrily Pat Thorn

SCHEDULING
- Pat Laurie

AWSNA DELEGATE
- Marc Merrill

NEWSLETTER COMMITTEE
- Lorey Sherry

Sample Proposed Mandate

_____ for _____ Committee

Chairperson: _____   Date: _____

Members:

A. Area of responsibility:

B. Area of responsibility (advisory):

C. Advice prior to decisions:

D. Accountability:

E. Recommendation for change:

F. Responsibilities to be added:

Appendix – Chapter 5

Sample Administrator Job Description

HIRED BY: Joint meeting of college of teachers and trustees
REPORTS TO: College and board

GENERAL STATEMENT OF DUTIES: Provides administrative leadership to the faculty, board, and office staff; responsible for hiring, evaluation, and firing of office staff and support staff; assumes responsibility for the fiscal life of the school, including current finances and development work.

DISTINGUISHING FEATURES OF THE POSITION: This position is a key faculty position, and as such requires the depth and commitment expected of all key faculty members. This means commitment to the study of anthroposophy and the striving to keep the spiritual foundations of the school intact. The essential nature of the work is resource management, including but not limited to money and nonteaching personnel. Direction comes from the college of teachers and the board of trustees, in the form of policies and procedures which must be executed. This position is frequently the link between the school and public agencies. Internally, this position is entrusted with responsibilities which are highly sensitive, such as interactions with parents regarding late payments of bills, referring angry parents to the right place, etc. This position has considerable influence in many areas, including the public relations image of the school.

EXAMPLES OF DUTIES PERFORMED: Depending upon assignment, duties may include, but are not limited to, the following:

(1) As a member of the college of teachers, participate in the development and direct implementation of goals, objectives, policies, and procedures of the school, including curriculum development, staffing needs and program modifications.

(2) Direct and manage the preparation and administration of the school budget.

(3) Interpret, analyze and explain policies, procedures and programs.

(4) Coordinate the work of the administrative committee; participate in meetings with the faculty, parent council and other groups and individuals having an interest or potential interest in the affairs of the school.

(5) Represent the school in community in professional meetings as required, and to other agencies and government.

(6) Respond to the most difficult complaints and requests for information.

(7) Select, supervise, train and evaluate non-faculty staff; participate in the selection and assignments of faculty staff.

(8) Administer all insurance plans.

(9) Oversee the Development function.

(10) Play a major role in fundraising and capital campaigns.

(11) Write grant proposals and reports to Waldorf affiliated foundations.

(12) Provide assistance to staff on computer problems.

REQUIRED KNOWLEDGE, SKILLS AND ATTRIBUTES: Considerable knowledge of Waldorf school philosophy, including administrative and educational principles, techniques, and methods. Knowledge of principles of school administration, including finance, budgeting, and personnel administration. Knowledge of principles of effective public relations and interrelationships with community groups, private and public agencies, parents, and the general public. Some familiarity with computers and skill with spreadsheet program. Ability to work in an extremely busy environment and to keep several projects going at once. Ability to analyze, interpret, summarize and present administrative and financial data in an effective manner. Ability to communicate effectively both orally and in writing. Ability to deal with people tactfully and courteously.

DESIRED TRAINING AND EXPERIENCE: Any combination equivalent to experience and education that could likely provide the required knowledge and abilities would be qualifying. A typical way to obtain the knowledge and abilities would be: *Experience*: Five years of progressively responsible experience in administrative, managerial or teaching capacity in a school organization involving responsibility for the planning, organization, implementation and supervision of varied work programs. *Education*: Equivalent to a Bachelor's degree from an accredited college or university. Completion of the two-year Waldorf teacher training course is desirable.

Appendix – Chapter 5

Sample Business Manager Job Description

APPOINTED BY: Board, upon recommendation from an ad hoc faculty/board group

TERM: Indefinite, with annual review by the faculty

AREAS OF RESPONSIBILITY:

(1) Ensure proper and efficient operation of all business-related matters to include:

- financial, legal and insurance matters,
- business office operation,
- overseeing plant manager in the maintenance of buildings and grounds,
- purchasing and contracting,
- staff personnel matters and liaison between faculty and business office staff,
- meeting all health and safety standards,
- maintaining student and staff medical records,
- annual review of all non-teaching & maintenance staff,
- maintain policy books and records of decisions.

(2) Make decisions based on existing financial policies and procedures as drafted by appropriate committees.

(3) Be sufficiently knowledgeable in the areas of insurance, state and federal regulations, legal and other matters to be in a position, along with other members with particular expertise, to advise the board and faculty chair in such matters.

(4) Serve on the board, the faculty and the faculty finance committee, investment, financial aid and on such other committees as may be appropriate.

(5) Review and implement school policies and practices as they effect or determine business and administrative functioning of the school.

(6) Monitor approved capital expenses and budgets.

(7) Insure dissemination of information where it would be important for overall school operation.

(8) Be involved with the formation of grant requests, bequests and fundraising.

AREAS OF RESPONSIBILITY (Advisory): Serve as resource for faculty chair, Admissions office, parents, Development office, faculty and staff personnel.

Appendix – Chapter 5

ADVICE PRIOR TO DECISIONS: Confer with faculty chair and other relevant persons/committees.

ACCOUNTABILITY: Business Manager is accountable to the board and faculty chair.

Appendix – Chapter 5

Sample Development Officer Job Description

Parent Relations:
Record relational activities, work toward smooth transition of leadership, maintain ongoing review of management systems to ensure they are meeting needs.

Volunteer Enlistment:
Track enlistment, provide background on prospects to enlisters, prepare job descriptions, evaluate volunteer job performance.

Alumni Relations:
Assist in planning, coordinating and evaluating events; provide catalyst to develop sense of family.

Solicitation, Annual Fund Campaign:
Track solicitation process, provide background on prospects to solicitors, prepare reports regularly to inform workers of progress, train volunteers, ensure effective interface with office, provide all necessary written materials; manage annual fund drive, develop donor lists, biographies, update giving records; receive, record and acknowledge all gift income; prepare annual report; monitor budgets of all events and notify of potential over-run.

Computer:
File management and maintenance.

Events:
Transition leadership, assist in planning, coordination, budget and evaluation.

Meetings:
Attend development, board and faculty meetings, as well as related committee meetings as needed.

Assist Admissions:
School tours, open houses, observation mornings.

Sample Admissions Director Job Description

HIRED BY: The college of teachers
REPORTS TO: The college and the administrator

GENERAL STATEMENT OF DUTIES: Provides first contact of Waldorf school to the public. Creates initial interview with the parents to explain the Waldorf philosophy. Generates interest in the Waldorf school by advertising and outreach.

EXAMPLES OF DUTIES PERFORMED: Depending upon assignment, duties may include, but are not limited to, the following:

(1) Take and return phone calls from prospective parents.

(2) Mail out school information packet.

(3) Arrange and conduct school tours.

(4) Arrange and conduct school interviews.

(5) Arrange subsequent interviews for class teachers and visits for students.

(6) Bring recommendations for admissions to the college.

(7) Keep track of applications in progress and overall awareness of the school's enrollment situation.

(8) Be responsible for re-enrollment and tuition aid.

(9) Conduct exit interviews with parents of children leaving the school.

(10) Plan and oversee in-house public events such as: open houses, talks on Waldorf education, parent orientation, parent education evenings, visitor's days, etc.

(11) Plan and arrange publicity for the above.

(12) Arrange ongoing advertising for the school in consultation with the Development Officer.

(13) Update and refine and order school public relations materials such as: brochures, flyers, posters, books, etc.

(14) Collect material for school displays for talks conducted outside of the school.

Appendix – Chapter 5

(15) Participate as a colleague in office, faculty, college, enrollment committee, tuition aid committee, board meetings, etc.

REQUIRED KNOWLEDGE, SKILLS, AND ATTRIBUTES: Considerable knowledge of Waldorf school philosophy, including administrative and educational principles, techniques, and methods. Knowledge of principles of effective public relations and interrelationships with community groups, private and public agencies, parents, and the general public. Ability to communicate effectively both orally and in writing. Ability to deal with people tactfully and courteously.

Appendix – Chapter 6

Admissions Process

The admissions process is handled by the appropriate members of the Admissions Group which consists of the admissions officer (Kindergarten, Lower School or Upper School), the school doctor, a remedial eurythmist, a remedial teacher, and the prospective class teacher. The various stages of the admissions process are as follows:

1. INFORMAL INTERVIEW: If the prospective parents are new to Waldorf education, they will be invited to an informal interview with the appropriate admissions officer or another member of the staff, who will explain our educational philosophy and show the prospective parents the school.

2. APPLICATION: Parents are then asked to fill in the application and medical forms and submit them to the school office together with the child's most recent school reports, a photograph, and the application fee.

    If all is well, the admissions secretary will then arrange for the prospective class teacher or guardian and a eurythmy teacher to interview the child.

3. INTERVIEW AND DECISION: When a child comes for an interview, the class teacher assesses the child's artistic and academic abilities, and the eurythmy teacher checks his or her coordination, balance and dexterity. In making their decision, the teachers will always consider the importance of maintaining a balanced group in the class. If necessary, a further assessment will be made by a remedial teacher and/or school doctor.

    Parents will be informed of the decision by the admissions secretary as soon as possible. Some pupils may be accepted only on certain conditions, for example, extra remedial work or language coaching. If there are any signs of difficulties, the Admissions Group will make the final decision.

FIVE IMPORTANT POINTS
- Admission from the Kindergarten to Class 1 is not automatic. An application must be made, and the child must be seen by the school doctor.
- Children with extra needs will be admitted only if the appropriate help can be provided.
- In some cases the Admissions Group may decide to accept a pupil for a trial period.
- All children coming on exchanges or visiting the school must go through the admissions process.
- Children who leave the school but wish to be readmitted must go through the formal admissions process.

Appendix – Chapter 6

Admissions Procedure for New Parents

An informal tour of Pine Hill while school is in progress can be arranged by calling the school.

Records of previous schooling should be sent to Pine Hill, along with a completed (nonbinding) application and an application fee of $35.00.

Admissions director interview: Upon receipt of records, the school will schedule an interview with the admissions director. This interview allows for a more in-depth discussion of the school's program and the child's educational background.

Class teacher interview: At the conclusion of a mutually successful admissions interview, a meeting may be scheduled between the parents and child and the class teacher of the class the child would enter. A day's visit in the class will also be arranged.

Class teacher and admissions will bring recommendation to accept the child to the college, where the final decision will be made. The Remedial Group may need to be included at this time.

A letter indicating whether a child is accepted or not will be sent by the school. A letter of acceptance will be accompanied by an enrollment agreement, to be signed and returned to the school with a non-refundable deposit. This will ensure a place will be held for the child.

Exit Interviews

The Director of Admissions will contact the parents of a child believed to be leaving Pine Hill.

It is the responsibility of the parents to inform the class teacher(s) personally and to communicate this intent to the school Admissions office in writing. A letter will be sent from the school confirming receipt of such notice and that a place will not be held for the child.

Each family with a child leaving or not re-enrolling an eligible child will be asked to meet with a designated faculty member. The college chairperson or other college member will also participate with exit interviews where there is a possibility of bad feelings or strong questions around the withdrawal. The interviewer should attempt to solicit information in a friendly manner and to record the parental views, to include:

Appendix – Chapter 6

- A brief history of the child's tenure at Pine Hill: the year entered, teachers, significant absences, etc.

- Achievements: how the child has progressed, where he/she is in comparison with peers, his/her strengths and weaknesses.

- The strengths/weaknesses of Pine Hill: What suggestions would they have as regards program, additions or deletions, teacher strengths, staff, communications, etc.

- Their reasons for leaving Pine Hill.

- Future plans for the student as regards education: where, what kind of school, etc.

Appendix – Chapter 6

THE PINE HILL WALDORF SCHOOL, WILTON, NEW HAMPSHIRE

Admissions Procedure for Class Teacher

1. The school admissions person will usually have met the family before the class teacher. School records will be in our hands (or brought by parents).

2. Please read the admissions person's comments and/or questions on the enrollment form. Any indications of learning disabilities will be noted. Also read the child's previous records/reports. A second teacher (usually B. Collen) should be present if problems are indicated.

3. During your interview you should get:
   a. A picture of the child's development/educational history
   b. A sense of the family situation (marital, siblings, TV, diet, etc.)
   c. A clear picture of the child's relative skill level
   d. An evaluation of the child's spatial orientation, dominance, etc. Please refer to the council letter attached.

4. Record comments and notes on the enrollment sheet

5. Schedule a class visit for the child if you wish to proceed with the process.

* * * * * * * * * * * *

You have an interview at _____ o'clock on _____

with _____ for _____

Enclosed:

[ ] School records

[ ] Application

[ ] Enrollment procedure form

[ ] Council letter on admissions

They are also scheduled for an interview with _____

at _____

Appendix – Chapter 6

THE WALDORF SCHOOL

Child's Name _____ Sex _____ Birthplace _____

Applying for (circle): K 1 2 3 4 5 6 7 8 Birthdate _____ Present Age ___

Fathers Name _____ Business Name _____

Address _____ Address _____

_____ _____

Phone _____ Phone _____

Mother's Name _____ Business Name _____

Address _____ Address _____

_____ _____

Phone _____ Phone _____

Parents: Married _____ Separated _____ Divorced _____

Names and Ages of other children in the family:

1. _____ Age _____   4. _____ Age _____

2. _____ Age _____   5. _____ Age _____

3. _____ Age _____   6. _____ Age _____

If child has had previous schooling, please answer the following:

Name of last school _____

Address _____ Dates Attended _____

Present Grade, or Last Grade Attended _____

Please state where you heard of the Waldorf School. _____

_____

Parent's Signature _____ Date of Application _____

(Please note: This application form is not a binding contract.)

Please write, and attach to this form, a biographical sketch of your child – describing the pregnancy, birth, early childhood, health & illness, eating and sleeping habits, social interaction and any other information which you believe will help us come to a better understanding of your child's needs.

APPLICATION FOR ADMISSION
The Waldorf School
739 Massachusetts Avenue Lexington, Massachusetts 02173 Tel 617-863-1062

An application fee of $30.00 is required of each applicant. Please enclose a check or money order payable to The Waldorf School.

Name of Child _____

Child's Birthdate _____ Birthplace _____ Citizenship _____ Sex ____

Desired date of school entrance _____ Child's age as of Sept. 15 of that year _____

Application is for:

___ Nursery (child must be 3 1/2 by September of school entrance)

   ___ Tuesday, Thursday

   ___ Monday, Wednesday, Friday

   ___ Five mornings

___ Kindergarten (child must be at least 4 1/2 by September of school entrance)

___ The Afternoon Program requires a separate application. Contact the office.

___ Grade (applicants for First Grade must be 6 by June 30 prior to school entrance)

Do you think you would need Tuition Assistance? ___ Yes ___ No

Mother's Full Name _____

Home Address (Street/Town) _____

(State/Zip) _____ Home Phone _____

Nature of Work/Place of Business _____

_____ Business Phone _____

Father's Full Name _____

Home Address (Street/Town) _____

(State/Zip) _____ Home Phone _____

Nature of Work/Place of Business _____

_____ Business Phone _____

If parents have separate addresses, child lives with ____ Mother ____ Father

Correspondence should be addressed to ____ Mother ____ Father

Other children in the family

Name	Birthdate	School Presently Attending

Child's previous group experience (include playgroup, daycare, Sunday School, etc.)

The Monadnock Waldorf School

98 South Lincoln Street
Keene, New Hampshire 03431
Phone: 357-4442

For office use only: _____
Date given to office: _____
Interview with teacher: _____
Deposit received: _____   Tuition form: ____
Accepted: _____
_____
_____

APPLICATION FOR ADMISSION
1988-1989

CONDITIONS OF ENROLLMENT

Each student who is accepted will undergo a one month period of evaluation. During this time the parents will have the opportunity to become familiar with the school, and the teacher will be able to observe the student's needs and abilities. At the end of one month, either the parents or teacher may terminate the enrollment contract, with no remaining financial obligations.

There is a growing body of research that supports the position of Waldorf schools, that children should remain in a play-oriented preschool until the age of six. We, at The Monadnock Waldorf School, recommend that a child be 6 years old prior to September 30 of the year of entry into first grade. We use this date as a guideline, with the understanding that special attention will be paid to summer birthdays especially with boys. It is strongly recommended that children entering the preschool program be 3½ years of age by September 30.

TO BE FILLED OUT BY PARENT OR GUARDIAN. (Please print or type):

Name of child: _____
                First   Middle   Last

Address: _____
              Street   City or Town   State   Zip

Telephone: _____   _____
                     Home   Daytime (or Alternate)

Application is for Grade: _____   Kindergarten: _____   Preschool (Mon.-Thurs.): _____

Child's age as of September 30 of year of entrance: _____yrs. _____mos.   D.O.B. _____
                                                                                    mo/day/yr

Birthplace _____   Sex _____   Transported by _____
                                                                      (carpool/bus)

Name and relationship of other adults and/or children living in household:
_____

Father's Full Name: _____   Home address (if different) _____
                                                _____

Mother's Full Name: _____   Home address (if different) _____

(Continued on back)   _____

Page Two

Occupation - Mother: _____

Occupation - Father: _____

Are there any extra curricular activities your child is now participating in (Scouts, 4-H, Dance, Gymnastics, summer camp)?

Has your child attended school before? _____ If transferring, please indicate previous school and address: _____

Has your child had any major difficulties? Are there any difficulties with vision, hearing, walking, speaking, other? Please describe general health:

What qualities would you like to see strengthened in your child in the coming year?

How did you hear of the Waldorf School?

We would like to have names and addresses of all grandparents for the school mailing list. These names will also be included in a yearly financial request called the Annual Giving Campaign, unless otherwise specified by the parent.

Grandparents' Full Names _____
    Home Address _____
Grandparents' Full Names _____
    Home Address _____

PLEASE NOTE:

    There is an application fee of $25.00 for all new students. Please submit this with the completed application. There is a $300.00 non-refundable deposit for elementary and $200.00 deposit for preschool, payable upon the student's acceptance into the school. The deposit fee will be applied towards the full tuition. A tuition agreement form must be signed by parents and school in order to complete the enrollment process.

    The Monadnock Waldorf School admits students of any race, color and national or ethnic origin.

****

I, the parent and/or guardian, give my permission to The Monadnock Waldorf School to take my child to the hospital in an emergency situation in the event that I cannot be reached by telephone.

                              Signature _____

I give my permission for my child to be taken on school field trips.

                              Signature _____

PARENT APPLICATION

(Attach recent photograph here)

The Waldorf School

Application for Admission (parent form)

DIRECTIONS: The following material should be forwarded to the Director of Admissions

1. Completed Application for Admission filled out by parents.
2. Completed Questionnaire filled out by student.
3. Non-refundable $25.00 application fee.
4. Two recommendation forms from present school (Math & English teachers preferred.)
5. Transcripts from present school.
6. Please call the school to arrange an interview date for student & parents.

Applicant's Name: _____ Date of Birth _____ Sex _____
                                                                                                                              Mo.   Day   Yr.   M/F

Applying to enter _____ th grade for school year 19____ - 19____. Boarding _____ Day _____

Home Address: _____ Tel. No. (____) _____
                      Street   Area

_____ Birthplace _____
City   State   Zip   Nationality: _____

                                                                           Occupation or
Father's Name: _____ Position: _____
                                                                                             (Please be specific)

Address and telephone (if different from above)   Employed by: _____

_____ Address: _____
                    Street

_____ _____
City   State   Zip

Tel. No: (____) _____ Tel. No. (____) _____
      Area   Area

                                                                           Occupation or
Mother's Name: _____ Position: _____
                                                                                             (Please be specific)

Address and telephone (if different from above)   Employed by: _____

_____ Address: _____
                    Street

_____ _____
City   State   Zip

Tel. No: (____) _____ Tel. No: (____) _____
      Area   Area

Stepparents (if any): Name: _____ _____

Address: _____ Tel. No. (____) _____
                                                                                           Area

Name: _____

Address: _____ Tel. No. (____) _____
                                                                                           Area

The Waldorf School

STUDENT APPLICATION

This is not an examination! It is an opportunity for you to discuss informally some aspects of your life. Please answer the questions fully and with complete frankness, using the blanks following the questions. Try to say what you really think, not what you feel we would like to have you say. There are no "right" or "wrong" answers!

PLEASE ANSWER IN YOUR OWN HANDWRITING

NAME _____ NICKNAME? _____

ADDRESS _____

_____

BACKGROUND: In a paragraph describe your former school: What was the size of your school? Your own assessment of your achievements, what you liked and what you didn't like.

SCHOOL SUBJECTS: Briefly describe your thoughts about the following school subjects:

ENGLISH:

MATHEMATICS:

FOREIGN LANGUAGES:

READING AND WRITING:

1. How often do you read on your own?

2. Mention a few books you liked very much.

Brothers and sisters, if any:

Names	Ages	School presently attending

School applicant now attends: Name: _____

Address: _____ Grades & Dates Attended: _____

If applicant previously attended any other secondary schools, please list them, with addresses and dates.

— —

Frank and complete answers to the following will best serve the applicant. Use the back of this form if more space is necessary.

1. Please give the reasons for changing schools:

2. What characteristics are you looking for in seeking a new school?

3. Has the applicant ever had any serious physical problems, illnesses, injuries? If so, please describe and give the ages when these occurred.

4. Please describe any circumstances in the applicant's home, family or environment which may have had supportive *or* negative effects on his/her personal, or school life.

5. If the applicant has had any significant learning, behavior or emotional problems, please describe.

DANCE

1. Do you like to dance? What kind do you enjoy the most?

THEATER, MOVIES, ETC.

1. Have you seen any plays? Which ones?

2. Do you like to act?

3. Do you see many movies? Mention some of your favorites?

4. How often do you watch T.V. or listen to the radio?

5. How do you think movies or television could be improved?

SPORTS

1. Do you like sports?

2. Circle any of the following you have done – underline or add any you like to do.

      TEAM SPORTS: (baseball, basketball, football, hockey, soccer, etc.)

      INDIVIDUAL SPORTS: (riding, swimming, skiing, running, etc.)

OTHER INTERESTS

1. How do you usually spend your free time?

2. Do you belong to any clubs or associations in or outside of school? Explain.

3. Do you have any regular jobs or responsibilities at home? What are they?

4. What would you like to do a year or two after graduating from high school?

ANSWER ALL QUESTIONS BELOW.

How do you see yourself relating to adults and people your own age?

The Waldorf School faculty and students work hard to create a healthy social life. The school does not support the use of drugs, alcohol, or tobacco and has policies against their use. Are you willing to abide by these policies?

Use a pencil and sketch a human being on a separate piece of paper and attach it to this questionnaire.

On a separate piece of paper, develop at least one well written paragraph on one of the following topics:

    a) Relate an incident in which you had to stand up for something you believed in. What did you do? How did you feel?

    b) Describe a person that has been important in your life.

Why do you want to come to the Waldorf School?

6. Within the last three years, has the applicant had any psychological counselling or psychiatric treatment? _____ (yes or no). If so, would you please list below the name and address of the counselor or doctor and arrange to have a report released to us. Briefly explain the reasons for counselling.

Name: _____ Tel. No. (_____) _____
                                                            Area

Address: _____
            Street   City   State   Zip

7. Please add any information you think would help us in reaching a decision on admission or in helping the applicant as a student here. (For example: special skills, interests, musical or artistic abilities, need temperamental characteristics, etc.)

8. From what source did you hear of the Waldorf School? (Please be specific as to the name of the friend, school, book, or other source.)

Give the name and address of the person who will sign the enrollment agreement and be responsible for payment of tuition fees:

Name: _____ Tel. No. (_____) _____
                                                            Area

Address: _____

Signature of parent or guardian: _____

Date: _____

The Waldorf School does not discriminate on the basis of race, religion, sex, ethnic background or national origin in admission of students, in financial aid grants or in any program offered.

Office Use Only	
Application Received	_____
Fee Received	_____

The Waldorf School

TEACHER RECOMMENDATION
ENGLISH

Name of applicant _____ Current grade _____

1. How long have you known this student, and in what context?

2. What are the first words that come to your mind to describe this student?

3. Please evaluate the applicant in the following areas: (check appropriate box)

		performance below grade level	performance consistent with grade level	performance above grade level
a.) Vocabulary	Oral			
	Written			
b.) Writing	Sentence structure			
	Clarity of style			
	Ability to organize ideas in a logical sequence			
	Spelling			
	Punctuation			
c.) Reading	Speed			
	Accuracy			
	Capacity for drawing appropriate inferences			
	Ability to move from literal to figurative interpretations			

4. How does this student's overall performance relate to his or her ability?

5. Describe this student's class participation and working relationship:
   a. with other students

   b. with adults

Academic Evaluation, please check appropriate response(s).

ACADEMIC POTENTIAL	limited	fair	average	good	outstanding
EFFORT AND PERSEVERANCE	does very little	some desire	well motivated	sets high goals	perseveres under pressure
STUDY HABITS	poor	fair		good	excellent
INTELLECTUAL CURIOSITY	limited	occasionally sparked	narrow	strong and varied	intense and varied
ABILITY TO WORK INDEPENDENTLY	needs much supervision	needs help frequently	needs help occasionally		always works well
USE OF TIME	poor	occasionally wastes	usually uses well		always uses effectively
ABILITY TO FOLLOW DIRECTIONS	needs much explanation	occasionally needs help			works quickly and effectively
ATTENTION SPAN	easily distracted	occasionally distracted	usually good		exceptionally attentive
CREATIVITY AND ORIGINALITY	tends to follow	occasional spark	generates ideas independently		unusually original
PERSONAL EVALUATION INTEGRITY AND HONESTY	cannot be trusted	questionable	usually trustworthy		highly developed
CONSIDERATION OF OTHERS	thoughtless	seldom considerate	usually considerate		unusually supportive
SOCIAL ADJUSTMENT WITH PEERS	serious problems	loner	scapegoat	friendly	leader	peacemaker
CLASSROOM CONDUCT	troublemaker	occasionally disrupts	usually good	always good	domineering
INITIATIVE	never initiates	rarely shown	occasionally initiates		frequent display
EMOTIONAL STABILITY	insecure	overly tense	attention getter		stable
SELF-CONFIDENCE	needs much reassurance	needs some support	appears overly confident		healthy self-image
FULFILLMENT OF RESPONSIBILITIES	rare	occasional	usual		regular
COOPERATION OF PARENTS/GUARDIAN	poor	fair	good		outstanding

In your opinion, what is this student's greatest need?

Date: _____

Teacher's Name: _____ Phone: _____

School: _____

Address: _____ Zip: _____

Thank you for your time and effort in this student's behalf.

The Waldorf School

TEACHER RECOMMENDATION
MATHEMATICS

Name of applicant _____ Current grade _____

1. How long have you known this student, and in what context?

2. What are the first words that come to your mind to describe this student?

3. Please evaluate the applicant in the following areas: (check appropriate box)

	performance below grade level	performance consistent with grade level	performance above grade level
Addition			
Subtraction			
Multiplication			
Division			
Decimals			
Integers			
Pos./Neg. numbers			
Fractions			

4. Title and author of text used:

5. Please list the topics covered in this year's course, or specify if Algebra I, Algebra II or Plane Geometry, etc.

6. To what degree has the student mastered material covered in the course so far?

7. Describe the student's ability in problem solving and in dealing with abstract concepts.

8. Describe the student's class participation and working relationship:
    a. with other students

    b. with adults

Academic Evaluation, please check appropriate response(s).

ACADEMIC POTENTIAL	limited — fair — average — good — outstanding
EFFORT AND PERSEVERANCE	does very little — some desire — well motivated — sets high goals — perseveres under pressure
STUDY HABITS	poor — fair — good — excellent
INTELLECTUAL CURIOSITY	limited — occasionally sparked — narrow — strong and varied — intense and varied
ABILITY TO WORK INDEPENDENTLY	needs much supervision — needs help frequently — needs help occasionally — always works well
USE OF TIME	poor — occasionally wastes — usually uses well — always uses effectively
ABILITY TO FOLLOW DIRECTIONS	needs much explanation — occasionally needs help — works quickly and effectively
ATTENTION SPAN	easily distracted — occasionally distracted — usually good — exceptionally attentive
CREATIVITY AND ORIGINALITY	tends to follow — occasional spark — generates ideas independently — unusually original
PERSONAL EVALUATION INTEGRITY AND HONESTY	cannot be trusted — questionable — usually trustworthy — highly developed
CONSIDERATION OF OTHERS	thoughtless — seldom considerate — usually considerate — unusually supportive
SOCIAL ADJUSTMENT WITH PEERS	serious problems — loner — scapegoat — friendly — leader — peacemaker
CLASSROOM CONDUCT	troublemaker — occasionally disrupts — usually good — always good — domineering
INITIATIVE	never initiates — rarely shown — occasionally initiates — frequent display
EMOTIONAL STABILITY	insecure — overly tense — attention getter — stable
SELF-CONFIDENCE	needs much reassurance — needs some support — appears overly confident — healthy self-image
FULFILLMENT OF RESPONSIBILITIES	rare — occasional — usual — regular
COOPERATION OF PARENTS/GUARDIAN	poor — fair — good — outstanding

In your opinion, what is this student's greatest need?

Date: _____

Teacher's Name: _____ Phone: _____

School: _____

Address: _____ Zip: _____

Thank you for your time and effort in this student's behalf.

Sample Request for Records

REQUEST FOR RECORDS

To the Principal or Headmaster,

With regard to: _____

The above named student is applying to the Waldorf school for entrance into the ____th grade. Would you please send us a transcript of record, including any standardized test scores that are available. If your policy permits, we would also appreciate a descriptive statement about this student by you or a counselor who knows the student well.

(Recommendation forms will be given to the student for his/her English and Math teachers.)

I hereby give my permission to _____ School to release the records of _____ and provide other requested information to the Waldorf school.

Signature of the parent _____

Date _____

1987-1988 ENROLLMENT PROCEDURES:
New Students

1. For each child, complete an Application for Admission and submit to the school secretary with a non-refundable application fee of $25.00.

2. If your child is transferring from another school, sign a Consent to Release Educational Records form.

3. After the Application for Admission, student records and application fee are received, interviews with the Admissions Director and Class Teacher will be arranged for parents and child.

4. A Payment Plan is chosen for the year's tuition, after which a Tuition Agreement is drawn up and signed. (For families who are unable to pay the full tuition fee, a scholarship may be applied for, no later than May 15, 1987.)

5. When acceptance has been determined, the family is contacted. A deposit of $300 (Elementary & Junior High) and/or $200 (Preschool & Kindergarten) is made toward the 1987-88 tuition. (This is due 15 days after acceptance.)

6. Confirmation of enrollment takes place upon signature of the tuition contract and completion of the above steps. Final acceptance is granted following a one-month trial period of attendance in the school.

7. Before school begins in the fall, an emergency card (to be filled out and returned), school calendar, and parent handbook will be sent to the family.

1987-1988 ENROLLMENT PROCEDURES:
Continuing Students

1. Complete a Continuing Application for each child (no fee required).

2. Choose one of three payment plans for the 1987-88 tuition and submit it to the school office <u>before</u> May 15th. (Scholarship applications must be returned <u>no later</u> than May 15th.)

3. A deposit of $300 (Elementary & Junior High) and/or $200 (Preschool & Kindergarten) is made toward the 1987-88 tuition (due <u>May 15, 1987</u>).

4. A Tuition Agreement is drawn up and signed.

5. A letter to confirm enrollment is sent to the family upon completion of enrollment.

6. Before school begins in the fall, an emergency card (to be filled out and returned), school calendar, and parent handbook will be sent to the family.

Mail your choice of payment plans to:

The Monadnock Waldorf School
98 South Lincoln Street
Keene, New Hampshire 03431

Phone: 603-357-4442

Clip out and return to school

Payment Plans for 1987-88 Tuition

(choose one)

FAMILY NAME _____

CHILDREN'S NAMES _____
_____

[ ] A. **Early payment plan:**
Payment in full by July 31. One percent of total tuition may be deducted if this option is chosen.

[ ] B. **Regular payment plan:**
Balance of tuition due after deposit(s) paid in three equal installments: August 15, September 15, and November 15.

[ ] C. **Extended payment plan:**
Balance of tuition due after deposit(s) paid in eight equal installments, July 15 through February 15. A $40 finance charge will be added to accounts of families who choose this option -- ($20 if only one preschool or kindergarten tuition).

Appendix – Chapter 6

Tuition Protection Plan

Virtually all independent schools require full payment of tuition for the entire school year because independent school expenses are incurred on an annual basis. We cannot, therefore, refund tuition paid or cancel unpaid obligations in the event of a student's separation from school during the year. We realize, however, that family circumstances can change, and in these instances it would be desirable to have some method to protect your financial commitment to the School. This is what the Tuition Protection Plan is designed to do. Here is how it works:

1. If a student is withdrawn voluntarily after July 15th, the Plan will pay 60% of the prorated tuition that is due for the remainder of the school year. The benefit formula is:

$$\frac{60\% \text{ of (weeks separated X annual tuition)}}{36 \text{ Weeks (full school year)}}$$

2. If a student is involuntarily dismissed from Pine Hill during the year, the Plan will pay 75% of the prorated tuition due for the remainder of the school year. The benefit formula is:

$$\frac{75\% \text{ of (weeks separated X annual tuition)}}{36 \text{ Weeks (full school year)}}$$

Example: A family electing the 10-payment plan moves to Duluth on November 21st (after one-third of the school year), withdrawing their third grader whose full-year tuition is $4500. The family would have already made five payments totaling $2250. The Tuition Protection Plan would cover 60% of the unused tuition of $3000 or $1800. The family would pay full tuition for the portion of the year their child attended Pine Hill ($4500 X 33% = $1500) plus 40% of unused tuition or $1200. Since they have already paid $2250, their remaining obligation would be $450.

Fine Print

- The school reserves the right to determine the reason for separation.
- The Plan does not cover temporary absences due to illness or other medical conditions.
- The Plan does not cover withdrawals or dismissals due to insurrection, rebellion, riot, civil commotion, war, toxic waste or nuclear accidents, epidemic, destruction of any school facility, or closure of the school for any reason.

Appendix – Chapter 6

The Pine Hill Waldorf School Policy on
Overdue Tuition Policy

The following policy concerning the process for handling overdue financial obligations to the school was developed jointly by the college of teachers and the board of trustees. It is intended to provide guidance to the finance committee of the board and the executive committee of the college and does not necessarily imply that rigid procedures must be followed in each case. The policy seeks to balance the school's need to seek payment from those who have promised their financial support and to ensure that pedagogical concerns are appropriately addressed in the process.

The policy has three phases:

- The business manager attempts to collect overdue payments in the usual way by calling, writing letters, securing commitments to pay by a specific date, following up on those commitments, etc.

- If parents are unwilling to make a firm commitment or do not honor the commitments they have made, they are asked to meet with the finance committee of the board. The class teacher is informed about the matter at this point.

- If an agreement cannot be reached between the parents and the finance committee, or if communication breaks down for any reason, the matter is taken for discussion to the full college of teachers. The final decision concerning whether a child can remain at Pine Hill in the absence of the committed financial support is made by a group made up of two executive committee members, two finance committee members, and the class teacher. The decision of this group is by consensus.

Appendix – Chapter 8

Sample Hiring Letter

Dear _____,   April 12, 199?

    The college of teachers at the _____ Waldorf School would like to offer you a position as a class teacher and other related duties as determined by the college for the academic year _____. We are excited about your joining us in this important work, and we hope that your upcoming years at our school will be rich and meaningful.

    We are prepared to offer you a salary of $_____, which is arrived at by taking our base pay $ _____, plus dependency allowance of $_____, plus an experience increment of $ _____ based on your ____ years of experience.

    Additionally you will receive as benefits medical insurance $ _____ per month, dental insurance of $ _____ per month, and a pension allotment of $ _____ per month.

    We expect that you will agree to participate in all aspects of our self-evaluation process. Enclosed is a Teacher's Handbook which details the tasks of teachers at our school.

    Please be so kind as to write a confirmation of your intention to accept this position which will acknowledge this letter and be kept as a permanent part of your personnel folder.

    We are all very happy to have you join us.

                                                                  Sincerely,

                                                                _____

                                                                For the college of teachers

Appendix – Chapter 8

Sample Teacher Contract

Dear _____,

On behalf of the college of teachers, we are please to offer you a position at the Waldorf school for the _____ academic year.

Your salary of $ _____ per annum is calculated as follows:

Base salary _____

Dependents allowance _____

Experience increment _____   Total: $ _____

In addition to this salary, you will receive the following benefits:

Tuition allowance for your children

Medical insurance

Dental insurance

Pension

Pay will be given monthly, in advance over a 12-month period beginning on September 1, _____.

The School's expectation is that you will follow the school work calendar which begins on the third Monday of August each year, two weeks prior to school opening, and includes all professional days, faculty meetings and workshops. Duties will cease one week after the closing of the academic year, upon submission of your grades and reports and main lesson books, or at such time as the college of teachers deems necessary.

It is understood that as a colleague in the Waldorf school you join a group of teachers who work under the direction of the college of teachers with the philosophy, purpose, and curriculum of Waldorf education and who seek excellence in the teaching of children. Further, a colleague participates in the life of the whole school and contributes to its working as required: meetings of the whole faculty, committee meetings, and other duties commonly expected of teachers, including activities such as self-evaluation, conferences with parents, faculty work days, participation in teacher conferences, recess duty, receiving colleagues into your classroom, occasional substitution, and the filing of student reports in good order and in a timely fashion. Main lesson teachers agree to be in their classrooms at least 20 minutes prior to the beginning of the academic day. It is expected that each January you will make clear to the college your intention for the upcoming academic year. Exceptions to any of the above must be agreed upon by the college chairperson.

It is further expected that you will fulfill any legal obligations required by the school, such as medical tests. Your performance as a teacher will be evaluated by the college of teachers, whose determination will be final and binding upon you. If you agree with the above expectations and conditions, kindly sign and return both copies of this letter. One will be returned to you for your records.

Accepted (signed)_____

Date: _____

Received by the college of teachers by: _____

Appendix – Chapter 8

Sample Teacher Evaluation Policy

1. All teachers should evaluate themselves and maintain a written record of their reflections, which is reviewed and updated once a year. These self-evaluations will be kept in the office personnel files in the college chairperson's office.

2. All teachers should have, as a required part of their schedule, time to observe other teachers at Pine Hill (or in other schools when appropriate) and to discuss their observations and questions with the teachers visited. Each teacher will have at least one such visit scheduled per year.

3. Outside observers—master teachers—will be invited to observe and evaluate the teachers and discuss their findings with them, based on at least two visits in the classroom. Records of these meetings should be kept as part of the teacher's evaluation file and should be signed by the teacher and the outside observer. Outside observers—either class teachers or specialist teachers—will be invited in alternate years.

4. Teachers should share their self-evaluations in the college of teachers at least once a year. Everyone in the college is free to comment on these presentations in the spirit of mutual growth, affirming strengths, and helping to improve weaknesses.

5. New teachers should have a mentor to assist them with self-evaluation and to serve as liaison with the college. They should meet with the college by Thanksgiving and Easter to review their work. If by Christmas of the second year, any significant problems have not been worked out, the college should decide by February whether or not the teacher should continue the following year. The mentor should arrange regular meetings with the new teacher and visit classes before Thanksgiving and Easter, in order to keep the college informed as to how things are going. In the case of a new class teacher, the mentor should also be a class teacher and, if possible, from the grade immediately ahead of the new teacher's.

6. The college of teachers is the form for evaluating teacher competence. Significant problems which raise doubts about competence should be presented in the college in the presence of the teacher concerned. An evaluative discussion should follow; whether or not the concerned teacher remains for that discussion should be left to the free decision of all. Either the teacher may decide to leave, or a college member may ask that he leave; otherwise, he will take part in the discussion. A written record should be kept of recommendations and decisions, and these should be communicated to the teacher if he was not present for the discussion.

Parents and/or teachers wanting to raise questions about teacher competence should address them to the college chairman or a college member, who will then arrange for a discussion to occur. Parents should be informed through the parent group and parent handbook that they have this avenue to raise questions.

7. The main criteria for teacher evaluation, which should be addressed by teachers in their reports, are the following:

    a. Classroom management and discipline
    b. Teaching style—voice, self-presence, authority, give and take, children's reception
    c. Teaching methods—form, order and content of the lessons (correct rhythms, content for age group, artistic handling of the subject)
    d. Children's work—care for materials, order and form of workbooks, displays, etc.)
    e. Aesthetics and hygiene in the classroom—order, neatness, displays, dress, room temperature, circulation of air, etc.
    f. Parent interaction—quality of communication
    g. Colleague interaction—Do you have ability to work in a cooperative way with colleagues? How else are you participating in carrying the overall organism of the school?

The self-evaluation report should be written with the above criteria in mind. If the report is insufficient either in length or in quality, the college chairperson will request that it be rewritten.

Reports should conclude with some mention of those areas being worked upon and of anything the teacher thinks that he needs to do to improve his work.

8. The college chairperson would serve as facilitator of the school evaluation plan.

Appendix – Chapter 8

Evaluation Criteria for Teachers

The aim of the college is to promote ever higher standards in teaching through conversations with colleagues, visitations, and continual self-evaluation. The areas listed below should be seen as "signposts"—applicable to varying degrees, depending upon the teacher, subjects taught, and grade level.

We ask that teachers speak with a colleague before and after a visit, using these criteria as a framework. Please also report to the Teacher Development Committee within a week of the visit.

I. Content of lesson

    a. Appropriate for age level?
    b. Challenges the student?
    c. Clarity of presentation
    d. Enthusiasm in presentation
    e. Responsiveness of students
    f. Is there a "sense for the whole?"
    g. Artistry in presentation

II. Form and discipline

    a. Is the lesson formed in a way that allows the students to receive the content?
    b. Teacher's authority and presence before the class, i.e., the whole group.
    c. Teacher's response to individual disciplinary problems, difficult situations.
    d. Threefold balance of head, heart, and limbs in lesson
    e. Appearance of room, students and teacher.

III. Teacher/student relationship

    a. Is there a "breathing" in the lesson?
    b. Warmth in teacher/student relationship?
    c. Student-to-student interactions
    d. Does the teacher promote positive social interaction within the class?
    e. Is the teacher available for one-on-one help, conversation, etc.?

IV. Academic, artistic and pedagogical standards

    a. Is the class as a whole working hard, performing at grade level, eager to acquire new knowledge?
    b. Does the teacher promote high academic standards?
    c. Quality of good book work
    d. Does the teacher follow through on homework, correction, etc.?
    e. Teacher's artistic work (blackboard paintings, singing, recorder)
    f. Does the teacher delve into the curriculum and thoroughly prepare his/her lessons?

V. Colleagueship

    a. Is the teacher easy to work with?
    b. Communicates regularly?
    c. Willing to help others?
    d. Take on non-teaching tasks?
    e. Promotes good will and fellowship among colleagues?
    f. Can the teacher take advice?

VI. Parent relations

    a. Regular conferences with parents?
    b. Accessible?
    c. Able to communicate goals and share program of students?

VII Teacher's relationship to anthroposophy

    a. Does the teacher appear to work out of anthroposophy?
    b. Participate actively in faculty study?
    c. Willing to ask questions and hear the advice of other?

Sample Peer Evaluation Agreement Letter

To the College of Teachers:

By signing this letter I indicate my agreement to participate in an evaluation of my teaching at _____ Waldorf School.

I understand that I will be visited by _____ and that I will meet with him/her after each visit for a conversation, during which I will get feedback about my strengths and areas in which improvement is needed.

I agree to write up my notes of this conversation and give them to the person evaluating my work to read and then sign. I also agree to read and/or share in a verbal report all of this content with the college of teachers at an agreed upon time and date.

This evaluation will then be placed in my personnel file in the office.

Signature: _____   Date: _____

Appendix – Chapter 8

In-House Evaluation Form

Teacher visited: _____   Date: _____

By: _____

I. DISCIPLINE:

    a. teacher's authority, presence before class, sympathy vs. antipathy in relation to children, holding the whole group
    b. children's behavior
    c. children's work habits

II. TEACHER'S SPEECH/ SPEECH WORK WITH CHILDREN:

    clarity   intonation   variation   projection

III. FORM AND CONTENT OF THE LESSON

    a. three-part lesson: head, heart and will activities
        How is the balance?
        Is it challenging?
        circle work?
    b. two-day rhythm
        presentation
        review
        book work (pictures, text)
    c. work with and attention to individual children

IV. APPEARANCE, DECORUM, HYGIENE

    a. classroom appearance, orderliness
    b. teacher's and children's dress, general appearance
    c. ventilation, etc.

V. EVALUATION OF CHILDREN'S WORK:

    a. oral
    b. written

continued

Appendix – Chapter 8

COMMENTS

STRENGTHS:

AREAS IN NEED OF IMPROVEMENT:

RECOMMENDATIONS:

Middle School Course Evaluation and Description

Student: _____
Main Lesson: Chemistry
Grade: 7
Teacher: _____

Course Description: Chemistry is the science dealing with the composition and properties of substances and with the reactions by which substances are produced or converted into other substances.

After an introduction to chemistry and a brief look at its historical background, the seventh grade looked at how substances combust or burn. We observed the opposition of light and weight and observed many different types of flames, smoke, and ash. We contrasted the burning of sulfur and phosphorus and studied the consuming ember within carbon. While we were doing this, the students were writing their accurate observations. These were shared the next day and conclusions were reached.

We explored the nature of crystallization. The limestone cycle was studied and this led us into an understanding of acids and bases, how they react and how salts are formed.

The children wrote up their observations of the many experiments that we did in class as well as original essays on the material we discussed.

Key: Outstanding, excellent, good, fair, poor, incomplete

Homework:	Class participation:
Ability to observe:	Behavior:
Spelling tests:	Final Chemistry test:

MAIN LESSON BOOK:

Appearance:	Aesthetics:
Completeness:	Quality of essays:
Comments:	

Final grade _____   Teacher's signature: _____

Appendix – Chapter 8

High School Student Progress Report

Name:_____   Date: _____

Advisor's Name: _____

    To all teachers:

In order to keep a close watch on this student's progress, and thus be able to help him/her in a timely manner, I ask that you answer in an appropriate manner the following questions. Please use the reverse side if you would like to make additional comments.

Name of class: _____

1. Has his/her effort been satisfactory? [ ]Yes [ ]No

2. Has he/she been attentive? [ ]Yes [ ]No

3. Are his/her assignments complete? [ ]Yes [ ]No

4. Has he/she reported for extra help? [ ]Yes [ ]No

5. Does the student use his/her time well? [ ]Yes [ ]No

6. Has the student been tardy to class within the last five days? [ ]Yes [ ]No

7. How many classes has the student been absent in the last five days? [ ]Yes [ ]No

8. What is the student's approximate grade thus far this term? [ ]Yes [ ]No

9. Can you determine if the student has been working adequately in study hall?

                                                                         [ ]Yes [ ]No

Teacher's signature: _____

Students: Please take one copy of this form to each of your teachers and then return to your advisor.

Appendix – Chapter 10

Sample Board of Trustees Committee List

THE GREAT BARRINGTON RUDOLF STEINER SCHOOL

I. Efficient means for board to do its work
    A. Delegation to committees
    B. Specialization by committees
    C. Ideally all trustees serve on one or more committees
    D. Representation of broader school community encouraged: Parents – Faculty – Friends
    E. Trustees should chair committees
    F. Develop committee mission
    G. Report at each board meeting
    H. All meetings are minuted

II. Committees
    A. Human Resources
    B. Development
    C. Executive/Finance
    D. Buildings and Grounds
    E. Educational Support

III. Human Resources
    A. Compensation
    B. Benefits: pension, disability, health, tuition remission
    C. Personnel policies
    D. Employee contracts

IV. Development
    A. Coordinator
    B. Annual Giving
    C. Capital Campaign
    D. Public Relations
    E. Alumni
    F. Long-Range Planning
    G. Parent-Teacher Association
    H. Publications
    I. Enrollment

Appendix – Chapter 10

SAMPLE LEGAL DESCRIPTION OF THE BOARD OF TRUSTEES

Article I
Board of Trustees

Section 1. Composition of the Board of Trustees.

The business and affairs of the Corporation, except as they be delegated to the Executive Committee hereinafter provided, or except as they be reserved to the Faculty as hereinafter provided, shall be controlled by a Board of not less than eleven (11) and not more than fifteen (15) trustees. The Board of Trustees shall be referred to in these Bylaws as *the Board*.

Four of the trustees shall be members of the College of Teachers of the Waldorf School, and shall be chosen by the College of Teachers in such manner as it may determine. These trustees shall be referred to in these Bylaws as *faculty trustees*.

The remaining trustees shall be determined by the procedure specified in Article I, Section 3 of these Bylaws, entitled "Selection of Trustees". These trustees shall be referred to in these Bylaws as *non-faculty trustees*, although there is no requirement that they not be members of the school faculty.

At least one-third (1/3) of the trustees must be members of the Anthroposophical Society.

Section 2. Terms of Trustees.

The terms of faculty trustees shall be determined by the College of Teachers.

Non-faculty trustees shall serve for a term of three (3) years, beginning in May. The terms of non-faculty trustees shall be staggered so that no more than half expire in any one year. Upon the completion of one term, a trustee shall serve a next term only if re-elected as specified in Article I, Section 3 of these Bylaws.

Section 3. Selection of Trustees.

Each year a Nominating Committee shall be appointed, consisting of

- Two (2) non-faculty trustees chosen by the Board
- Two (2) faculty members chosen by the College of Teachers
- Two (2) non-trustees chosen by the School's parent body or an organization representative of the School's parent body, in a manner specified by the Board

Section 5. Powers and Duties of the Clerk.

The Clerk shall:

a. Keep the minutes of all meetings of the Board of Trustees and of the Executive Committee.

b. Attend to the giving and serving of all notices for the Corporation.

c. Attest the signatures of the proper officers to all contracts, securities and other obligations of the Corporation and affix the seal of the Corporation thereto.

d. Perform all duties incident to the office of the Secretary, subject to the control of the Board, and such other duties as may from time to time be required of him by the Board, the Executive Committee, or the President.

Article III

Executive Committee

The President of the Board of Trustees shall appoint an Executive Committee of three (3) to five (5) members, who shall be charged with conducting such affairs and business of the Board as is deemed necessary and proper by the Board between meetings of the Board. The President of the Board shall be a member of said Executive Committee. The other members of the Executive Committee may be any members of the Board. The Executive Committee shall be responsible to the President and shall engage in no action which is specifically reserved by these Bylaws to the Board as a whole or to any officer thereof.

Article IV

Committees

The Board of Trustees may establish such Committees as it sees fit, and may delegate responsibilities and authority to them, subject at all times to the ultimate authority of the Board. Committees established by the Board may have members who are not trustees.

Article V

Membership

The members of the Corporation shall be those persons from time to time constituting its Board of Trustees. The vote and acts of the Trustees shall constitute the vote and acts of the members of the Corporation for all purposes in which action by the members, as distinguished from action by the Board of Trustees, is required or permitted by law.

Article VI

Amendments

New Bylaws may be adopted or these Bylaws may be amended or repealed by a a two-thirds (2/3) majority of the total membership of the Board, including not less than two-thirds (2/3) of the faculty trustees, except that Article I, Section 7, paragraph (f) may not be amended or repealed.

Appendix – Chapter 10

The Nominating Committee shall prepare a slate of candidates for the non-faculty trustee positions which will become vacant in the May of that year.

At the April meeting of the Board, the Board shall vote to accept or reject the slate of candidates prepared by the Nominating Committee. If the Board rejects the slate, then the Nominating Committee shall prepare a new slate for consideration at the next Board meeting; and this process shall continue (with the terms of the existing trustees being continued if necessary) until a slate is approved.

If a non-faculty trustee resigns or is removed before the expiration of his or her term, the Nominating Committee shall meet to nominate a trustee to serve out the remainder of the term, who must be confirmed by the Board.

The Nominating Committee shall recommend candidates, and the Board shall approve or disapprove them, in accordance with the following requirements:

1. Trustees shall have a commitment to Waldorf education in general, beyond Pine Hill and the education of their own children.
2. Trustees shall recognize that Waldorf Education is based on the life work of Rudolf Steiner and shall have a respectful openness to Anthroposophy and a sympathy for social and cultural renewal as expressed in Anthroposophy.
3. Some members of the Board should have applicable business and legal experience.
4. Trustees shall have demonstrated their willingness to work for the school, including the expenditure of personal time and energy.
5. Trustees shall have a commitment to the long-term development of the school.
6. Trustees shall have an interest in generating funds for the school.

Section 4. Meetings.

The Board shall specify the schedule of its regular meetings, but must hold at least one meeting in the Spring and one meeting in the Fall of every year. Meetings shall be held at the   Waldorf School in   or at such other place as shall be designated by the President of the Board.

A special meeting of the Board may be held at any time and place upon the call of the President of the Board or, in the event of his absence or inability to act, the Vice President of the Board or any three (3) trustees.

Section 5. Notice of Meetings.

No decisions or actions of any regular or special meeting of the Board shall be valid unless written notice shall have been mailed to each trustee at his or her last known residence or place of business no less than ten (10) days before the meeting.

However, if every member not so notified signs, either before or after a meeting, a written waiver of notice or consent to the holding of the meeting or an approval of the minutes thereof, then the decisions and actions of the meeting shall be as valid as though proper notification had taken place. All such waivers, consents, or approvals shall be filed with the corporate records or made a part of the minutes of the meeting.

Section 6. Quorum.

A quorum for the transaction of business shall consist of at least one-half (½) of the faculty trustees and at least one-half (½) of the non-faculty trustees. A majority vote of such quorum present at the time and place of any meeting of the Board shall determine any proposition that may come before the Board, provided that no other provision of these Bylaws be violated.

Section 7. Powers of the Board of Trustees.

The trustees shall, in addition to the general powers conferred upon them by these Bylaws, have the power to:

a. Elect the officers of the Corporation annually, at the April meeting of the Board.

b. Receive and hold by purchase, gift, devise, bequest or grant, real or personal property for educational purposes connected with the Corporation or for the benefit of the School.

c. Sell, mortgage, lease or otherwise use and dispose of the property of the Corporation in such a manner as the trustees shall deem most conducive to the prosperity of the Corporation.

d. Declare vacant the seat of any trustee who is absent from any three (3) consecutive regular meetings of the Board; or, by a vote of a three-fourths (3/4) majority of the total membership of the Board, declare vacant the seat of any trustee for any other reason.

e. Make and amend all Bylaws necessary and proper to carry into effect the powers of the said Board of Trustees as necessary and desirable in the advancement of the interests of the School, as provided in Article VI of these Bylaws, provided that no Bylaw shall conflict with the Constitution or laws of the United States of America or of the State of New Hampshire, or with the provisions of Article II, Section D of the *Articles of Association of the   Waldorf School*.

f. Close the School and dispose of its assets in accordance with Article II, Section E of the *Articles of Association of the   Waldorf School* if, in the judgment of the Board, the School no longer adheres to and promotes the purposes as stated in Article II, Section A of the *Articles of Association of the   Waldorf School*.

g. Annually approve the operating budget for the School. The College of Teachers will recommend to the Board the gross salary figure for incorporation in the annual operating budget.

Section 8. Powers Withheld from the Board of Trustees.

Specifically excluded from the powers of the Board of Trustees and reserved to the Faculty of the School are all matters pertaining to the conduct of the educational program of the School, including, but not restricted to, the formation of the curriculum, the engagement or dismissal of faculty or staff members, and the allocation of gross salaries and wages as set forth in the operating budget.

The College of Teachers has the right to veto any action or decision of the Board of Trustees which violates this provision. The College of Teachers must notify the Board of Trustees in writing, no later than the seventh (7th) day following the day of the meeting at which an action or decision is taken, that it is exercising its right to review that action or decision, and must make a final decision no later than the thirty-first (31st) day following the day of the meeting.

Appendix – Chapter 10

Article II
Officers of the Corporation

Section 1. General.

The officers of the Corporation shall consist of a President, a Vice President, a Treasurer, and a Clerk, all of whom shall be members of the Board of Trustees. The Treasurer may also be the Vice President or the Clerk, but not both; otherwise, no individual may hold more than two offices.

Other officers, not necessarily members of the Board, may be appointed at the direction of the Board.

Section 2. Powers and Duties of the President.

The President of the Corporation shall:

a. Be the President of the Board of Trustees.

b. Preside at all meetings of the Board and of the Executive Committee at which he is present.

c. When directed by the Board, sign with the proper officers of the Corporation all contracts, securities, and other obligations of the Corporation in the name of the Corporation.

d. Do and perform such other duties as may from time to time be assigned to him by the Board.

e. Have a general oversight over the business affairs and finances of the school.

Section 3. Powers and Duties of the Vice President.

The Vice President shall exercise the powers and perform the duties of the President in case of the President's absence or disability.

Section 4. Powers and Duties of the Treasurer.

The Treasurer shall:

a. Have custody of the funds and securities of the Corporation which may come into his hands and shall, if required by the trustees at any time, give such bond as the Board of Trustees may require.

b. Perform such other duties as the President or the Board may require of him.

c. Prepare or cause to be prepared, and present to the Board of Trustees at its October meeting, a complete financial report and balance sheet showing the assets and liabilities of the Corporation as of the close of the preceding fiscal year, together with a profit and loss statement showing the gross and net income and operating expenses of the Corporation for the same period.

d. Whenever required by the Board of Trustees or the President, render to them or to him a statement of the finances of the Corporation.